A Practical Guide
to Forensic Psychotherapy

Forensic Focus 3

Forensic Focus

This series, now edited by Gwen Adshead, takes the currently crystallizing field of Forensic Psychotherapy as its focal point, offering a forum for the presentation of theoretical and clinical issues. It also embraces such influential neighbouring disciplines as language, law, literature, criminology, ethics and philosophy, as well as psychiatry and psychology, its established progenitors.

Gwen Adshead is Consultant Psychotherapist and Honorary Senior Lecturer in Forensic Psychotherapy at Broadmoor Hospital.

Forensic Focus 3

A Practical Guide
to Forensic Psychotherapy

Edited by
Estela V. Welldon and Cleo Van Velsen

Forewords by
Fiona Caldicott DBE, *immediate past President of the Royal College of Psychiatrists*
Helena Kennedy *QC*

Jessica Kingsley Publishers
London and Bristol, Pennsylvania

First published in the United Kingdom in 1997 by
Jessica Kingsley Publishers Ltd
116 Pentonville Road
London N1 9JB, England
and
325 Chestnut Street, Philadelphia,
PA19106, USA

Second impression 1999

Copyright © 1997 Jessica Kingsley Publishers

Forewords copyright © 1997 Fiona Caldicott and Helena Kennedy

Library of Congress Cataloging in Publication Data
A CIP catalogue record for this book is available from the Library of Congress

British Library Cataloguing in Publication Data
A practical guide to forensic psychotherapy
1. Psychology, forensic 2. Forensic psychiatry
I. Welldon, Estella V. II. Velsen, Cleo Van
616.8'914

ISBN 1-85302-389-2

Printed and Bound in Great Britain by
Athenaeum Press, Gateshead, Tyne and Wear

Contents

Part III Society, Law and Psychiatry

Part IV. Audit and Research

Foreword

It is fitting that a new book in the series should take the form of essays focused on the 'intricacies and complexities encountered in working with the forensic patient' (p.1). This will complement the broader horizons of theory and practice delineated in *Forensic Focus 1*.

In these pages the trainee will find the shape of things to come, whereas the trainer will be glad of promptings for informed debate and demands for elucidation. The vignettes, presented as case studies in Part II, thus provide excellent catalytic material on which to base a sequence of seminars.

The editors rightly stress the indubitable fact that forensic psychotherapy is a 'team effort' (p.14). It is largely left to the reader's self-questioning as to whether an issue under consideration can safely be dealt with in a non-secure setting, or whether secure facilities are mandatory. Each setting has assets and liabilities. '*Where* can the proposed therapy best take place?' is always a pivotal question. Fortunately, for much forensic psychotherapy an open setting is ideal. But for many patients at the psychotic and psychopathic end of the population spectrum, concerns about external security prevail.

This book is appropriately placed in the *Forensic Focus* series and will augment its relevance.

Murray Cox

Foreword

This is an important book which I hope will be read by all those whose work may bring them into contact with mentally disordered offenders, and who seek practical guidance.

It should also be of interest further afield as policy makers and politicians try to respond to the widespread concern in society at large about criminal behaviour, its management and its causation.

The field of forensic psychiatry has become of increasing importance in psychiatric work worldwide, and its practitioners are now developing increasingly specialized expertise at its interface with other areas of clinical activity. Forensic psychotherapy is one example of these welcome developments, with one group of specialists finding that another group has much to offer in terms of the understanding and treatment of their patients.

There are too many examples in medicine of specialization leading to rigid separation from other specialist areas, which impoverishes clinical work and deprives patients of comprehensive care. It is good to see this tendency being addressed at several interfaces such as this one. It has been particularly gratifying to be President of the Royal College of Psychiatrists while the joint training programme for senior and specialist registrars has been developed in forensic psychotherapy.

This does not mean that mentally disordered offenders should all be offered psychotherapeutic treatment, just as this is not appropriate for many seriously mentally ill patients. However, the understanding which emanates from the theories underpinning the psychotherapies of proven efficacy can assist those who work with individuals who suffer from the most severe forms of disabling and tormenting mental disorders. Such understanding can help the practitioner to sustain work which is always challenging, and often gruelling.

There are chapters in this book addressing most of the commonly encountered problems in the field, and practical guidance on clinical management permeates it.

The issues of containing and holding people who have had extremely abusive experiences which have greatly traumatized them are frequently highlighted. Dynamic administration (Foulkes 1975) is revisited.

Another theme is the impact on staff of trying to care for such damaged individuals. Provocation, aggression and seduction are only some of the responses which can try the therapeutic alliance to its limits, illustrating the importance of supervision for all staff, and personal therapy for most.

Systems for helping staff to continue to work in secure settings, from the nurturing of a delicate therapeutic relationship to its survival in the face of murderous rage, including the fear of this being enacted, are frequently referenced.

Maggie Hilton, in her chapter on *Violence and Alcohol* encapsulates much of this as follows: 'For instance, patients may be labelled as untreatable with no recognition that it is the limits of our knowledge and ways of working which results in failure.

In my view such work requires an ability to stay with very difficult experiences and material and struggle to foster an understanding and working through of very complex damaged aspects of the personality. It also requires an ability to struggle to maintain a dialogue with those who may long since have lost any belief that they can be understood or that their lives can be different.'

Although the book is concise and the chapters short, they are well referenced so that the interested reader is led further in understanding a particular topic.

In summary this book is a most welcome addition to the growing literature on forensic psychotherapy.

Fiona Caldicott DBE
October 1996

Foreword

When I was invited to address the 1995 conference of the International Association for Forensic Psychotherapy in Glasgow, I overheard my elderly Scottish mother say quite innocently that I was there to speak to a group of Forensic Psychopaths.

I reported this malapropism to my audience and they took it on their chins, inured to the brickbats received by their profession, particularly in Britain where until recently the prefix psycho evoked either terror or scepticism and certainly created confusion. However, the tide has turned and there is growing recognition that the psychological sciences have a crucial role to play in the understanding of profound social problems and in seeking solutions.

This cultural shift, acknowledging professionalism, skill and specialist knowledge, has been particularly noticeable in the courts. There is now a greater willingness to admit expert testimony to explain human responses and states of mind, which may be outside the tribunal's experience, and to assist in presenting therapeutic options when it comes to sentencing offenders.

Traditionally the law was anxious to keep the role of psychiatry limited because it was not deemed sufficiently scientific. The map of the human mind might be as singular as a fingerprint but it was not susceptible to the same display of process and evidential rigour that the courts thought necessary. While psychiatric symptoms might huddle together in recognizable clusters, they were not measurable like temperature or a blood group. Too much depended upon the history given by the patient, which raised questions as to whether the information might be self-serving. It was one thing for men in white coats to come and tell us that someone was barking mad by applying the M'Naughten Rules, but anything short of that was quite another story. It was not for experts to usurp the function of the judge or jury.

The first real breakthrough in recent years came in the field of family law where psychiatric experts helped courts deal with the difficult issues of child welfare. The exposure of child sexual abuse on a wider scale than had been previously recognized enlarged this role. The courts realized that there was much to learn about the silence and guilt which surrounded such abuse and the dynamic which was created between abused and abuser. In the lead-up to the Children Act, psychiatrists, psychologists as well as paediatricians and social workers were invited to seminars to interact with judges on the subject of children and the law. Increasingly in child care cases the courts sought assistance from psychiatric experts.

In criminal cases, the areas where psychiatric evidence was admitted was carefully circumscribed. Reports could be used in mitigation and to help with the appropriate disposal of a case at the point of sentencing but in the trial itself it was only in homicide cases, where the defence of diminished responsibility was being run, that psychiatrists usually testified. Occasionally psychiatrists would be called to attest to a psychiatric history or automatism.

In the past, classic judicial response when lawyers made applications to call psychiatric evidence was that an understanding of the human condition was all a matter of common sense and jurors were perfectly capable of deciding whether a person was slow-witted or impressionable or attention-seeking without the need for fancy labels or clever specialists. However, the miscarriages of justice which were exposed in the last decade radically altered that perspective. Jurors and judges seemed perplexed and unwilling to believe that people would confess against their own interest. There were human behaviours which were counter-intuitive and made no sense at all until a psychiatrist or psychologist lent us their expertise. In appropriate cases experts in the field were able to show how the vulnerability of particular people could lead to false confessions, especially if they had low intelligence or other susceptibilies.

Psychiatric evidence is also being admitted to support the defence of provocation, e.g. informing the courts about the effects of domestic violence upon women: the profound sense of shame, the inability to leave their abusers, the belief such women can come to have that their partner is omnipotent. I have also called expert evidence in cases where the accused was sexually abused as a child to explain the experience of flashbacks to the original violation, as part of an ongoing post traumatic stress disorder.

Psychiatry is having a significant impact on legal discourse and a recent wave of case law testifies to a radical departure from the past.

In this more receptive courtroom environment, the new discipline of Forensic Psychotherapy has an important role to play in confronting the ignorance which exists about many kinds of offender and in providing an alternative to the simplistic response of locking them up. Incarceration alone never confronts the roots of antisocial or aberrant behaviour but the political jockeying for primacy on law and order means that those who argue for therapeutic responses, either within or outside of a prison setting, receive little public support. It is all the more imperative that the work of practitioners is shared and that within our different professions new perspectives are debated.

I have learned enormously from my collaboration with other professionals but I have a lot more learning to do. It is therefore with great enthusiasm that I congratulate the editors and authors of this fine piece of work which was informative, challenging and proof that the law and psychiatry share very fertile soil.

Helena Kennedy Q C
October 1996

Introduction

The term forensic psychotherapy is a new one and the purpose of this book is to introduce and explore what is a new discipline. Through a series of clinical essays we present readers with the intricacies and complexities encountered in working with the forensic patient – that is, those who are in contact with the law. The authors suggest that effective, impressive and constructive work is achievable with a difficult and disturbed population. Our main priority is to provide the interested reader with a flavour of what happens in the inner world of the forensic patient, indeed to show that such patients have an internal world with a kaleidoscopic quality. We seek to address the intellectual laziness of public figures and their belief that 'we must understand a little less and condemn a little more'. Our authors belong to the 'brave new world' necessary in the present political climate with its return to the 'short sharp shock'. The emphasis of this volume is clinical and by no means claims to be all-inclusive. Last year the first major textbook of forensic psychotherapy, looking at theory and practice, was published (Cordess and Cox 1996) and we see our volume as part of an expanding written body of knowledge. The contributors are all women who have been associated with the editors in the context of a study group for quite some time and they reflect the significant number of new female professionals in the field. Most of them are associated with the Diploma Course on Forensic Psychotherapy, either as faculty members or as students, and they represent a range of core professionals.

The ways in which public authorities approach the management and treatment of offenders sometimes seems capricious. Take the fall-out from the Cleveland child abuse case. This event produced a considerable public shock, so it was not surprising that various authorities felt they had to do something urgently. There was an immediate reaction, with long term destructive consequences for both the families and the different professionals involved. The unthinking midnight raids were the result of stereotypes based on prejudices in which the public expulsion and punishment of the assumed perpetrators was thought to be the magical solution. Here is a powerful illustration of the general wish to split offenders from victims which leaves the system unable to use what has been learnt about cycles of abuse. This was well understood in the enquiry after Cleveland with its injunction that professionals must work together in an integrated way (HMSO 1988).

1

A more recent enquiry, namely that into the case of Jason Mitchell who murdered an elderly couple and his father (Blom-Cooper *et al.* 1996), specifically comments on the fact that the patient's 'inner life was left unexplored by all the clinicians'. It further states:

> Psychiatrists managing offender patients also need skills in psychodynamic assessment. The clinical knowledge on which the management of patients like Jason Mitchell is based should include as far as possible an understanding of their personality development, self-image, and emotional life. The need for psychodynamic assessment is not confined to the relatively small group of patients who are suitable for psychodynamic psychotherapy. Psychodynamic assessment is needed for the wider purpose of contributing to an understanding of the patient's inner world, and the nature of their personal relationship with others, including clinical staff. Adequate training in this area of practice is essential, both for general and forensic psychiatrists. (p.244–245)

Another example of a common stereotype is that of male sexual badness contrasted with the goodness of women. In real life it is not always men who are perpetrators and women who are victims. Easy lies, instead of uncomfortable truths, help neither understanding nor treatment.

The theoretical orientation of this book is psychoanalytic, although in an applied sense. It is beyond our scope to examine the considerable body of work within forensic psychology, with its emphasis on cognitive–behavioural approaches to assessment and treatment; we see the two as complementary (Perkins 1996). Forensic psychotherapy is a new field but psychoanalysis, and an interest in crime and criminality, are no strangers. Freud himself did not write much about criminality apart from a paper on guilt (Freud, S. 1916) but, perhaps more importantly, he struggled in his later work to come to grips with the nature of aggression and destructiveness. Since then psychodynamic thinking has evolved techniques over many years of practice which avoid the need to go in for crash methods of treatment. Offenders in analytic psychotherapy are treated like other patients except for certain modifications of technique designed with the patients' welfare in mind.

The UK has, from a very early stage, been at the forefront of forensic psychotherapy. The Association for the Scientific Treatment of Delinquency and Crime was founded in 1931, the title being proposed by the eminent psychoanalyst Dr Glover, who became the first chairman of the Portman Clinic, an NHS out-patient clinic for the treatment of social and sexual deviancy.

From the start, the founding members of the Association, from which eventually the Portman Clinic sprang aimed to:

(1)   Initiate and promote scientific research into the causes and prevention of crime.

(2)   Establish observation centres and clinics for diagnosis and treatment of delinquency and crime.

(3)   Co-ordinate and consolidate existing scientific work in the prevention of delinquency and crime.

(4)   Secure co-operation between all bodies engaged in similar work in all parts of the world, and ultimately to promote an international organization.

(5)   Assist and advise through the medium of scientific experts the judicial and magisterial bench, the hospitals and government departments in the investigation, diagnosis, and treatment of suitable cases (this aim was revised somewhat in 1938).

(6)   Promote and assist in promoting educational and training facilities for students in the scientific study of delinquency and crime.

(7)   Promote discussion and educate the opinion of the general public on these subjects by publications and other means.

These original seven points remain valid and constitute a satisfactory outline description of the objectives of forensic psychotherapy today.

In more recent years there has also been rapid expansion of forensic psychiatry as a speciality within psychiatry. With the Butler report in 1975 the numbers of consultant posts and beds in medium secure units has been significantly increased, although demand continues to rise. The special hospitals have ceased to be hidden containers of forgotten patients and doctors: they have developed and become more integrated within the National Health Service.

There has been a significant increase in the research of so-called mentally disordered offenders with figures of between 15 per cent and 34 per cent (Gunn *et al.* 1978) of all prisoners being identified as current psychiatric cases. In many ways the concerns and preoccupations of those in forensic psychiatry are not so different from those early psychoanalysts; for example how can a crime be understood and a criminal appropriately punished and/or treated?

As Professor Bluglass (1990) indicates, forensic psychiatry arises from a complex interaction of disciplines and diverges from the rest of medicine since its concern involves the law or matters pertaining to the law. Three different but interrelated areas have to be dealt with: (1) society, (2) the crime, and (3) the offender. Forensic psychotherapy is concerned above all with the offender; all other elements are to be examined and investigated primarily in order to understand better the offender patient, and to enable us to provide the patient with suitable treatment programmes. There has been resistance to forensic psychotherapy, partly because it is profoundly misunderstood. While our work is often in the news, the distortion of reporting tends to obscure both what has already been achieved and what could be achieved with a better use of resources.

Psychological situations which may lead to crime and antisocial actions are deeply associated with sociological, cultural and historical conditions and these, of course, help to shape the law and mental health care. Many offences have roots which go back into the structure of society and/or the earlier experiences of the mentally disordered offender. There is always a complex interaction between personality and environment with protective factors being as important as pathological ones. As Gallwey (1991) puts it, simplistic explanations are unsatisfactory as they take 'insufficient account of purely destructive, sadistic and revengeful feelings in much criminal behaviour'. There are many questions that need to be asked: Why are individual differences so great? Why do some survive environments better than others? Why do some offenders have a capacity to make use of a therapeutic relationship to learn and grow psychically, while others can only launch destructive attacks on anything good? How can we begin to sort out such factors in our assessments of patients? How can we help psychotherapists and other teams to achieve the right combination of hopefulness and energy and yet avoid the therapeutic evangelism which can so often lead to retaliation born from hopelessness and despair? These questions will not be completely answered but illuminated by many contributions in this book.

We need, too, to rethink the purpose of prisons, and an essential element in such reassessment is to recognize the nature of the disgust, turned into denial, aroused in ourselves by some offences (for a recent discussion see Gilligan 1996).

There has always been a wish for punishment and retribution and policies of tougher sentencing remain very popular 'solutions' even in the face of research quoted even by those institutions not noted for being anti-establishment: 'there is no convincing argument that prison effectively reduces the level of crime, nor does there seem to be a convincing cost benefit argument' (Economist 1996). There is the tendency to associate forensic psychiatry, and particularly forensic psychotherapy, with being 'soft' or 'lax' and excusing offenders. In fact the task of forensic psychotherapy is to help to locate responsibility, by means of understanding, within a person rather than in the environment. Many prisoners feel at home in a prison with its walls, guards and macho culture as it actually matches their internal world so well; thinking is still unavailable and impulses are acted out rather than addressed. The forensic psychotherapist can give meaning to the criminal act: for the sake of the patient and not for his own intellectual satisfaction.

No subject provokes so much confusion and misunderstanding as the problems relating to the mentally disordered offender patient. These include assessment, management, the suitability for treatment and indeed which treatment. There are many dilemmas about treatment indications, and problems of communication can arise between the different professionals dealing with such offenders. It is the responsibility of the therapist to pay as much attention to such communications as he or she pays to what is happening in the treatment room.

Forensic psychotherapists are concerned with the psychodynamic understanding of the particular offender patient and, in this context, the crime becomes important as a means to understand better the psychopathology of the offender. Psychoanalysis, particularly in this country, sees the mind as having an internal world inhabited by internal objects (formed from constitutional factors in addition to early environmental experiences) which act as touchstones for the perception of a patient's reality. The iller a patient is, the more distorted are the internal objects and thus the more distorted the external world becomes. Forensic patients uniquely demonstrate their internal worlds as with their crime they act out something of their internal object relations.

Forensic psychiatry has until recently concentrated on the epidemiology of 'mentally disordered offenders' and concern is now increasingly felt about treatment. Offenders can remain as inpatients for many years, even a life-time, and there is uncertainty as to what to do with them. Psychiatric diagnoses are often of somewhat limited benefit as questions remain unanswered: why does one person with a diagnosis of schizophrenia or depressive illness commit a violent assault and another not? What is it about a particular person, suffering from a particular mental illness that leads to the crime?

Many of those labelled as mentally disordered offenders in the prison and health systems have a diagnosis of schizophrenia or other major mental illness such as manic depressive psychosis or major depressive illness. These are the patients that are most obviously seen to fall in the remit of forensic psychiatrists and, when in acute states of psychosis and disturbance, need immediate treatment, for example transfer to a hospital and medication – in other words the prompt treatment of psychotic illness is the first priority.

Psychoanalysis is a model of mind that can be of assistance in trying to understand a person's internal world although it is by no means all inclusive. It is a model which allows notions both of nature and nurture to co-exist although there are arguments in the field about the relative importance of each. When it comes to a patient suffering from a major psychotic illness it can be more helpful to think of psychodynamic thinking as expanding and opening up phenomenology, rather than the area of aetiology or cause. Thus a forensic psychotherapist can be of great assistance in comprehending the nature of a particular offender and his crime in the context of an institution. Working with such patients has an impact on staff and understanding how the dynamics of the patients are played out amongst staff is essential for the effectiveness of the team. An example was the admission of a man who had violently murdered a baby. Not only he, but also the professionals, had to struggle to face the enormity of this action.

As is well known, 'pure' psychoanalytic psychotherapy with psychotic patients is limited although it has been described (Sohn 1995) and is vital in helping others to understand psychotic phenomena in more depth.

Apart from patients diagnosed with a major mental illness, other groups of patients such as sex offenders or those diagnosed as 'personality disorders' are often heartily disliked by general psychiatrists (and sometimes by forensic psychiatrists), and there is a debate about whether or not they come under the remit of psychiatry at all. Clinicians and units vary in the number of such patients they will attempt to treat. One of the main reasons for this is the skilled nature of the psychological work that is needed to work with such patients. It is also complex to have a mixed population of psychotic and non-psychotic patients in a ward or medium secure unit. Some would argue that forensic psychiatrists must be modest in their scope and concentrate only on those people to whom a clinical diagnosis of a major mental disorder can be given. There is a suggestion that others, inhabitants of prisons, or those with a personality disorder or a perversion should not be the responsibility of the forensic psychiatrist or psychotherapist and hence may remain unassessed and untreated. It is heartening to see the new requirement for sexual offenders with a sentence of over four years to have treatment of some kind, but this is largely being left to the prison service. We would even argue that our interest should not only be in patients (both psychotic and non-psychotic), but should be broad enough to enable professionals to be interested in criminality *per se.*

The assessment of dangerousness, or as it is now called risk assessment, is another area in which forensic psychotherapists have a role. The view we hold is that there is a meaning to the criminal act from the standpoint of the patient which might be discovered, however irrational the assault may seem initially. The law requires somebody to have a guilty mind (*mens rea*) before they can be found guilty of a crime. Similarly, in forensic psychotherapy and forensic psychiatry we are interested in the state of the mind of the person who committed the act, not just the act in itself. This use of the act to gain understanding of the patient's internal world is one of the features that makes forensic psychotherapy different from other branches of psychoanalysis and psychotherapy, where actual behaviours are viewed more metaphorically. The point about forensic patients is that internal scenarios are acted out concretely; fantasies, nightmares or dreams become concrete reality.

Crimes and misdemeanours are directed against society, or so society believes. We must therefore consider the relationship between the offender and society or individual members of society. Recognition of the social system is of vital importance in the institutions where patients are housed. In this professional field society is embodied by the criminal justice system which necessarily affects the patient–therapist relationship. Legal definitions such as 'disorder of mind' do not match clinical ones. Similarly, the term 'mentally disordered offender' is a legal concept applying as it can to any psychiatric diagnosis ranging from dementia through psychosis to personality disorders. It is confusing because even if mental disorder is not raised as a defence or in mitigation it doesn't mean that clinically a psychiatrist would not make a diagnosis of mental illness. One of the purposes of this volume is to facilitate a shared idiom and more understanding. The range of titles reflects the shorthand that has evolved in order for law and medicine to have a common language. It is for this reason too that the volume includes lawyers' points of view. It is vital that forensic psychotherapists have a knowledge of social context because, if not, their presence in court will be unhelpful and treatment will be jeopardized. Courts are, on the whole, hungry for simple explanations, considered opinions and treatments that can actually be implemented. Clinicians also need to be aware of their limitations: namely, what they can and can't comment on and what they must leave for the court to decide.

The therapist must be trained and equipped with insight into his or her own internal world and its motivations, or he/she may unwittingly react to a situation as if he was a normal member of the public. This is natural but inadequate, since we must be concerned not primarily with society's problems but with the patient's. Proper training of the treaters is also essential since we have to be aware of the potential danger of being caught in the transferential process, which can become perverse or violent in no time at all. In the words of Murray Cox 'there is a constant need to distinguish prudential fear from countertransference. A forensic psychotherapist who has never been frightened, is like a surgeon who has never lost a swab' (1992).

Whereas we would like to stress the importance of treatment, it is crucial to recognize that successful treatment rests not only with the professional psychotherapist but also with a multi-professional team in an inpatient setting and the team of helpers, including the clerical staff in an outpatient setting. The total surroundings from the character of the building to the welcome of the receptionist *matter*.

The bulk of this book, then, constitutes a series of clinical chapters examining a range of psychopathologies associated with different criminal, or potentially criminal behaviours (for example attacks on self are often forgotten precursors of violence and cruelty against others). Also there are areas of pathology much neglected in psychiatry, namely crimes against property such as burglary as well as cheating, stealing and fraud.

Many patients that we meet have histories of childhood victimization and for this reason the clinical cases begin with two chapters exploring the dynamics of sexual abuse in the family and the precursors of antisocial behaviour as seen in children. References from all the chapters point the way to writings which discuss theoretical issues in more detail.

Aetiology of the criminal behaviour is explored but the cases emphasize the problems of management and care in the here and now – in other words there is an emphasis on phenomenology as well as aetiology. At a time when work has to be justified and shown to be effective the volume includes chapters on audit and research, an area neglected by psychotherapists and psychoanalysts for too long.

Much of the work described by the authors is courageous; patients like those in this book can stretch therapists to their utmost with their impaired capacity to think and their tendency to act out in a destructive way. Via the transference and counter-transference, a therapist can so easily be pushed into enactment. Conversely, forensic patients can also make remarkable progress, if properly assessed with clear selection criteria and adequate treatment programmes that are implemented with the support and co-operation of the rest of the team. Forensic patients cannot be seen in isolation.

Violence, crime and 'societal disintegration' are topical issues in these years approaching the end of the millennium. It has taken *only* sixty-five years for the seven original aims to be partly accomplished, yet in 1996 there seems once again to be a prevailing notion about an increase in natural evil and badness, a return to harsh fears with a concurrent rise in a desire for punishment and retribution. At the same time there is a push towards evidence-based medicine and rational solutions to problems. What is politically expedient does not always match up with the most effective or efficient solution to a problem. Understanding seems to enter societal thought for a period of time, as reflected in enlightened treatment regimes such as the Portman Clinic, the Henderson Hospital and Peper Harow. However, such periods are often followed by others where there is a return to incarceration as a solution. The Portman Clinic lives, but the Henderson has been under serious threat of closure and Peper Harow has actually been closed down.

Our book demonstrates, however, that there is another trend; a trend amongst professionals to acknowledge the work in trying to understand the criminal mind and to implement this kind of understanding in a practical way.

A major cross-disciplinary effort should be made to understand and eradicate at least some of the more correctable reasons for crime in our societies. This obviously involves political scientists, sociologists and community leaders as well as forensic workers. To judge from what is currently appearing in the press, a major effort is required to promote discussion and to educate the opinion of the general public. Forensic psychotherapists can, and must, play a crucial role in this, but the main burden must fall on those in the media and in politics who have special communicating skills.

These efforts cannot and should not be confined to individual countries. The problems are universal even if they take special forms in different societies, and we shall make more progress more rapidly if we cooperate internationally. With this in mind the International Association for Forensic Psychotherapy was set up in 1991 during the XVII Congress of the Academy of Law and Mental Health. The objectives are, amongst others, to develop interest in and support for forensic psychotherapy internationally, to provide a means for colleagues to cooperate more easily, to facilitate the flow of information, and to encourage communication with members of the legal profession and others involved in the management of offenders. With this in mind we meet annually.

At this formative stage in the development of our subject there is a need for rigorous thinking to ensure that the discipline of forensic psychotherapy is genuinely disciplined.

This means starting from basics and asking crucial questions: What is forensic psychotherapy? What are its objectives and its limitations? How do we see our profession evolving? Given the many systems of law and society world-wide, is the profession to develop in national cells? Or should we rather stress the international dimensions of our profession?

This book seeks to shed light on some of the questions raised in this introduction and the editors hope it will be of interest to colleagues and other professionals involved in these difficult problems.

PART I

Forensic Psychotherapy
The Practical Approach

Estela V. Welldon

INTRODUCTION

Forensic psychotherapy is a new discipline, being the offspring of forensic psychiatry and psychoanalytical psychotherapy. Its aim is the psychodynamic comprehension of the offender and his consequent treatment, regardless of the seriousness of the offence. It involves understanding the unconscious, as well as the conscious, motivations of the criminal mind, and of particular offence behaviour. It does not seek to condone the crime or to excuse the criminal. On the contrary, the object is to help the offender acknowledge responsibility for his acts and thereby to save both him and society from the perpetration of further crimes. One of the problems in achieving this object is that the offender attacks, through his actions, the outside world – society – which is immediately affected. Hence, concerns are rarely focused on the internal world of the offender. It is time to re-focus our concerns, at least in part.

Forensic psychotherapy has gone beyond the special relationship between patient and psychotherapist. There is a triangle – patient, psychotherapist and society. As Professor Bluglass (1990) points out, 'The role of the forensic psychiatrist in confronting and trying to reconcile the differences between the interests of the law and those of psychiatry is a crucial and important one' (p.7).

If forensic psychotherapy is the handling of three interacting positions – the therapist's, the patient's and society's criminal justice system (de Smit 1992) – it follows that treatment of the forensic patient population should ideally be carried out within the National Health Service, and not within the private sector. Forensic psychotherapy has to be considered in the overall context of health care for people involved in the criminal justice process. Its aims, however, are not identical to those of the criminal justice system. There is an inevitable, and indeed necessary, conflict of values (Harding 1992). Evaluations should ideally be conducted independently, according to criteria which correspond to health based values (Reed Report 1992).

A discipline such as this needs explanation. For example, society instinctively views sexual offenders and their victims in distinct and reflex ways. Whereas the treatment of victims is encouraged and everyone is concerned about their welfare, the same does not apply to the perpetrators who are believed to be the products of 'evil forces'. Lip service is paid to the fact that victims could easily become perpetrators but emotional responses tend to be biased. A split is in full operation.

Another recurrent stereotype is that in which women are victims and men perpetrators. When men are sexual abusers all sorts of different agencies, social and medical, intervene and very soon the police are called in. By contrast, the female 'offender' finds it very difficult to get a hearing (Welldon 1988). Nobody wants to hear about her predicament, and nobody takes her too seriously. Until recently a lack of legislation on female perversion reflected society's total denial of it. There is no getting away from the fact that the offender's actions are blatantly carried out against society or those principles society values, and which we all share. Accordingly, a wide range of people are inescapably involved.

A crucial point about the discipline of forensic psychotherapy is that it is a team effort and not an heroic action by the psychotherapist alone. Successful treatment rests not only with the professional psychotherapist but also with a team of helpers, including psychologists, social workers, administration and the clerical staff.

For the general public it is, no doubt, society which matters most, but for the professional forensic psychotherapist the prime consideration must be the patient. If forensic psychotherapy is concerned above all with the patient, it should be scarcely less concerned with the 'treater' and his training.

The UK has, from an early stage, been in the forefront of forensic psychotherapy and, within the UK, the Portman Clinic has been the leader. The history of the Clinic goes back to 1931, when a small group of men and women psychoanalysts met in London and established an Association to promote a better way of dealing with criminals than putting them in prison. Much later, in 1991, the original aims of the Portman Clinic were adopted by the newly established International Association for Forensic Psychotherapy. Barely a year earlier, in 1990, the first Course on Forensic Psychotherapy based at the Portman Clinic under the aegis of the BPMF and presently under the CPMD (Continuing Professional Medical Development) University College London began to train national and international professionals in the techniques of this special branch of psychotherapy.

THE CRIMINAL ACT

The criminal action is the central fact. Sometimes it has the capacity to become explosive, violent and uncontrollable with attendant profound consequences for society. At times, it is the equivalent of a neurotic symptom. Pfäfflin (1992) describes the symptom as a constructive and healthy reaction. He adds that it is 'conservative', meaning that the patient needs it and keeps it until it can be properly understood and then he can give it up. At other times, it is the expression of more severe psychopathology; it is secretive, completely encapsulated and split from the rest of the patient's personality, which acts as a defence against a psychotic illness (Hopper 1991); at still other times, it is calculated and associated with professional, careerist criminality. The criminal action always appears understandable as an action against society and yet, at the same time, it is a self-destructive act, with harmful effects for the offender.

The action may be characterized by a manic defence, created against the acknowledgement or recognition of a masked chronic depression. Alternatively it may include compulsion, impulsivity, inability to intersperse thought before action and, as mentioned earlier, a total failure to understand it.

THE FORENSIC PATIENT

The forensic patient, identified in the legal system as a mentally disordered offender, can have a psychopathology ranging from dementia to overtly psychotic, including psychopathic personalities. They all share an inability to think before the action occurs because they are not mentally equipped to make the necessary links (Bion 1959). The thinking process is not functioning in the particular area of psychopathology, for example the psychosis in someone with schizophrenia and the perversion in a sex offender (often encapsulated from the rest of his personality) Hopper 1991. The work of therapy is to help links to be made but at times the patient's tendency to make sadistic attacks on his own capacity for thought and reflection is projected and directed against the therapist's capacity to think and reflect, and it is then that the therapist feels confused, numbed and unable to make any useful interpretations.

It is important to make a basic distinction between offenders who are mentally disordered and those who are not. Some offenders have a professional orientation towards their criminal activities. For example, they calculate the consequences, even going so far as to engage in a cost-benefit planning of their actions, involving such matters as how many months or years in prison they are prepared to risk. In other words, such offenders may not differ in important psychological traits from careerists generally. These two seemingly different categories do at times overlap or succeed one another. It is not unusual to find patients who have been criminal 'careerists' for a number of years but who on reaching their thirties begin to question the validity of what they are doing and express a deep interest in seeking professional help to change their life-styles.

An important group of offenders mentioned before are those suffering from psychotic illness. Some may be amenable to individual treatment (Sohn 1995) but in general psychodynamic thinking can be helpful in understanding management by investigating the impact of such patients in an institution such as a medium secure unit or a special hospital.

The patients I shall explore in more detail, with regard to assessment, are those seen in outpatient clinics with a diagnosis of personality disorder or sexual perversion.

Most forensic patients have deeply disturbed backgrounds. Some have criminal records and very low self-esteem which is often covered by a façade of cockiness and arrogance; their impulse control is minimal and they are suspicious and filled with hate towards people in authority. Some rebellious and violent ex-convicts have long histories of crime against property and persons. Others may refer themselves and in these cases are often insecure, inadequate and ashamed people. They enact their pathological sexual deviancy, such as exhibitionism, paedophilia and voyeurism, in a very secretive manner so that only their victims know about their behaviour. Some patients have a great capacity for expressing anger, yet seem shy and awkward in showing tenderness or love to anybody.

Often, forensic patients are deviant both sexually and socially. For example, some sexual deviations present themselves as criminal activities by definition, although some patients who indulge in these actions may never have been caught. This is a secret or secretive population who apparently lead normal lives, sometimes in both work and domestic situations. However, the links between criminal actions such as 'breaking and entering' and sexual deviations are not always obvious, at least not until the unconscious motivation is revealed.

THE ASSESSMENT

The psychodynamic assessment requires a wide understanding of all factors concerning that particular person; his psychological growth, his family – taking it back at least three generations – his own sub-culture, and other circumstances. The psychotherapist needs to investigate the 'crimes' in detail, especially the sequence of events leading up to the action as well as the offender's reaction to it. This can give clues to early traumatic experiences, and to the unconscious ways through which an individual tries to resolve conflicts resulting from these experiences. In this way, even during the evaluation itself, the psychotherapist is able slowly to uncover layers of primitive defences and the motivations behind them – enabling us to learn about the offender's capacity or incapacity for psychodynamic treatment, as well as initiating a process whereby the offender might acquire insight into the nature of his crimes.

In order to assess treatability for psychotherapy accurately in these patients we must modify terms and concepts from those used in assessing neurotic patients. For example, when the criminal action is committed clumsily, the person is especially susceptible to detection. The criminal action has become the equivalent of the neurotic symptom. The offender may also express fears of a custodial sentence, which may denote, in his own terms, motivation for treatment. This could signal that it is the appropriate time to start treatment, since the patient is susceptible, however much under implied duress. He is now ready to own his psychopathology and this may indicate an incipient sense of capacity for insight. From this therapeutic standpoint, it is not unfortunate that a patient has to face prosecution, but what is unfortunate is that just when he is ready for treatment he may instead have to face punishment. The patient may actually acquire a criminal record for the first time while in treatment or on the waiting list. Ironically, the very success of our treatment may produce this result. It is when the patient who has hitherto escaped detection starts to acquire some insight into himself that he becomes clumsy and is detected. So, in a way, it may be said that psychotherapy results in a higher rate of official, statistical criminality!

THE CIRCUMSTANCES OF ASSESSMENT

Setting and surroundings are important – especially since the forensic patient has usually had previous experience of the judicial system, having been caught, detected and judged. In his dealing with the psychotherapist, he is prone to feel judged, charged, persecuted, and subject to prejudice. Institutions should provide structures to protect the therapists from the inherent anxiety produced by working with forensic patients. If the diagnostician is not well trained, a new confrontation could easily be experienced by the prospective patient as a further condemnation of his/her illegal action.

Because of their fears of intimacy in the one-to-one situation these patients form a strong transference to the Clinic as an institution. The institution treating them can become as important as, or more so, than the therapist himself. A safe and containing atmosphere in which the patients feel secure and acknowledged from the moment of their arrival is essential.

INSTITUTIONAL SETTING

The institution reinforces a sense of boundaries and so acts as a container for all tensions involved and allows the emergence of trust and a collective awareness of, and sensitivity to, the recrudescence of violence, reducing its likelihood.

The topic of forensic psychotherapy and its contribution to forensic psychiatry in an institutional setting has been described by Cox (1983). The failure of psychotherapy to thrive within specifically the British Special Hospitals is critically examined by Pilgrim (1987).

TRANSFERENCE

It is necessary to understand the personality traits of forensic patients since they lead directly into an understanding of the transference and counter-transference phenomena, which appear from the beginning of the assessment and during the psychodynamic treatment. The following points are essential.

(1)   The need to be in control, which is apparent from the moment they are first seen and also during treatment.

(2)   Early experiences of deprivation and subjection to seductiveness make them vulnerable to anything which in any way is reminiscent of the original experiences.

(3)   A desire for revenge expressed in sadomasochism as an unconscious need to inflict harm.

(4)   Erotization or sexualization of the action.

(5)   Manic defence against depression.

There are very elaborate and sophisticated unconscious mechanisms which these patients have built up in themselves, which operate as a 'self-survival kit': this is 'turned on' automatically in situations of extreme vulnerability when they experience being psychically naked or 'stripped'.

COUNTER-TRANSFERENCE

These patients act out sadistic and intrusive attacks on therapists and on their treatment in many different ways, including on their capacity to think: this leaves therapists confused and unable to offer adequate interpretations.

Money matters are important both in concrete and in symbolic terms. This is obvious with patients whose day to day living is provided by their own or close associates' delinquent or perverse actions. A frequent problem is the offer or 'pushing' of a gift which could at times render the therapist a receiver of stolen goods.

The therapists' inner knowledge that the State is paying for their professional services becomes invaluable while working with this patient population, since they are also aware of this basic fact. It reinforces both parties in the contractual agreement on which the therapy is based. The therapists are debarred from blackmail and the patients feel neither exploited nor able to exploit anybody about money matters.

The psychotherapist must listen to the patient carefully, without interrupting, however difficult or painful the material may be. Some supposedly 'unusual' or 'rare' predicaments are not that unusual: the so-called rarity is often due to the clinician's inability to listen because of the psychic pain involved. This is frequently the case with incestuous relationships. It is important to be aware of how our own feelings may be the origin, for example, of the under-recording of female perversions – such as female paedophilia and maternal incest. Patients may be ready to talk about these urges but diagnosticians generally are not ready to listen to them. The requirement of personal therapy for future treaters is of basic importance – in order to be able to discern what belongs to the treater's internal world and what to the patient. Most of these patients' material can disturb profoundly because at times it feels like dealing with 'dynamite'. Sometimes, if unprepared, the therapist could easily become irate, as if he or she is being 'taken for a ride', and indeed the patient often tries to be in total control of the situation. In other instances, patients succeed in making their therapists become their true partners in their specific perversions.

Alternatively, the treater may feel flattered by the fact that whatever positive change may have been achieved, the patients may ascribe to the practitioner's own professional efforts. However, the flattery won't last for long; it will soon be replaced by complaints and dissatisfaction about relapses or re-offending assumed to be due to the practitioner's inefficiency and lack of 'skills', just as before the 'cure' of the problem had to do with his/her excellence.

In other words, there is a constant switch between idealization and denigration. This happens because psycho-pathological predicaments and offending behaviour are the result of a deep, chronic, hidden depression. This turns into a manic and at times bizarrely funny acting out. There is so much pain underneath that the patients barely manage at times to confront it. They try at all costs to avoid their real feelings. The therapist could easily be caught in the counter-transference process, assuming an omnipotent role in the patient's actions regardless of whether they are law abiding or not.

CONCLUSIONS

In short, the assessment is to be carried out like any other assessment but, if anything, with even more care and sensitivity. With forensic psychotherapy in action it is foreseeable that the more we understand about the criminal mind the more we can take positive preventive action. This, in turn, could lead to better management and the implementation of more cost effective treatment of patients.

2

Management and Treatment

Caecilia Taylor

INTRODUCTION

The forensic psychotherapist can be asked to contribute to both clinical and legal decisions that need to be made about mentally disordered offenders at almost any stage of the criminal justice process. This involvement often encompasses much more than simply whether or not to accept an individual into conventional therapy: assessment can be extremely valuable for diagnostic purposes, for recommending a treatment disposal to the court, or for providing an understanding of the patient's personality for colleagues planning or struggling with approaches other than the purely psychodynamic. An opinion may also be requested on the suitability of this model for a particular patient, whether in an individual or a group setting – and by no means all are sufficiently self-reflective, or able to lower their rigid defences without succumbing to florid psychotic breakdown. Sometimes less intensive, supportive work will serve a more beneficial (and less dangerous to the patient or others) 'propping up' function; sometimes the focus might most usefully be on a specific problem closely related to the offending behaviour, such as substance misuse or sexuality. Having gained detailed and intimate knowledge about the inner world of patients in such treatment, either personally or via supervision, the forensic psychotherapist will have perhaps the most legitimate grounds for expressing optimism or pessimism about its success. He or she therefore has a valuable role to play too in an assessment of the risks involved in any plans for release into the community.

Whatever the decision, it is especially important with offender patients, as well as being a formal requirement of the Care Programme Approach (Department of Health 1990) that all those contributing to their management are aware of the specific aims, progress and outcome of each other's contact. While the issues of confidentiality are complex, knowledge that others might be exposed to serious danger can never be sacrosanct. The forensic psychotherapist therefore has a responsibility to ensure that at the very least basic information about attendance and progress, and sometimes evidence of acting out, or the possibility that the patient has actually become involved in further offending, is exchanged speedily and reliably. It will be helpful, therefore, to have an understanding of the structure and workings of the criminal justice process and how these relate, both externally and symbolically, to the individual who is subject to it.

PATHWAYS TO TREATMENT

Self-Referral

It is by no means inevitable that patients come to attention simply because they have been 'caught in the act' or subsequent to it. Some will seek referral themselves, because of their increasing concerns about internal longings to commit illegal acts, or their actual commission, or a realization that the one is increasingly leading to the other. While on one level there is a deep need for enactment, and an anticipation that this will provide relief, on another there is the acknowledgement that it can never bring lasting satisfaction. Such individuals will often present with neurotic symptoms such as anxiety, depression, or difficulty sustaining what they see as normal sexual relationships.

Clinical vignette

A young Italian man was referred by a youth counsellor in whom he had confided his increasingly violent fantasies of rape. Although he had never yet committed this offence, it emerged that he frequently stalked young girls in parts of town where he knew he would not be recognized, and exposed himself to them. It was his fear that he would one day be caught, rather than compunction, that led him to seek help, although he also suffered from depression and panic attacks, and was deeply confused about his sexual orientation. At the heart of his wish to humiliate women in the worst way possible, was his rage and longing towards his bullying yet provocative mother, whose love was tied up in the memory of his dead twin and her unfaithful husband. In sessions his need to punish declined as his anxieties and confusions were acknowledged, contained and above all respected.

A similar example of the type of preventive work done in a forensic out-patient setting includes an ex-army sergeant referred by his GP whose recurrent, irritable depression led to impulses to commit extreme acts of violence in response to minor irritations in his interactions with strangers that he could only just control, but was keen to rid himself of.

Arrest

Many patients, however, are unable or unwilling to intervene on their own behalf to put a stop to their offending. The manner in which it (sooner or later) comes to the attention of the police can give extraordinarily interesting clues about key, habitual patterns of functioning – or malfunctioning – of the unconscious mind. The young man on a spree of burglaries who forgot to wear his gloves; the battering husband who repeatedly disobeyed injunctions banning him from his wife's house; the teenage girl who strangled her new-born baby and hid it in the wardrobe – all made it possible, even easy, for society to step in, like some all-embracing parent figure or externally-represented super-ego, and say 'no'. All also denied some aspect of the reality of their behaviour.

There is an argument that much, if not all, offending behaviour has its roots in psychopathology, but in practice it is often a matter of chance as to whether individual clinical need is recognized or responded to. The initial contact of an offender following arrest is of course with the police, and even they have a responsibility – by no means easily fulfilled – under the Police and Criminal Evidence Act 1984 (Home Office 1985) to recognize mental illness, and to provide an 'appropriate adult' to be present during their interviews with anyone whom they suspect of suffering. This may be a relative, probation officer, social worker, psychiatrist or someone similar. The alleged offender must also be given access to a solicitor, who may themselves be sufficiently experienced to ask for a psychiatric assessment, either then – or later, if the problem has not been recognized immediately.

Being arrested and questioned, sometimes for hours, is a bewildering experience for many offenders. It could be the first time for months or years that a young delinquent is confronted with limit-setting, or mean the dawning of realization on the part of an older person as to how seriously he has betrayed himself and others. Most will feel frightened, confused, intimidated or angry; occasionally, the predominant emotion of the recidivist whose crimes are escalating is relief, because they know they might well have gone on to do something so much worse. Tape-recordings are always made of police interviews, and may be made available to psychiatrists later on request. These are well worth listening to, as they give clinicians the closest 'live' account of the patient's mental state at the time of the crime, and how he reacted to his offending being both detected and curbed.

THE INITIAL COURT APPEARANCE

If charges are to be pressed, the individual will be held in the police cells overnight and produced in the local magistrates' court the following day. Depending upon the seriousness of the purported crime, and his plea, he may either be dealt with there and then, given bail, or be remanded into custody. Some magistrates' courts now also have one or two members of a psychiatric 'diversion' team (see James and Hamilton 1992 for an account) in attendance, who will screen those due to appear, and if appropriate make initial recommendations to the court and/or arrange their admission to hospital. With few staff, little time and often no independent informants, however, they may only be able to detect the most severe mental illness, and even this is not always possible.

REMAND INTO CUSTODY

For the more serious offender remanded into custody, imprisonment almost always represents a severe stress, even if is not for the first time. This is important for the therapist to realize, whether he or she is holding regular sessions in the prison, making a special visit to assess an individual, or only becomes involved in treatment at a later stage, because the experience often remains vivid in the memory. Family and social relationships (positive or ambivalent) are suddenly severed, and income or employment often threatened. Remand prisons tend to be severely over-crowded and busy, with a rapid turnover of inmates, making it difficult to get to know, much less trust, fellow prisoners or staff. Bullying and violent attacks are common enough to engender a legitimate sense of paranoia. Sex offenders are the traditional target (or, in women's prisons, child abusers), and are thus often placed at their own request on 'Rule 43', or in a separate wing for their own protection. Many prison officers are very supportive, but nevertheless a 'them' and 'us' culture usually reigns.

What tends to preoccupy inmates above all, however, is the injustice – as they perceive it – of their situation: at this stage it can be hard to direct a discussion to any topic other than that of their complete innocence, their guilt of much else but not this crime, the 'unfairness' (and occasionally alleged brutality) of police tactics, or the trumped-up nature of the evidence against them. The defence mechanisms of splitting and projective identification described by Melanie Klein (1940) operate with particular force in prisons, leading to disownership of the bad parts of the self and the location of guilt and responsibility in the object: hence the almost traditional resentment on the part of inmates towards the authority figures responsible for their custody and control.

These defences also serve to protect against the sense of emotional inadequacy and awareness of dependency needs, since they 'rely, via omnipotent fantasy, on self-idealization, with devaluing of qualities within essential relationships, and deny the necessity for real adaptation, reparation or the management of suffering' (Gallwey 1990). Such patients will find it hard to submit to the feelings of vulnerability inherent in, and necessary to, the therapeutic process. By the same token, they will tend to split the staff of any team caring for them into bad (those experienced as hated, feared and attacking) and good (those there is a need to placate). In the case of the latter, there may even be an attempt to bring the object down to the patient's own level, by seducing that figure identified with parental introjects, in order to 'reduce one's own sense of unworthiness' (see Rycroft 1968 for a useful definition of 'corruption of the super-ego').

It can take many months, and occasionally over a year, especially if the plea is one of not guilty, for those more serious cases that are referred to crown court (including the Central Criminal Court or 'Old Bailey') to come to trial. Inmates therefore have much time to think about themselves and their frequently very damaged lives. Feelings of guilt and failure can be overwhelming, and the risk of suicide among remand prisoners is very high. The commonest methods are the most violent, including hanging and setting fire to one's cell (often not recognized as an act of deliberate self-harm). Strenuous efforts have been made in recent years to improve the detection of those at risk. Some will have access to Samaritans' schemes, while the most vulnerable, if recognized as such, are admitted to the health care centre for a period; since those facing a murder charge fall into this category, they are often placed there automatically on reception. Unfortunately, the policy of *not* placing suicidal inmates in bare strip cells for their own protection (the idea being to deprive them of anything they might conceivably use to harm themselves) is still not widely implemented. As a result, prisoners will often keep their distress to themselves, rather than face this brutal form of isolation.

Clinical vignette

A woman charged with the murder of her husband was received into the prison health care centre, where she was noted to lie on her bed for hours at a time but to be sleeping poorly. During an interview with the prison medical officer, she expressed suicidal ideas. Her two young children had been placed in emergency foster care. She was – unusually – completely compliant with the prison regime and even 'obeyed' an invitation to meet weekly with the visiting psychotherapist. She talked superficially of a 'near-perfect' marriage, and seemed to want her therapist (who was aware of forensic evidence that she had been raped) to be able to 'extract' from her details of its darker side. Interpretations to this effect gradually enabled her to begin to take responsibility for what she wished, and did not wish to 'give'. It was her decision, eventually, that her account of her husband's behaviour should be incorporated into a report for the court.

The importance of recognizing acute mental disorder, such as depression or psychosis, during the remand phase is obviously that immediate treatment can then be given, either in prison, or by transferring the patient out to a psychiatric hospital (under the terms of the Mental Health Act, 1983 prison health care centres are not recognized as places where treatment can be given against a patient's will). If personality disorder (a diagnosis that is often missed in the prison setting; Brooke, Taylor, Gunn and Maden 1996) is suspected, an in-patient assessment period of up to six months is allowed so that clinicians can determine whether the individual is 'treatable'. This is a requirement of the current Mental Health Act, but is a controversial area involving difficult judgements about a person's motivation and ability to change. In either case, the patient usually stays in hospital until the time of the trial, but will still have to attend court; if necessary, the case is delayed until the defendant is recovered sufficiently to be, legally speaking, 'fit to plead and stand trial' (see Bowden and Dooley 1995 for an account).

Whether or not actual transfer is necessary, it is also important to gather evidence of mental disorder for presentation to the court, since this may substantially affect the outcome of the trial. This evidence can be used in two ways: first, to support the argument that the defendant is not guilty because he was not fully responsible for his actions. The plea here can be one of insanity (rarely), diminished responsibility, or infanticide; all but the former apply to charges of murder, and must be established if the mandatory life sentence is to be avoided. Second, evidence can be presented, after a finding of guilt, in mitigation; in other words to reduce the severity of the sentence and/or to persuade the judge to include a treatment component in it. The decision to introduce evidence of mental disorder can be made by the defence, the prosecution, or the judge, and usually two psychiatrists (one for each side) are instructed to assess the patient by visiting him in prison, where he is living on bail, or while he is in hospital. It is almost always best for a forensic psychotherapist who is already involved at this stage to avoid also being the author of the report, so as to ensure that the boundaries of the therapeutic relationship, as well as its confidentiality, are kept as clearly delineated as possible. This need not mean, however, a complete prohibition on his or her contributing to the thinking behind its conclusions and recommendations, in which the patient can, indeed should, participate.

THE TRIAL

The trial is a highly important event for any offender, especially when the charges are grave and the outcome stands to affect his life for a long time to come. Defendants usually take it very seriously, and I have seen even the most hardened and anti-authoritarian dress in their smartest, cleanest, newest clothes (although not necessarily a suit and tie!), which seems to be symbolic of the respect they feel the proceedings deserve. Any perceived miscarriage of justice will be resented and brooded upon for years; attempts to appeal (almost always legally aided) against conviction or sentence are common. Others, however, look to the punishment meted out to assuage their enormous sense of guilt, and any sense that it is insufficient for the payment of retributive dues can seriously delay a patient's ability to 'move on', in therapy, from some terrible past act towards a future.

DISPOSAL

While the term conjures up images of getting rid of rubbish, it actually refers to what fate the judge decides is in store for an individual who has just been convicted. At the time of writing, unless the offence is murder the judge has complete discretion as to sentencing, and practice varies widely depending on his or her views of the case, and knowledge as to what health care services are available.

Treatment can, of course, be undertaken voluntarily (although in prison it is hard to get), but there are also several options that include a mandatory component. Even some very serious offences such as infanticide (where the contribution of psychopathology is considerable, and the risk to the public negligible) can, and often do, lead to a probation order with psychiatric supervision as a condition; this may be anything from regular hospital out-patient or community psychiatric care, to psychological approaches (such as cognitive behavioural work) or, of course, psychotherapy. The patient also has to see a designated probation officer at the required intervals, who should report any failure to obey the conditions of the order to the court. Theoretically, a prison sentence can then be imposed, but in practice even non-compliant individuals do not often seem to be formally 'breached'. The maximum duration of a probation order with psychiatric treatment as a condition is three years.

If the crime and the illness are more serious, after hearing psychiatric evidence the judge can impose a 'hospital order' (Section 37 of the Mental Health Act 1983) *instead* of a prison sentence. The patient is sent to a psychiatric hospital for treatment and can be discharged at any time the consultant responsible for his care judges him to have recovered. If it is judged that the risk to the public could be great for quite some time to come, a 'restriction order' (Section 41) can also be recommended (by two psychiatrists), although its actual imposition is entirely at the discretion of the judge. It can be for a designated period (say five years), or, much more commonly, and because of the difficulties of predicting treatment outcome in the long-term, unlimited in time. Patients under a restriction order can only be discharged from hospital with the agreement of the Home Office, or by a special Mental Health Review Tribunal, which must be chaired by judge, or a recorder who is a QC. Discharge can be 'conditional' – on the patient's accepting continuing psychiatric and social work supervision in the community, and liable to instant recall to hospital if he does not – or 'absolute'.

SERVING A SENTENCE

Convicted prisoners have far fewer privileges than those on remand, and together with prior vulnerability, the institutionalization and isolation produced in those serving a long sentence (most lose all contact with their wives or girlfriends), plus the high prevalence of drug misuse, mean that many become ill some time after the trial; depression and anxiety are particularly common. 'Lifers' are particularly prone, being 'almost by definition mentally abnormal or sexually deviant' in a series of studies by Sapsford (1983). If identified, mentally ill prisoners serving a sentence can also be transferred out into a hospital for treatment under the Mental Health Act (1983).

There is little in the way of psychiatric treatment offered to sentenced prisoners, even when it is thought appropriate (and again, opinions on individual cases vary widely). HMP Grendon offers, on a voluntary basis, both acute psychiatric care and therapeutic community-style treatment (described by Selby 1991) with a considerable group psychodynamic component, for those with personality disorder, but the number of places is very limited and no such facility exists for women. The Sex Offender Treatment Programme (described by Thornton and Hogue 1993) has been operating for the last few years in a number of designated prisons. Depending on the nature and frequency of the offending, and length of sentence, prisoners undergo a core or extended programme, with a 'booster' prior to release. Although not strictly compulsory, the consequence of choosing not to take part may be loss of remission or parole. It is implemented by prison officers with a basic training, supervised by prison psychologists, and is largely cognitive-behavioural in approach.

It is commonly supposed – almost assumed – by many members of the public that offenders will malinger mental disorder as an excuse for their crimes, or in order to get sent to hospital rather than prison, where conditions are much less punitive. This does sometimes happen, but in practice ignorance of the subtleties of psychiatric symptoms makes them hard to feign successfully, especially for any length of time. The culture amongst the majority of offenders is, however, one of enormous stigma against anyone who seems in danger of getting 'nutted off'. Of a series of 203 men remanded into custody on a range of charges from serious violence to lesser non-violent offences, not one of the subsample of 121 men who *were* in fact psychotic offered 'madness' as an excuse (Taylor 1985). Much more common is a profound fear of madness, which often stems from a complete lack of understanding or awareness of the inner precipitants of what they know is 'abnormal' behaviour, which is therefore frighteningly beyond their control.

FORENSIC PSYCHIATRIC HEALTH SERVICES

Special Hospitals

Hospital services for the mentally disordered offender exist across a range of levels of security. At the maximum secure end of the spectrum, there are currently three special hospitals in England: Ashworth, Rampton and Broadmoor; these have very recently become self-managing special health authorities. A new high security psychiatric commissioning board has also just been established, which may in future decide to purchase these services from new providers, such as those already running medium secure services, or the private sector. Special hospitals take the most serious offenders (including a small number of women) who are considered a grave and immediate risk to the public, and rely on a high degree of both perimeter and internal security. The nursing staff are not only trained in control and restraint techniques, but how to deal with dangerous untoward incidents such as hostage-taking.

The special hospitals are increasingly offering treatments focused upon particular problem; at Broadmoor, for example, units exist for substance misusers (described by McKeown *et al.* 1996 *et seq*), and for young 'psychopaths' (Reiss, Grubin and Meux 1996), and there is an expanding forensic psychotherapy department with academic and clinical interests. The hospital also has excellent workshop, training and education facilities. In the past, conditions in the special hospitals, and the treatment meted out to their patients, have been heavily criticized (eg: Department of Health 1992); but much was done in the early 1990s to improve outmoded practices such as the over-use of seclusion (which used to be universal at night), and to reduce professional isolation.

Medium Secure Units

Previously called regional secure units, when regions were still in existence, these are locked, self-contained buildings with a moderate degree of internal security, but no perimeter wall. They take patients from special hospitals who are thought to be ready for gradual rehabilitation into the community, or, conversely, patients from general psychiatric wards or prisons who need assessment and treatment at a higher level of security, usually because of a worrying degree of violence in the context of their illness. The risk to the public must be perceived as less than would qualify them for a special hospital (and the Home Office has a say in the decision), as escape *is* possible given sufficient determination. Moreover, patients can abscond once they are well enough – and trusted enough – to be given escorted or (eventually) unescorted leave, and it is impossible always accurately to evaluate the risk of this happening. Most, however, do not, and are rehabilitated into flats or supported hostels. The idea is that this should be achievable in about two years, so that beds do not become 'blocked'.

Medium secure units vary greatly in size, from about 15 patients to over 60. They cater largely for psychotic patients, as those with a personality disorder are perceived as far more difficult to treat, and requiring input over a much longer period. They are mixed, but are almost always dominated by men, which, although all have single rooms, can be difficult for a lone woman patient. The small size of some of the units means that a wide variety of occupational therapies cannot be provided, let alone work training. Once a patient has been discharged, he or she will usually be offered out-patient follow-up, social work supervision (both mandatory if the discharge is conditional and a restriction order remains in place) and, increasingly, a community forensic psychiatric nursing service. There is still a considerable short-fall in the number of beds actually required in this sector, and most have to operate a waiting list; increasingly, patients are admitted temporarily into private medium secure units (often some distance away) until space becomes available. Many units are currently expanding in a government initiative to try to cope with demand, but there is also a great shortage of qualified professionals of all kinds to staff them.

Locked Wards and Intensive Care Units

These tend to be specialized wards within district general hospital psychiatric units. They are designed to manage patients with 'challenging behaviour', who may or may not have a criminal history or be facing current charges. Ironically, they tend to have to cope with higher levels of 'disturbed' behaviour than some medium secure units, and even many wards in special hospitals. Not infrequently, an opinion is sought from the forensic team at the local medium secure unit, or a referral made for a patient to be admitted there for a period until stabilized on treatment. These smaller, 'low secure' units are not ideal for patients who require a long admission as they often lack large day areas or grounds in which the patients can be taken out on parole. On the other hand, they are likely to be nearer the homes of partners and family, making visiting, and if indicated, joint work, more practicable.

In addition, there are a few centres around the country which are unique in the service they offer: the Portman Clinic, for example, provides out-patient psychotherapy for those with problems of sexual deviancy; the Henderson is an in-patient therapeutic community for young, personality-disordered men and women who undertake treatment on a voluntary basis; there are also a few assessment centres specifically for remandees.

Multi-Disciplinary Teams

At maximum and medium levels of security, and frequently on intensive care units, patients are managed by a ward multi-disciplinary team with special forensic expertise. A consultant forensic psychiatrist heads the team, working alongside forensically trained nursing staff, a social worker, psychologist and an occupational therapist. The approach to assessment and treatment is, and has to be, eclectic, since for many patients both biological and psychological problems have aetiological significance. Most are treated with a combination of medication, cognitive-behavioural techniques, and group or individual interpretive work, in which at least one of these professionals usually has a special training and interest. Often overlooked, but equally important, is the 'milieu therapy' (reviewed by Wolf 1977) offered by forensic in-patient facilities. This term refers to the beneficial effects of an environment that emphasizes containment, structure, involvement and a practical orientation to individuals whose lives have hitherto been chaotic and unpredictable.

PART II

Case Studies

3

The Psychodynamics of Incest

Judith Trowell

INTRODUCTION

Once sexual abuse has been suspected or disclosed very powerful feelings arise such as shock, horror, fear, anxiety, rage, revulsion, distress and sadness. But at the same time there is both a denial, 'it cannot be true, these things do not happen, and not in this family that I know quite well', and a wish not to know, a desire to walk away and not become involved. At every stage, with cases of child sexual abuse, there is this same conflict, the wish to rescue and protect and the wish to ignore in the hope it will go away.

The consequences of suspecting abuse or hearing a child disclose means there needs to be action. The person told must inform social services or the NSPCC, there will be strategy meetings, investigative interviews and case conferences. The child and his, or her, family are likely to be split up one way or another, the alleged abuser may leave, or the child may be removed. Shame, confusion, guilt, doubts, disbelief are further emotions aroused.

If the abuser is the father, or stepfather, mother is precipitously placed in a conflict of loyalty between her partner, her emotional support and bread-winner, and her vulnerable child in need of protection. If mother's relationship with her child has been poor, the decision to believe, and support, the child may be difficult or impossible. Extended families can become drawn in, taking sides with 'their daughter', or 'their son' or the grandchild. Ripples spread into the community; school is likely to be involved, neighbours, the GP and community links. Inevitably child sexual abuse with obvious uncontrolled sexuality, aggression and abuse of power provoke very strong feelings in all those around.

The inter-agency professional networks that must assess the case and then carry through any legal action are always subjected to this emotional barrage – their capacity to hold on to clear rational objective thinking is imperative, but is all too frequently lost. Different agencies and professionals easily become identified with different members of the family. This process is known as mirroring, and if not expected and anticipated, can lead to inter-professional and inter-agency conflict. Police want evidence for a criminal prosecution, social workers want to protect the child and to keep the child's world as undisturbed as possible and health workers want to care, make it better/treat. All too often these different professional aims lead to heated conflict and fragmentation of the network. No one wants to work, or have dealings, with the alleged abuser, except to convict. There is revulsion, disgust and outrage. All the professionals ostensibly want to 'help' the child and they may become rivalrous for this role. What can also happen is that the social worker who is working with the mother becomes so involved in supporting her that sight is lost of her parenting inadequacies. Often these mothers have themselves been physically and/or sexually abused and do need a great deal of help and support (the abusers may have also been physically or sexually abused). The needs of the child, once the abuse has stopped can be lost in the greater needs of the mother. It may well be that the health visitor, the GP, the child health or child mental health worker or the school teachers, are the professionals that are in touch with the child's pain and distress after the initial matters of child protection have been dealt with, because the social worker has had to work so hard to engage and work in partnership with the mother.

In case conferences these divergent views can lead to very heated and, at times, acrimonious discussions. The professionals speaking for the child feel ignored, put down, or attacked and the professionals speaking for the mother feel misunderstood. No one speaks for the abuser except to express the wish to punish.

With good supervision throughout the assessment and investigative work, and with skilled chairing at case conferences these difficulties can be anticipated and dealt with so that the decisions made are not too biased, or distorted, by those identifications. If the decision is to go for Court action civil and/or criminal, sadly all too often these conscious conflicts and unconscious dynamics can be reactivated and dominate the legal process unless this phase is handled with sensitivity, care and awareness.

Once decisions in court are made there is then the full assessment of treatment needs. Again the dynamics can be acted out. Whose need dominates in a time of limited resources? Agreeing a treatment plan for parents, abuser, abused child and siblings can be skewed unless there is constant vigilance and monitoring of the process of decision making, because once again the identification with the different family members and their needs is so powerful.

In order to understand why sexual abuse can be so disturbing, one needs to consider the process of psychosexual development, a process that occurs in all of us.

INFANCY

Infants come into the world with a primitive sense of self capable of very powerful emotions; Love, and in opposition to this, Hate and Envy. It is to be hoped that the infant learns quite soon that no-one is all good, to be given all the love; and others all bad, to be hated, envied – against whom all the anger and aggression should be directed. He or she brings the two sides together and realizes painfully that we are all shades of grey, to be loved and hated, and are both loving and hating.

Alongside this it seems there is, from the beginning, an awareness of sexuality and sexual differences. Little boys are aware of their penis as a source of pleasure and excitement (the erections when their nappies are changed) and are also aware of desire to thrust forward, penetrate, a wish to get inside. Little girls are likewise aware of sexual pleasure from their external genitalia but they also have a sense of something valuable; an awareness of their insides, of a space that is important, and a wish to be entered. Both, it seems, are aware of an incompleteness, and there is a turning to others due to this awareness of differences; equal but different. This then is the beginning of infantile sexuality.

We need to consider psychosexual development in the pre-school phase, at primary school age and then secondary school age. I cannot include here biological and physiological developmental changes, but am focusing on the emotional development. How this assists our understanding of children and the impact on them of sexual abuse will be explored.

PRE-SCHOOL CHILDREN

Children of this age are dominated by a sense of omnipotence that they control and rule the world. Giving this up is a slow painful process. In addition, they have magical thinking, believing that a thought is translated into action. They have animistic thinking, their own understanding of time and a lack of impulse control, finding frustration difficult to tolerate and wanting immediate gratification. Their sexual feelings and interest are very intense including intense sexual feelings for both parents. In their fantasies boys wish to enter their mother and fear father's rivalry, they also wish to be entered by fathers to have babies. Similarly, girls wish to be entered by father and have babies, and fear rivalry with mother. They also wish to enter mother and make babies.

Both boys and girls, I think, are aware of the goodies, the 'source of life' inside mother. The major anxiety is not, only, in boys the fear of castration, and in girls the acceptance of their lack of a penis. It is, also, a recognition of Mother as the powerful one. Mother, who has inside her the womb, the father's penis and all the babies. Boys and girls fear mother (woman). Boys fear their penis will be trapped inside mother (vagina dentate) and girls fear that mother's envy will lead her to attack them as potential rivals.

How this fear and anxiety is dealt with depends on:

(1)   The mother's capacity to go on loving, despite the child's rage and fear.

(2)   The father's capacity to appropriately support the child and support the mother.

(3)   The children's sense of mother and father as nurturing, caring and supporting; that is, *not* attacking or destroying each other. The implications for children with warring parents or a single isolated unsupported parent, are obvious at once.

(4)   The child's capacity to tolerate being left out of the parental couple's relationship, usually turning to masturbation with fantasies of a simple kind.

These young children have a number of confusions which are entirely normal arising from all this. They are:

(1)   How are babies made? Does the penis enter the mouth, anus, wee wee hole or where; which is the vital one?

(2)   Are babies made from food and therefore are they really rubbish – pooh?

(3)   Boys and girls believing they can make babies all by themselves and therefore not need anyone else.

(4)   Boys longing to have babies, girls longing for their penis to grow.

Given that all this is normal, it is not surprising that child sexual abuse in these small children and babies can be emotionally seriously dangerous (never mind the physical damage). To be subjected to actual sexual experience can lead to emotional chaos. Boys and girls sexually abused by their father, stepfather or elder brother do not have the maturational space to do all the developmental work required to be ready to move ultimately to normal adult sexuality.

Oral or anal penetration fits in with, and reinforces some of these confusions. Actual vaginal penetration in girls is an attack, not a loving acceptance. Anal intercourse can lead on to homosexuality for boys and, furthermore, if it is violent the boy may become passive or identify with the violence and become very aggressive. Fantasies and longings, if actually enacted, leave them stuck with their magical thinking and omnipotence.

But perhaps the most damaging aspect for these children is linked with their perception that mother wishes to attack or destroy something precious and potentially rivalrous, (particularly for girls), thus leaving them with a sense that the sexual abuse was in some way done on behalf of, or with, mother's agreement. She wanted it to happen and could have prevented it. This in no way is to diminish the responsibility of the adult male for his actions, but instead is an attempt to understand how the child perceives what happens and how it involves both parents.

This can be seen particularly clearly in children in foster placement, who in treatment become increasingly enraged, defiant and difficult with the foster mothers, to the extent that placements break down unless the child and foster mother can be helped to handle this fury. This illustrates the importance of understanding the dynamics of the whole system.

The perception of mother's involvement in their abuse by men is of course as nothing compared with the cases of sexual abuse *by* women. These do seem to be particularly damaging to children's emotional development. If the mother is the central emotional figure and she herself actively abuses, the experience then can only be described as mind-blowing. There is nothing to hold onto, no possibility of help, of rescue, or of being protected.

I am aware that the literature does not describe severe emotional consequences following sexual abuse in the pre-school years. I would suggest that this is because children who still lack verbal capacities have difficulty in thinking about what has happened. What they are left with are sensations and feelings. Working with clinical samples it is only late on in treatment that they begin to develop an awareness and an understanding of these sensations and feelings that have troubled them, perhaps for years, without being able to clarify what caused them or put them into words.

JUNIOR SCHOOL AGE

Children of this age are rapidly acquiring skills and gaining considerable satisfaction from this. They have logical concrete thinking and have learnt impulse control. However, their emotions, although hidden beneath a calmer exterior, are very intense and powerful.

They are capable of a greater range of emotions in addition to love, hate and envy; namely – joy, hope, concern, depression, shame and guilt. Their sexual identity is more developed. Doubts and fears are dealt with by 'rude' jokes, sniggering or by sublimation, for example football, bikes and so forth.

The responses of the adults to them, and their function as role models as a basis for sexual identity, remains very important. These children masturbate frequently and have elaborate private fantasies. The direct link to their own parents is displaced onto Prince Charming, Superman, a Princess, Superwoman, or some other cartoon or 'real' super-hero or heroine.

There is a vulnerability about children of this age as they struggle to tolerate/accept differences between boys and girls, men and women, children and adults (the generational gap). If it is mishandled by those around it is very easy for these children to tip over into derision, hostility, contempt and then sadism or, conversely, an increased vulnerability, offering themselves up as victims, in other words masochism with the loss of self-esteem, self-blame and acceptance of guilt that we see so often.

Therefore, sexual abuse in this age group can very easily lead to the child adopting a masochistic victim position and, particularly in the boys, a sadistic attitude and a frightening identification with and wish to emulate the abuser. Their sexual development can be halted or they may espouse a homosexual orientation.

SECONDARY SCHOOL (11–16 YEARS)

I believe the sexual development of girls faces a crucial phase somewhere between 10 and 12 years. With the onset of puberty and emerging genital sexuality girls, having been close to their fathers during the activities of primary school, move into a phase when they are very close to their mothers. The onset of menstruation must inevitably have immense consequences, the bleeding giving rise to fears of being damaged or injured inside. As I have indicated earlier the fear of mother's attacks on their insides was a concern in their early years, and now it re-emerges. If a girl is to pass successfully through this phase her mother needs to be sensitive and supportive. Girls seem particularly to need the 'blessing' on their emerging sexuality from their mothers – that is, a need for mother's approval, pride and pleasure in their daughters. This means mothers have to accept there may shortly be two sexually active women in the house at the same time, and also recognize their daughter's ascendency and their own inevitable decline. Mothers also have to help fathers admire their daughter and let her go.

Boys are rivals with their fathers, and mothers may be possessive, but usually both parents take pride and pleasure in their son's developing physique and prowess.

In both sexes there is extensive masturbation. The peer group is important but in early adolescence the masturbatory fantasies are usually directed at older adolescents or 'superstars' for example pop figures. Sexual experimentation, homosexuality, love and hate and intense relationships, with peers of both sexes and other adults, are the norm.

Sexual abuse at this stage in a vulnerable young person can grossly distort and stop the normal experimentation and evolution of their sexual identity. It can drive young people to take up a homosexual position, become sexually indiscriminate or retreat into mind-blowing activities – alcohol, substance abuse, suicidal behaviour and violence or anorexia.

If girls experience sexual abuse around the time of the onset of menstruation they have considerable problems in negotiating this phase because the damage of the sexual activity and the 'bleeding' leave external reality and internal fantasies in a confused muddle.

THE EFFECTS ON THE CHILD

The way to understand the impact of sexual abuse is, I am suggesting, to see it as an impingement, where the child's (unconscious) mind is penetrated, regardless of what happened in the actual sexual abuse, what actually happened to their bodies.

In the external world the child has to handle a split. The apparently normal, perhaps caring adult; and then the bizarre experience of the intrusion, the secrecy, the fear, the lack of acknowledgment of what is happening. There is a 'madness'. The abuser forces the split, the 'madness', into the child. The unconscious fantasies that dominate the child will depend on which stage the child has attained at the time of the abuse, and how they and those around them react to the events. These secret experiences are split off in the unconscious and can become encapsulated. How much of the child's mind is taken over depends on the combination of the state of the child developmentally, as well as the severity, duration and degree of coercion. The child therefore may not 'know about', be aware of, or be able to recall the abusive experiences. Or he or she may remember in part and have forgotten (split off) other aspects. The split off part can become very deeply embedded and difficult to contact. We call this encapsulated 'madness'. This is not a psychiatric diagnosis but describes, as well as we can with inadequate words, the bizarre, distorted, world of the child with these experiences. In childhood sexual abuse the child may be forced to believe that what is happening is 'normal.' Not surprisingly there can be interference in thought, in thinking, making links and in remembering.

Where children have had good enough parenting early on and there is a reasonable degree of integration, the personality is formed but immature and the encapsulated area of the child's mind does not appear to be obvious. Sexual abuse, for example involving a step-father, a relative, or a family friend, that was of brief duration can be survived, and the child's psychosexual development may not be too distorted. In the main, there are almost invariably changes in self-esteem, in the level of functioning and in the capacity to relate, and establish intimacy. Children may become aggressive and defiant, or timid, isolated and withdrawn. It needs to be stated that usually these children have to cope as best they can. If they are fortunate they are offered a community resource, an educative group, short-term group therapy, or individual counselling, and many do well enough or manage. But there are numbers of children who are profoundly traumatized, in need of specialist help, who present serious management problems. These children are the ones whose lives were in emotional, if not material, chaos and where there has been persistent emotional abuse, deprivation or neglect. The sexual abuse may have been violent or of long duration, or both. The child's early parenting was almost certainly erratic and inconsistent, not meeting their basic needs. The child may be of itself a vulnerable child with erratic psychological and emotional development with some areas that were static and others of pseudo maturity. Their psychosexual development is overtaken by actual sexual knowledge, leaving them no space to explore or experiment, in order to discover themselves. These children present in a range of ways with the splitting and denial affecting different aspects of functioning.

(1)   The child can switch off feelings to avoid any close emotional relationships, ie. the 'refrigerator' child no-one can get through to. They can be quite competent, do well academically and use this as a means of escape. But many coping this way are out of touch, detached, drifting, isolated and aimless. They can, when provoked, erupt into unexpectedly violent behaviour over which they have little insight. Or they may wrist-slash, overdose or prostitute themselves.

(2)   The child can switch off its mind, its intellect, and behave as 'stupid' not knowing, unable to learn anything. A number of children with learning difficulties or assessed as mildly or seriously learning disordered, if investigated have been sexually abused.

(3)   The child retreats – does not have contact with reality for part of the time, living in a world of his/her own. However, often the fantasies with which they live have monstrous terrifying qualities which can lead to violence to others or to fear of a violent attack on themselves. There is little chance of escape, or real peace for the child preoccupied with their fantasies.

GENDER IDENTITY

Infantile sexuality has only been acknowledged in the last one hundred years and was one of Freud's most significant contributions. By this is meant the recognition that children themselves have sexual feelings and sexual sensations that are focused on particular body areas: mouth, anus and genitals.

As the children grow and develop, their feelings change and evolve and the area of the body they find most pleasurable also changes. Children have to negotiate, therefore, a path through an emotional and physical highly charged minefield. By the time the emotional and mental work is well developed, their bodies have bound them into adolescence and the whole process is reworked repeatedly until adulthood is attained with mature sexuality. The topics that have to be tackled include 'am I male or female', both a bodily recognition of gender and also a mental recognition of maleness or femaleness. Next, there needs to be exploration of possible sexual objects, the other one might turn to for sexual satisfaction; this may be same sex, opposite sex or both – heterosexual, homosexual or bisexual. There is then further work on more specific matters, with regard to the type of person and age (older, same age group or much younger). The remaining work to be done is around intimacy over a prolonged period and the development of ideas, thoughts and feelings about having one's own children – becoming a parent.

WHAT DOES INFANTILE SEXUALITY AND THE PSYCHOSEXUAL DEVELOPMENT TELL US THAT HELPS UNDERSTAND CHILDHOOD SEXUAL ABUSE?

For all children, their psychosexual development and emergence of gender identity ebbs and flows as other aspects of development take more or less emotional, and mental, time and energy. There may also be external events that intrude or deflect events such as bereavements, physical or mental illness in family members, life events of all sorts.

It is important to consider these matters because some children traumatized by child sexual abuse can behave or react emotionally in ways that are puzzling and confusing. The children's perceptions of themselves can disturb those around.

The child who is highly sexualized and masturbates is well known, as sadly are the children whose sexual excitement leads them to engage in sexual activity with other children. But children whose premature sexualization takes more bizarre forms are less easily understood. Some children retreat into a cut off state without any obvious external sexual activity and they can too easily be labelled as learning disabled or developmentally delayed.

Therefore, an understanding of the power and intensity of sexuality, conscious and unconscious, can make sense of the extent of the splitting denial, projection and omnipotence that are the familiar dynamics that so easily take over the families and then the professional network. Sexual abuse which involves sexuality, violence and the abuse of power inevitably produces strong reactions, but awareness can, one hopes, lead to thoughtful reflective responses.

4

Precursors in Childhood of Anti-Social Behaviour, Delinquency and Crime

Christine Bradley

It is widely acknowledged that the delinquent and criminal personality has its roots in early childhood experiences. If there has been severe emotional disruption and the early external environment has been experienced as abusive, then the stage is set for the developing child to view the external world with mistrust and hostility. Their 'inner world' has already become infiltrated with fears and anxieties which have felt monstrous. The children are rendered helpless to experience life in anything other than the self-destructive pattern which has been established for them. If this pattern is not interrupted, and replaced with primary experiences, which offer the child a feeling of being nurtured and provided for in a safe and contained way, then their need to survive painful, overwhelming memories becomes paramount. This survival mechanism can take on a perverse and primitive form. It does not allow for creative thinking to develop in the child, and nourishing relationships are not able to grow. The seeds of the anti-social tendency are sown.

I may appear to be painting a bleak picture, but my experience of working with such children over the past 25 years is that by the time such a child reaches a situation where help can be offered, this pattern is often well established. It takes committed, well informed and long suffering carers, who can withstand the rage and despair of such children, if change is to take place. Hoxter (1990) explained that in her experience of working with such children: 'Many of them have a pervading pre-occupation with the complex of experiences relating to their sense of deprivation, which left little space in their lives for anything else, thus diminishing their capacity to benefit from ordinary maturational experiences'.

In the earliest days of an infant's existence, there is a fusion between their emotional state and that of the world around them. Winnicott (1960) described this as 'symbiosis', a crucial stage for healthy emotional development, where the infant is able to experience a period of 'total dependence' without anxiety. This can only be facilitated if there is a primary carer who is able to be pre-occupied with the infant unconditionally, and is able to enter into the spirit of this relationship with a sense of creativity and playfulness; it is in this area of being that the earliest communication is established. From this experience the infant is able to emerge with a sense of emotional well-being. An inner reality has been established which will always feel protected from the pressures and emotional demands of the external world. It is this safe inner reality which has been called 'the stuff that dreams are made of' (Docker Drysedale 1990). As they begin to separate from this stage of development, a necessary step if a genuine way forward into reality is to be discovered, they begin to view the world with their own eyes, and with a newly found interest in the external environment. As this narcissistic phase is given up, both by the infant and the primary carer, a new and challenging stage of life begins.

With this developing separateness comes a realization that the person whom they once experienced as an integral part of their inner world is also separate. This loss is made bearable because of the quality of that first experience, which has facilitated their interest and transition into a new reality. This is enhanced through enriching play experiences. The loss of the original object is dealt with through the use of a transitional object, an item of affection and love, never to be lost, and to form the bridge between inner psychic reality and the external world (Winnicott 1969). As the ego develops and the child becomes an individual so they are able to tolerate frustration, acknowledge ambivalence and to become aware that it is possible to love and hate the same person without destroying them. With this increasing individuation, and strengthening self, the child begins to develop a genuine desire to show concern and guilt. Through this they can acquire a sense of responsibility and a desire to repair that which they feel they have damaged. Depressive feelings can be withstood, and they are able to be rational and think about the consequences of their actions.

With the onset of social relationships, the concept of the world not being a 'fair place' has to be understood and accepted, and the idea of sharing the world with others taken in. It is only if there is a self which is true to its own intentions, and feels satisfied with its own existence that this can happen. Otherwise envy rears its ugly head, and all hell is let loose! The result of the former is the ability to form friendships and to feel comfortable with imaginative and creative thoughts, whereas in the latter there can be increasing social isolation and often developing destructive fantasies, which at extreme can be acted out with catastrophic outcomes.

Time is moving on, and as children begin to explore their peer relationships, so they make decisions as to whose culture and society they wish to belong to. The children they move towards will be the ones whose ideas and values about life reflect their own, for better or for worse. Those whose sense of well being is nourished will look for situations to develop that in creative ways, whilst those who feel burdened with hopelessness and helplessness will unconsciously seek to recreate that, thereby finding it increasingly difficult to find a pathway into the mainstream of living. The prevalent culture seems unattainable, and so a sub-culture is developed which carries its own life, and acquires its own set of rules which may be perverse and prevaricating.

Of course most of us have spent a part of our lives veering in and out of both these areas, attempting to find a way through for ourselves, and our families, which carries some satisfaction and meaning. In this context Winnicott's concept of life and parenting as being 'good-enough' is most reassuring! But what of the child for whom these experiences have simply not been 'good-enough', where there was a severe breakdown in the early emotional holding relationship, and the environment was not reliable? Too many emotional demands on these children leads to panic, a state of unthinkable anxiety relating back to their earliest experiences when their primitive needs remained unnoticed, and were possibly even punished. They have felt annihilated by the outside world, and have had to build a protective shell to prevent such onslaughts. Because this shell is not rooted in true satisfactory experiences, it acquires a falseness or compliance, split off from the rage and fury which lies at the centre of baby's existence, and which is located in a time when the struggle to communicate its needs was abandoned, and energy was put into surviving rather than creating. As the child begins to develop, reality, rather than being experienced as challenging, is seen as threatening and overpowering. The main impulse is to disrupt anything or anybody who attempts to interrupt their own little world, which they have by now created to the exclusion of all others. It does not allow for creative thinking or communication in a way which is attached to other people. The difficulty is that by the time they reach school, they are difficult to reach, withdrawn and uncommunicative (a social isolate), or disruptive, uncontainable and not able to learn. It is quite possible that these are the children who will be excluded from school, making it even more possible for them to fall into sub-cultural ways of living. In my experience of working with children in residential care, the majority of whom fall into the category of what is termed the 'unintegrated' child (no inner togetherness) very often they have reached the point of exclusion several times before reaching secondary education. This renders the adolescent process extremely difficult and the anti-social tendency is well established, leaving the young person especially vulnerable to the hazards of their time namely, alcohol, drugs, sexual perversion and promiscuity. Laufer (1974), said that 'mental illness refers to a state where the adolescent has lost touch with reality, where the creations of his own mind are felt to be determined by, or operating in, the outside world'. One can see the precursors of that as lying in what I have outlined above. Indeed many of our prisons, secure units and mental hospitals are filled with these 'unintegrated' children, where institutionalization has become the only option. I would qualify the above statement by noting that good nursery provision can offer a great deal to such children and it is some gratification to know that in many situations, workers with under fives are putting considerable thought into how best to respond to their needs without over-reacting to their disruptiveness.

What can be offered to these children, which will make their road through life more tenable? It is possible, as I said at the beginning of this chapter, to effect change as long as those caring for them are prepared to withstand the pain of their inner despair, and to find ways of meeting these primary needs with appropriate provision. From this it may be possible to communicate with the trapped little self and for the worker to be allowed access to its world, from where the child can become dependent on the worker. Through this relationship the child may be able to find a starting point for themselves. As reality becomes more bearable, it is important that they have good models of identification to strengthen their position in relationship to the world. The role of the worker will move from offering ego-provision to being ego-supportive. As the child slowly realizes the creative potential in living and is able, with support, to withstand depressive feelings, so he may feel able to give up the anti-social tendency and identify with cultural opportunities offered to him.

Of course this is easier said than done; workers need to be supported and the necessary skills given, to achieve it. Unfortunately, time and space does not allow me to explore this more thoroughly. I thought it may be useful, to offer a few small vignettes, illustrating how such children are experienced by those around them, and how certain responses from grown-ups can be helpful to their understanding of the world.

Clinical vignette 1

Paul has an ability for getting under everyone's skin. His constant rapid talking, accompanied by frenetic movement exasperates both adults and children and he makes constant demands by screeching into faces or tugging at clothing. If met with a reprimand or a plea to show patience, he merely increases his hold, by putting pieces of clothing or flesh between his teeth.

Paul is certainly tiresome and the adults wonder how one little boy can render them powerless, angry, and defeated. He has the look of a premature child, talks often of his cherished powers and warns of the massive violence he is capable of, should he ever be called upon to use it. He needs us to be totally preoccupied with him in order for him to survive, and his best guarantee of this is for him to be always at the centre of our vision and our hearing. His teeth in our skin is painful but an illustrative reminder of his need of bonding and attachment. His flamboyant gestures lock us into noticing Paul, but they could also tell us more. Paul seems to have no beginning and no centre, but rather bits of him are scattered everywhere. His cartwheels are a circle repeatedly turning over and over, as if Paul is trying to unravel himself and find a beginning experience of reassurance in his feet hitting the floor, but this reassuring landing is fleeting, so he turns again and again in active fashion. Paul is like a ball of wool where the beginning has become lost in the middle; he is an unstarted child.

This vivid account of an encounter with an unintegrated child as described by Jo Richardson, teacher at the Caldecott School, graphically describes the difficulties of finding a way into working with such children. With Paul it was through his language and constant squeaking that Jo was able to identify his little self as an 'Eek' which was squeaking for its existence. Jo made contact with the 'Eek' and made a place for it in the classroom. She provided a desk in the classroom next to Paul's, where the 'Eek' symbolically represented by a troll doll could sit. Later she writes

> Paul communicates to us in many ways, none of them straightforward. Through his screech he hints of the abandoned baby within and dares us to accept him. By surrounding himself with trolls, monsters and orphans he showed the dependence of his own kind, and demonstrates his need of love by putting himself at risk. His constant need of food speaks volumes about his needyness. He masks a deep sadness by never appearing to cry and our work is to begin to understand these various communications and to check our responses to them. Discovering what we are working with is only the first step, but finding the growing point gives us the place to start. (Richardson 1993)

Clinical vignette 2

Mark, 14 years old, was waiting for me as I stepped out of my car when I arrived at the Caldecott Community and he looked sad and lost. 'How many cars do you have Christine?' he asked me. Responding to the lack of aliveness in his face 'Seven', I said 'I have three Rolls-Royces, two Daimlers, a helicopter and a horse and cart.' 'Where do you keep them all?' he asked. 'In my imagination,' I replied. 'What do you keep in your imagination?' I asked him. He breathed a deep sigh 'I don't have any imagination. I only have the reality I live with.' 'That's a shame,' I responded. 'Why is it a shame?' he asked. 'Because with an imagination reality doesn't seem so hard.' 'Reality has always been hard,' replied Mark. 'May I have some of your imagination?' he asked me, with a tear in his eye. 'Of course,' I said.

'You may have the use of one of my Rolls-Royces.' 'Thank you,' he said. 'Now I feel a little better.'

These two small examples describe the plight of these very deprived children, who have been devoid of early satisfactory experiences, and have been unable to feel that other people are engaged with them in a non abusive way. If we are to prevent them from becoming entrenched in the anti-social tendency, it is crucial that workers are enabled to reach them in truly creative ways.

[5]

Adolescents who Sexually Abuse

Eileen Vizard

INTRODUCTION

Although it is now at least 15 years since the sexual victimization of children became recognized as a phenomenon in the USA (Kempe and Kempe 1978) and in the UK (Mrazek, Lynch and Bentovim 1981), acknowledgement of the existence of child and adolescent perpetrators of sexual abuse is relatively recent (NCH 1992). There are few clinical projects in the UK (Monck and New 1995) which have evaluated or even described their work with young sexual abusers in any detail and therefore the basic facts about this group of young perpetrators are not well known to many clinicians or academics. In addition, theoretical approaches to work with young abusers have tended to polarize practitioners into groups using one or other approach with little attempt to integrate thinking about the origins and nature of this complex problem (Hawkes, Jenkins and Vizard 1996). Good practice (Home Office/Department of Health/Department of Education and Science/Welsh Office 1991; NCH 1992) with adolescents and children at risk of inflicting significant harm through the sexual abuse of other children makes it clear that professional practitioners need to integrate their endeavours (i.e. talk to each other) to protect children and to develop services. This chapter will discuss definitional and theoretical issues, will briefly mention a structured approach to assessment (Vizard *et al.* 1996) and will describe themes emerging from treatment of young sexual abusers.

DEFINITIONAL ISSUES

The many complex definitional dilemmas with children and young people who sexually abuse other children have been discussed elsewhere (NCH 1992; Vizard, Monck and Misch 1995). Clinical definitions of sexually abusive behaviours by children have tended to be pragmatic and to focus on acts committed – for example, 'Any sexualised interaction between an adolescent and a much younger child whether or not force is used' (Davis and Leitenberg 1987). However, such definitions do not help in assessing younger sexualized children who may also be showing sexually abusive or sexually coercive behaviour. Indeed one of the greatest definitional problems lies in distinguishing abusive behaviour in young children from 'over sexualized' behaviour and from 'normal' sexual experimentation with child peers. This situation is exacerbated by the complete lack of acknowledgment by existing psychiatric classificatory systems of the existence of sexual arousal and sexually abusive behaviour in children under 16 years of age. In order to address this deficit and to keep up with research findings which indicate that children under 16 years of age do show sexually aroused and abusive behaviour (Ryan 1986; Vizard *et al.* 1995) it has been suggested (Vizard *et al.* 1996) that a new category of 'sexual arousal disorder of childhood' could be created. Rather than seeing this as yet another 'label' to be applied, it should be argued that this description would allow the child's need for specialist assessment and treatment services to be addressed at a much earlier point with the opportunity of preventing patterns of sexual offending.

THEORETICAL ISSUES

One of the difficulties in writing about theory in relation to young sexual abusers is that opinion about which model to support is divided and polarized with few practitioners feeling able to advocate an eclectic or specifically integrated approach. Research (NCH 1992; National Research Council 1993; Vizard *et al.* 1995) and clinical experience (Vizard *et al.* 1996; Becker 1990; Bentovim 1992) suggest that there is little evidence to support the use of one theoretical model to the exclusion of others despite strongly held views. Existing theoretical models in relation to adolescent sex offending are based on work with adults, and seldom take into account the physical, emotional, and social developmental factors which are an integral part of the psychopathology of child and adolescent sexual abusers. In reviewing these dilemmas, Hawkes *et al.* 1996, point out that the roots of sexual violence in adolescence are nearly always multifactorial and that familiarity with the main theoretical schools allows practitioners to select explanatory concepts and to tailor clinical interventions for individual young abusers based on a sound understanding of the underlying theory. It is clear that no single theoretical approach can span the whole range of issues arising in clinical work with young sex offenders and the dangers of a single factor approach to work with victims have already been clearly articulated (Finklehor 1986).

With notable exceptions (Bentovim 1992) little has been written from a psychodynamic perspective about the origins of sexual offending taking into account both family and individual dynamics. Psychoanalytical writers have focused on the psychopathology of the individual (Stoller 1986; McDougall 1990; Glasser 1979) and have frequently identified early problems in the mother–child relationship leading to later difficulties in forming trusting adult social and sexual relationships. Bentovim's 1992 model of traumagenic dynamics in the families of abused and abusing individuals draws on research findings (Monck and New 1995) which show that transgenerational patterns of child abuse are only too common in clinical populations. An impressive attempt has been made (Scharff and Scharff 1994) to integrate a range of psychoanalytical perspectives, particularly object relations theory (Fairbairn 1944; Klein 1946; Winnicott 1965) with recent research relating to child development, trauma and sexual abuse. The Scharffs' 1994 work links clinical practice with abuse victims showing Post Traumatic Stress Disorder (PTSD) and traditional psychoanalytical thought in a way which is unusual in the UK at present.

ASSESSMENT MODEL FOR ABUSING ADOLESCENTS

All assessment and treatment of young people under 18 years who abuse other children should be undertaken on an interagency basis and within a child protection context (Home Office 1991). This may have implications for traditional notions of patient therapist confidentiality but it must be remembered that the best interests and safety of the child come before clinical preferences. In practice, a policy of open confidentiality works well; that is, minute details of conversations or sessions with young abusers are kept confidential but issues suggesting that child protection action should be taken are shared on a need to know basis.

Recent clinical experience in working with over 80 young sexual offenders has suggested that a semistructured approach to assessment (Vizard *et al.* 1996) is the best way to start discussing difficult, embarrassing and dangerous behaviour with young people. Through drawing up an integrated abuse cycle, a pictorial representation of the thoughts, feelings and fantasies as well as the actions of the young person is generated (Figure 5.1) and this has been proved very helpful in the assessment of risk and treatability.

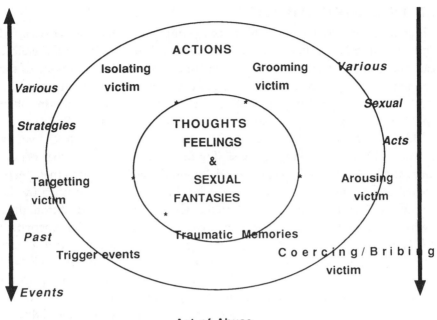

Source: Vizard, Wynick, Hawkes, Woods and Jenkins (1996)

Figure 5.1 Integrated abuse cycle: actions and thoughts

CLINICAL CASES AND THEIR TREATMENT

In Appendix 5.1 the cases of two young people referred to the Young Abusers Project are summarized and give a picture of the type of problems which a specialist team is asked to assess. In *clinical vignette 1,* 'Anthony' showed very serious disturbance, sexualized behaviour and poor impulse control which would have excluded him from group treatment. However, after two years in individual therapy, Anthony has started to make slow progress towards more acceptable social behaviour and has not re-offended although he still experiences intrusive sexual fantasies about other children and about animals.

In *clinical vignette 2* 'Daniel', despite his aggressive and challenging behaviour, was supported so well by his carers (a residential school) that he was eventually able to attend a full 30 week group work programme and subsequent follow up groups for some two years. During treatment and on follow up Daniel did not re-offend sexually or in any other way and was able to take on a college course and protected employment, something which would have seemed impossible both to Daniel and his carers at the point of referral.

THEMES EMERGING FROM GROUP
AND INDIVIDUAL THERAPY

Three treatment groups involving fifteen young people have so far occurred and ten young people have been seen in individual therapy. It is still therefore early days in terms of treatment outcome findings and although none of the young people in group or individual therapy re-offended during the treatment, this is not an unusual treatment effect (Vizard 1995) with recidivism often appearing several years post treatment and follow up (Grubin 1996).

In group work the themes emerging were related primarily to the young person's difficulty in taking responsibility for sexual abuse and other behaviours, the bitter sense of rejection by adults and the lack of trust in their peers. Denial of responsibility for abuse and other behaviours was justified by the young people as being the approach to life which they had learned from their own abuser and from neglectful parents. Self pity about past victim experiences nearly always had a substantial grounding in reality (the majority of this population have been seriously abused or neglected) which was acknowledged but not allowed to dominate and distract from work on the young person's own responsibility for abusing victims. Angry feelings stirred up when therapists or other group members challenged denial usually led to fruitful discussions about moral issues relating to the rights and wrongs of abuse, personal responsibility and so forth. Some very disturbed and angry young people found the developing cohesion of the group almost unbearable (both suffocating and too positive) and behaved destructively towards themselves and others in between sessions. Interestingly, only one of these young people behaved really aggressively within the sessions (trying to light a fire and throwing lighted papers out of the window) with most young people managing increasingly to contain and control their behaviour during the sessions. However, delinquent behaviour between sessions was common and could increasingly be connected to the preceding group session by the young person.

The transferences towards the therapists of either sex were often highly sexually charged with sexualized or flirtatious body language during group sessions sometimes so obvious that an interpretation or observation about the behaviour needed to be made. Such interactions often led to memories of the young person's own abuse being discussed and lessons learned about the vulnerable image projected to others by the young person's current sexualized behaviour.

Themes of separation and loss were crucially important for this deprived group of young abusers and were constantly addressed at the outset of therapy, at the beginning and end of each session and during sessions when relevant. Young sexual abusers like other deprived youngsters have intensely mixed feelings about becoming attached to adults and in the group sessions, both denigratory and idealizing views about the therapists were expressed. Towards the end of the group process, one or two very angry and disturbed patients felt unable to complete the sessions and did not return. For some of the other young people support from the carers and local authorities started to founder, for example, transport arrangements to group sessions would suddenly fail; accompanying carers would go off sick; professional communication would become confused. However, the majority completed the programme and returned for regular follow up some two years after the end of the group.

In order to support group work with the young people, a concurrent group for carers is run to allow for the young person to be escorted to the group and for feedback on the intervening week's behaviour to be given to the Project staff. The carer's group also allows a much needed opportunity for those looking after these dangerous young people to discuss their feelings about the work and to get professional and personal support. Since the work is extremely anxiety provoking and difficult to process, supervision of assessment and treatment work is essential for all workers including the most experienced.

Themes emerging from individual work have been similar to those described above for group work. In addition, it is worth noting that individual therapists working with young sexual abusers describe the intensely sexualized nature of the transference and the need to interpret this situation constantly. The possible risks for female therapists working individually with young sexual abusers, many of whom are misogynistic and sexually aroused to both women and to children is an important consideration. For male therapists working individually with young sexual abusers, many of whom have been homosexually abused, the fear of abuse by the therapist and the simultaneous wish to please the therapist by being sexualized, can combine to produce an erotically charged treatment situation. Apart from specific sexual issues, the main themes emerging from individual work with deprived young abusers are very similar to those described in other work with extremely deprived children (Boston and Szur 1983).

Young people assessed and treated by the Young Abusers Project have apparently benefited from individual and group psychotherapy, and research into treatment outcome is presently being undertaken. For those young people who cannot attend a specialist resource for treatment, perhaps for geographical or logistical reasons, it is essential that consultation and advice is given to referrers on how to provide treatment using the skills of local mental health colleagues.

CONCLUSION

It is now apparent that the proportion of young people and children who abuse other children is much higher than previously believed. The themes arising from group and individual work with abusive young people suggest that their overwhelming sense of rejection by adults also stems from a real rejection of their treatment needs by professionals in the field. The great advantage of targeting scarce resources towards young abusers as opposed to victims is that three needs are addressed at once – new victims are prevented from being created, the protection of existing victims is ensured and the treatment is given to the needy and dangerous young sexual abuser. True primary prevention of abuse is when we stop the young abuser from abusing in the first place.

— Appendix 5.1 —

Clinical vignette 1

'Anthony' is a boy with a history of sexual abuse by his father from the earliest age. This emerged when Anthony was five; he was rejected by his family and went to live in a children's home where he was again sexually abused. Throughout the following years he was moved from children's homes, different schools and foster placements where he could not be managed because of highly sexualized behaviour with younger children, adults and animals.

When referred to the Young Abusers Project for assessment at the age of 14 years Anthony was in a foster home where he had sexually assaulted his foster mother and sexually abused the family dogs and visiting children. The Project was asked to assess: (1) Whether Anthony would continue to abuse other children; (2) Where he should be placed and (3) Anthony's treatment needs.

The assessment showed that Anthony had been extremely damaged emotionally and psychologically by his experiences. However, he showed great remorse and a desire to repair the relationship with his foster mother. His emotional deprivation had produced a sexualization of all his relationships that would continue if not actively treated. The hunger for contact and nurture made it seem possible to work with him therapeutically. Since it seemed he had formed a close relationship with his carer, it was felt that the placement could hold if Anthony were to receive long-term help.

Individual therapy began and quickly Anthony used the opportunity to communicate his traumatic feelings from the abuse and rejections. After two years Anthony has moved on a great deal in his understanding that sexuality is no substitute for the kind of emotional contact that he needs. An important aspect of the therapy has been the close contact maintained with Anthony's carers who report steady progress in his behaviour.

Clinical vignette 2

'Daniel' is a boy from a neglectful and abusive background who had been rejected by his mother, put into care and then abused in care. Following his own abuse 'Daniel' started to target younger boys for abuse from within the care system and his behaviour gradually became more aggressive towards potential victims and towards adults. Since 'Daniel' was a large well built boy, there were real concerns about containing him and controlling aggression in treatment. In addition, 'Daniel's' level of arousal and excitement towards children meant that he often did not listen to instructions from adults, appearing constantly distracted, speaking rapidly when necessary and generally preferring action to words.

Nevertheless, 'Daniel' expressed interest in group treatment and with the active support of an excellent residential placement, 'Daniel' was able to attend the full course of group work and all follow up meetings for two years after the end of the group. Despite superficial scepticism about the group process, 'Daniel' became attached to his peers and to the therapists and slowly started to listen to what was being said.

By the end of treatment, 'Daniel's' rapid garbled speech had slowed down, his responses were thoughtful and even helpful (sometimes) to his peers. Daniel was able to move out to a community setting at age 18 years, into protected employment and to attend College, which he enjoyed.

On follow up, when asked what he had learned from the group treatment, 'Daniel' responded 'I think I can see things from the other person's point of view if you know what I mean...' 'Daniel' has also expressed an interest in starting individual therapy.

6

The Learning Disabled (Mentally Handicapped) Offender

Valerie Sinason

'And Eddy was put on probation
the longest word he could say'

Inkstains and Stilettos, Valerie Sinason 1986

Cognitive deficit, whether caused by chromosomal abnormality, organic illness, birth injury, violence (Buchanan and Oliver 1979; Ammerman *et al.* 1989), sexual abuse (Sinason 1986), lack of attachment, poor schooling, malnutrition or a combination of factors, erodes the psyche. To have a learning disability, however mild or severe, is a double deprivation. Not only is the individual deprived of the ability to think, read, write, discuss at the same level as their non-disabled peers, but also the individual has to experience the loneliness of being different in a way that people would not choose to be.

In psychoanalytic individual or group psychotherapy at the Tavistock Clinic, St George's Hospital and the Anna Freud Centre child and adult patients have expressed the fantasy that they must be the product of a damaging intercourse (Sinason 1986, p.88). When coupled with environmental deprivation and lack of attachment this can create extra vulnerability to being abused and, in turn, abusing. Both these states reduce cognitive functioning further. As one abused and abusing learning disabled adolescent in therapy said, throwing a pen at me: 'Smell sex – I mean spell it'. Traumatic experiences break through the containment of words. In an attempt to work through the shame, sadness, anger, and guilt that comes from being different many develop defensive secondary handicaps (Sinason 1986) by which they exacerbate their disabilities. The tragedy of this defence is that it depletes their emotional and intellectual functioning even further.

However, before we even begin to consider the emotional experience of severe or profound learning disability (which is likely to include some physical disability too) the sole impact of not being able to read, of mild disability, can make an individual more vulnerable to disturbance and offender behaviour.

On a crowded London bus a rather awkward and rough looking teenager asked for a 50p ticket and gave the harassed driver a £5 note. The driver pointed to the notice by his side: 'NO NOTES – Please give the driver the correct change'. Whilst the crowded bus watched this interaction the driver added 'Can't you read English?' rather tiredly. The young man froze for a moment and then started shouting 'Fuck off can't you. Leave me alone'. He snatched his note back from the ashen driver together with the loose small change left on the counter by the last passenger and leaped off the bus. After experiencing a moment of fear and shock – as I was sitting nearby – I realized that the teenager must be mildly learning disabled, illiterate. He could not read the sign. The tired insensitive words of the driver had therefore been an extra humiliation.

One young man I treat who steals following similar humiliations said 'I prefer being charged in court than going to a training centre for thick people. I prefer to be a criminal'. A criminal record and the specialized jargon that comes from being involved with the penal network provide a new vocabulary and a new identity. 'Probation', 'Section', 'Parole', 'police station' can be experienced as higher status words and concepts as they apply to 'normal' people too. Police statements and confessions, however, which require reading or writing skills, do not get mentioned, although body searches, which are experienced as brainscans – something that will highlight and prove the nature of the wrongness – are spoken of. Being regularly picked up or questioned by police can be a defensive secondary handicap. By being singled out for 'badness' the individual can take refuge from his unworked-through fears and fantasies concerning the reasons for being disabled.

It is, however, comparatively rare for this group to be considered as offenders. It is an ironic fact that in not being considered viable witnesses, in losing that essential legal legitimacy, severely handicapped people also lose the right to be seen as bad, as deviant, as perverse. Instead of feeling liberated by this exemption, the guilt leads to further crime and further cover-ups by the network. It was Freud (1923) who suggested that guilt itself can cause a crime and Klein (1932) who saw that guilt could heighten sexual desire and cause further sexually disturbed behaviour. Where individuals have suffered unfairly, being born with or acquiring a cognitive deficit, there can be a network dynamic that joins in with the strong wish to imagine people as either ennobled by suffering, or too 'simple' to be capable of offending.

Clinical vignette 1

Mr Smith, aged 28, was referred urgently for his 'challenging behaviour', a new euphemism for what would be described as self-destructive behaviour or suicidal behaviour if he were not handicapped. The social worker said she was concerned that Mr Smith was in danger of killing himself if he was not treated. When I arrived at the hospital to assess him she rather nervously told me she would be leaving her job in a month. Handicapped adults are often referred at such a point. On meeting the psychiatrist I was told that Mr Smith behaved in a sexually inappropriate way as a result of his severe mental handicap. I asked what that meant and was told that Mr Smith had a mental age of three and did not understand the difference between men and women.

A psychiatric Registrar added that Mr Smith stole women's underwear and liked to wear it. 'It's like dressing up to be like his mother. He does not really understand he should not'. The charge nurse said, 'He's a dirty little bugger. He's got his hand up his bum all the time and you'll smell him a mile off' and an art therapist commented that he often used to expose himself to little children. This progression of painful information that is often omitted on a referral letter is still common, although less than ten years ago.

It was after my first meeting with him that I was told he had masturbated two little children as well. After an initial police presence the case was closed as Mr Smith was considered to be so severely handicapped he was 'merely' responding in the way little children do to each other sexually. After my second meeting with Mr Smith the social worker informed me 'I didn't tell you. The hospital is closing down and we have found a lovely home for Mr Smith. It will be his first proper home and he is near the shops. It will make all the difference to his quality of life'.

Without even taking you close to poor Mr Smith whose miserable traumatic life of abuse and loss and perversion was depleting the small cognitive resources he had to begin with, we can get an idea of the layers of stupefaction that handicap gets surrounded with. There is such a strong desire to 'sanify' – especially when there is an ideological/economic push to the community in which mental illness and perversion are supposed to miraculously disappear – that the serious issues of deviance and perversion are unbearable to face. Watching someone bash his head, anally masturbate, steal underwear and approach little children is a frightening and numbing experience for staff – it stupefies. The professional network for the non-handicapped offender finds it hard to avoid splitting in which the worker who uncovers proof of abuse/abusing is seen as the perpetrator. In the field of handicap, the therapist who stands for the sane realization of the existence of an offence, a crime, can be denigrated as the mad idiot. The rest of the network will see the client as either dirty and stupid or improvable and deprived. It is unbearable to hold the splits together.

Clinical vignette 2

Miss Jones, aged 22, was referred for her despairing addiction to stealing. Despite her mental handicap, all her intelligence was hijacked into crime. She was capable of forgery, embezzling and stealing money and cheque books from other handicapped people as well as professional workers. Each time she was found out and nothing happened she grew more and more desperate, stealing larger and larger sums. Still nobody did anything. Finally, she broke into a block of flats and in one weekend stole hundreds of pounds as well as small electrical items.

She was complimented on the intelligence she had shown. No-one took it seriously. In the therapy group she asked a sex offender what the police cell was like. 'It's cold' said the man concerned. 'It is very cold and you lie on something hard and cold and it is a long time you are cold but then they give you a lovely breakfast'. Miss Jones said 'I wish I could be in a place like that. Then I couldn't steal'. We discussed her fantasy prison, a place of asylum with nothing she could steal and her longing to know if I or anyone could stop her. One of the most therapeutic things I could do for her was to report her to her social worker when she stole in the clinic.

Nothing happened. By this time Miss Jones was stealing several times a day. She was worn out with it. In an accelerated sequence she stole at her college and was expelled, stole at her work placement and was expelled, stole at a voluntary job and was sacked and then stole in a shop so dramatically that she was found and the police came and she was finally arrested. Her parents felt the hours she spent in the cell were the most peaceful in her life. She was then, however, sent to hospital where she stole remorselessly and when that caused nothing to happen she took to hiding knives and then was sent to a locked ward where she continued stealing. I am hoping she will be sent to prison. Her sense of guilt (Freud 1923) that has so fuelled her criminal career was too great for the meagre once-weekly psychotherapy available, given that her living accommodation was unsupportive.

DISCUSSION

In my review of learning disability and sex offending (Sinason 1993) I noted that Bronya Booth and Maria Grogan (1990) in examining sexual offences by adults with learning disabilities in the North West Region found that out of 76 sexual offenders, 73 were male and 3 female. The majority were in the 16–25 age-range and almost half were in the mild to moderate learning disability group. Only 15 per cent lived in hospital or prison and most lived in the parental home. Booth and Grogan point out that in the region concerned the main area of expertise was in the mental handicap hospital yet 83 per cent of those needing treatment lived in the community. This points to the inability of professionals to consider adequately the meaning of offender behaviour. Minimizing the nature and meaning of the offence threatens the success of community care as it can unsurprisingly arouse vehement neighbourhood concern. Whilst there can be primitive fears in any community concerning rehabilitative group homes in residential areas it is important not to dismiss community protests that are based on an accurate perception that particular projects contain individuals who are not safe for the community or in the community.

It is commonly agreed (Griffiths, Hingsburger and Christian 1985) that the nature of deviant sexual behaviour is similar for both handicapped and non-handicapped offenders but the sex offender with learning disabilities is less likely to reach the courts and therefore treatment (Breen and Turk 1991) and his crimes are more likely to be detected. However, there is some evidence that learning disabled offenders can become more violent (Gilby, Wolf and Goldberg 1989) and are more likely to find male than female victims (Griffiths et al. 1985). In the University of Canterbury research project on abuse and disability Hilary Brown and Vicky Turk have found that 41 per cent of their sample of abused adults were abused by another person with a handicap (Cooke and Craft 1995).

In a psychoanalytic group we run for sex offenders who are learning disabled at St Georges Hospital, Professor Sheila Hollins and I have found that all such offenders have experienced major past trauma themselves. We consider that until such offenders receive empathy for what they themselves experienced as children they cannot be expected to have concern for the children they hurt or wish to hurt or the houses they wish to break and enter. However, once such a process is underway the very fact of their deficit might, ironically, make treatment more effective. As a result of a failure to adequately process past trauma by symbolization the central disturbance of the learning disabled offender can be more visible.

In one particular group the male offenders had become movingly aware that their desires to offend, in both the build up of masturbatory fantasies and in action, followed loss or humiliation. In one mutative session, after a year of therapy, one man was able to document how, faced by painfully humiliating situations engineered by a nurse he left his ward driven by the need to commit an offence. 'I sat on a bench where I usually sit near a playing field where the children play, you know, and thought, you know, what I would do, something bad. And then the longer I sat there the more I thought about how angry I was with the nurse and so I went to the police station and told them about the nurse and they were very sympathetic.' The group applauded him. They all recognized the power of that different option.

If we allow ourselves to acknowledge the offence properly and not minimize it but also allow ourselves to acknowledge that the offence is not the whole of the individual who is carrying it, we do well for victims and offenders who are, after all, often the same person.

7

From Troubled Families
to Corrupt Care
Sexual Abuse in Institutions

Caroline Garland

The man I shall describe was caught as a child in a grossly abusive régime. A Social Services-run Children's Home, under a corrupt Director, was organized to provide the daily opportunity for the gratification of the staff members' brutal and perverse sexuality. Thus children taken in the name of 'care' from extremely difficult backgrounds were put into a system that was worse in many respects than that from which they had been rescued. When after more than a decade the Director was arrested and the Children's Home closed down, efforts were made to trace the boys – by then young men – and to encourage them to bring a legal action against the Authority in whose care they had lived for some years. It was a difficult task, because very few of the boys could bear to be identified: many had led lives in which frequent changes of home, job, and even name were commonplace. Those who could be traced found it hard to believe that this would not turn out to be a further trick. Of the several seen by me and seen by colleagues in the Tavistock Clinic, I am going to describe one particular history and experience; but many of the cases interviewed revealed similar outcomes in certain crucial respects.

For some children, the sexual abuse had been accompanied by physical brutality; for others, by a seductive suggestion that the child was the favourite, picked out from among the rest by virtue of special qualities and appeal. However different the nature of the conditions in which the abuse took place, the effect upon their adult development is marked. Trusting relationships with others are difficult or impossible; no one of these men could be said to have a stable sense of his own value and worth. Although BJ, the man I describe, has achieved relationships with women, these relationships are deeply troubled. A profound sense of shame and rage permeates his life and his contacts with the world. He suffers from a barely contained paranoid personality disorder. Paranoid states, involving the risk of an explosive violence, are evoked in him by any sense of being trapped or confined; equally by the suspicion that he is being looked at in a belittling way. The prognosis remains bleak – not least because he has already been consistently and enduringly betrayed by a State-approved and supported system purporting to offer 'care'. The possibility of trust in further 'treatments' is very low. To work with this man, and with individuals like him, requires an ability to tolerate being feared, hated, mistrusted and let down or avoided for long periods at a time, however available and accommodating such men may appear at first interview.

Clinical vignette: BJ: On the Run

BJ was a solidly built dark-haired man, with a slightly rough and ready appearance, who looked somewhat battered, and older than his 30 years. He told me at once that he had mislaid the questionnaire I had sent him. When I did not respond he went on rapidly to say that actually he had not wanted to fill it in, because he didn't know where it was going; and even more important, who would be reading it. He is anxious about 'authorities' of all descriptions, mistrustful for at least two reasons: first that he has been in serious trouble with the law since he was an adolescent; second that at heart he trusts no one, ultimately relies on no one to have his interests at heart.

I learned something of BJ's childhood. He was the second in a family of seven children. There was constant quarrelling and violence between his parents, which rebounded on the children – especially the two oldest, BJ and his older sister, who were knocked about by their father because they were blamed for the bad behaviour of the little ones. He could remember being kept off school and given a fiver by his father to go and buy a pair of sunglasses to hide the black eye he'd been given. But, BJ stressed, he could also remember good times, when there were periods of harmony and some family feeling was generated: he remains in touch with both parents and his siblings, and has powerful if ambivalent feelings of attachment to his mother.

The parents split up when he was 10 years old, and all the siblings were taken into care. He played up from the start partly because he didn't know why his parents had split up; no one told him anything. He was tested by a psychologist and he threw the patterned blocks all round the room – probably, he said disarmingly, because the tests were getting more difficult. The five younger children went home to mother some weeks later, but BJ was kept behind, because he was, as the Director frequently told him, a problem child, and this meant that he was singled out for the Director's 'special care' programme. He knew that he had been separated from his sibs, but did not find out that they had gone home for some months. When he found out that he alone was still in care, he went wild – 'there was no stopping me.' However wild he felt, much of this violent turmoil remained internal. He couldn't blow up in the home because of the reprisals from the Director and the other staff; he couldn't run away because there was nowhere to go.

BJ's mood shifted constantly throughout the interview. It was clear that the prospect of going over his childhood experiences at the hands of the Director disturbed him, making him restless, extremely claustrophobic and at certain points shaken by feelings of rage. This rage seemed to me important. It appeared to have a defensive function, and was therefore not only a primary reaction to the memory of the violation he had been subjected to. Feelings of anger enabled him to feel large, powerful and in control, unable to be pushed around as he was when a child, when he suffered acutely from feeling small, helpless and entirely without support. Thus being angry or acting violently has an organizing function for a personality that for much of the time has to remain split into separate compartments if it is to function at all without being overwhelmed by terrifying memories. When, as in the interview with me, these memories are opened up, a state of anger appears to hold BJ in some kind of equilibrium, helping him avoid disintegration and breakdown. However, when the memories are triggered off inadvertently, they sometimes have the quality of an experience taking place in the present, rather than an experience recollected from the past, and become quite overwhelming. When anger or fighting have failed as a defence, however, this is the point where BJ is driven to seek oblivion in one form or another, usually through alcohol, which leads to fights.

It seemed that what was called 'therapy' by the staff involved inducing a total breakdown of the child's defences, via verbal abuse, humiliation, (being made to wear pyjamas all day, slapped, having to listen to denigration of the child's relation with the mother, made to cry, made to cuddle a teddy and jeered at for it) and finally sexual assault. And, he said in the interview with some real distress, BJ didn't think he could go home because by then he was already being abused: both with physical violence, and with anal rape by the Director (he was then aged 11). He came to believe that these things were happening to him because he was 'not like other kids', he was far more difficult. He had only one visit home during the next several years; his mother visited very rarely. The violence to him was endless. Here in the interview he became quite agitated, and it was my impression that he found being alone in a room with one other person extremely stressful. He felt claustrophobic, trapped. He wanted to smoke, but I said that if he could manage it, it would be more helpful if instead he could try to put into words the sorts of feelings that were making him want to smoke. The violence progressed from being slapped around, to outright beating up: his head was battered until he became semi-conscious on many occasions. I felt – and I tried to describe it to him – that this linked with the way he fights or drinks himself into unconsciousness now, since to lose consciousness is a way of blotting out a terrifying, humiliating (wetting himself with fear) and painful series of events; and of course, the memories of such events, and the feelings about them, when they get stirred up in the present. He called it 'knocking them on the head', meaning drinking to the point of oblivion.

As he grew older, and was attending day school, BJ's behaviour at school became increasingly unmanageable and he was in constant trouble. He was trying to get himself arrested. At one point he tried to tell the Headmaster what was going on at the Home, and what was being done to him: he was called a liar, given a harsh caning, and suspended from school for six weeks. A paradoxical feature of this period was that as he became increasingly delinquent and difficult to manage, increasingly in trouble with the police, so also did he become increasingly afraid of the Director. The aggression and delinquency seems to have been an attempt to assert some kind of independence faced with his fear of and dependence on the Director, comparable to the kind of dependence that hostages develop in relation to the terrorists who hold them in their power. The Director, he said, was frightening, but also seductive – 'he could get you round to his way of thinking'. He continued to feel in thrall to the Director precisely because he had been so terrorized by him when a dependent child.[1] This power was so striking that when giving evidence at the Director's eventual trial, BJ had asked if he could sit behind a screen. There was a way that the Director had of looking at him, he said, that could still frighten him – he then ducked his head and looked at me from under his brows with a fixed unblinking gaze – 'like this'. In the event, he had had the screen taken away, and had faced the Director while giving his evidence, with his heart pounding. He felt frightened when the Director turned to face him in the courtroom and gave him 'that look'. 'You'd know at the Home when he looked at you like that you were for it.'

As a young adult, after leaving the Home, BJ rapidly developed a criminal history. He combined the tendency to feel let down and persecuted with an equal capacity to fall in with and trust what he called 'heavy villains'. To some extent it was the seductiveness of easy money and a flash way of

---

1   This behaviour is characteristic of survivors of prolonged and repeated trauma (see Herman 1992).

life, but I felt that a deeper reason was that large powerful men, who appeared to him to be able to run the show, tapped into something vulnerable and dependent, even helpless, in him, and he became an easy prey, just as he remained hypnotized by and frightened by the Director even when it had become clear that the man's behaviour to him had been deeply corrupt.

BJ was in trouble with the police from the age of 18, and in and out of prison from 21 onwards. The charges included burglary, theft, fighting, assault, the possession of firearms and the threat of serious harm. This last involved the cornering of a girl-friend whom he thought had been seeing another man. He had become frantically jealous and upset, and went round to scare them both with a gun that 'wasn't a real one'. I thought that the intensity of BJ's response to the threatened loss of someone who felt necessary to his well-being showed something of his underlying dependence and vulnerability. His history of abuse at the hands of those who were ostensibly caring for him makes him vulnerable to abuse from people on whom he depends; this is linked to his susceptibility to 'heavy villains'. In effect, people who present themselves as 'in the know', or women who provide him with some modicum of tenderness or care, tap into his deprivation and need for stability and can then use him for their own ends. He remains helplessly attached, while knowing that things aren't right between him and this person.

The one element in BJ's presentation that offered a less than bleak prognosis was that over the last few years he seemed to have found himself one or two reliable figures (an early probation officer, one particular girl-friend and her parents) whose ability to stick with him through thick and, in particular, thin he can put constantly to the test. He has an unexpectedly appealing and attractive side to him which has no doubt contributed to his capacity to engage women in wanting to help him – as he was succeeding in doing with me in this interview. My feeling was that this connected with his having had some sort of unarticulated good early experience with his mother, something without which he would have been entirely done for by now. One way of looking at it might be to say that he has the rudiments of a capacity to tell a good figure from a bad one, even if he then gives his good figures a hard time. This capacity is unstable, however, and he is likely to jump at new and tempting offers however unsuitable they prove to be, because he has not internalized something strong and stable enough to enable him to keep his head in the face of something tempting. He spoke of his girl-friend with affection and a kind of respect for her ability to put up with him, but there was a glimpse of the persecuted state that can develop even in relation to her, as he described her becoming pregnant with his child as 'her trap'.

When I saw BJ his girl-friend was pregnant for the second time and he spoke with some feeling of his wish to provide some kind of decent future for his children. Since his first-born's birth, he had given up his 'Jack the Lad stuff, flash cars, thieving and that – '. He also linked the change in his behaviour to the emergence of the facts about the Director's régime, and the subsequent verdict and prison sentence. Thus one possible factor that has contributed to the change is the recognition by society and by the law of the wrongs that were done to him. He has been somewhat relieved of the sense that he is the only wrong-doer, and this has reduced some of his need to attack society, including that bit of society represented by his own family, through stealing back from it some of what was stolen from him – namely his childhood and the good things that should have accompanied an ordinary childhood. However, less thieving has meant more fighting. Fighting has some of the defensive function I have already touched on, that of helping him to feel strong and in control rather than powerless and humiliated, evocative of the abuse he suffered. He usually manages to avoid physical violence to his girl-friend, however, and breaks 'things' (furniture, windows) up rather than people; and in this respect, and so far, he differentiates himself from the parental couple.

BJ suffered a severe breakdown once the Director's case came to light. He had been talking to his probation officer about the way he consistently got into trouble soon after each prison sentence was ended (this recidivism is, incidentally, often a feature of the behaviour of men sexually abused as children.) His probation officer asked him about his history in care, but he refused at first to say anything. After several weeks, and with some unhurried and sensitive help from her, he began to speak about it, very reluctantly and with deep shame, convinced that he would be shunned by anyone who knew about it. He was told of the discoveries concerning the Director's régime in the Homes, and eventually persuaded to cooperate and give evidence. As the trial eventually began, BJ began to suffer the breakdown he had so far avoided. He felt, particularly when cross-examined by the Director's defence, that all his worst fears had come true. Coinciding with his deep-rooted fear of the Director, was the official world accusing him of being a liar. He felt he, not the Director, was the criminal – who was going to believe him, a man with a criminal record, against the Head of a Children's Home? He tried to flee the courtroom (he described himself actually running down the street), but was brought back for the next day's trial. The police did their best to reassure him, but, BJ said ruefully, they'd never been his friends, nor he theirs. The intensity of the trial had brought back the events with an intolerable force. I suspect that this was the first time he had ever had to face quite what had been done to him, and for how long. It did not seem surprising, and could even be felt to be potentially constructive that he should have broken down at that point. ('Constructive' in that the extent of the abuse was no longer denied, either internally, inside himself, or externally within society; 'potentially' because merely to open up a deep wound, without the opportunity to work through the traumatizing events in a safe setting, is inadequate.)

The legacy of these experiences is an easily triggered tendency to develop a paranoid state. In this state he goes into hiding, paralyzed with fear. The alternative is a noisy aggression, and a violent temper. This second is of course a defence against the first, and is used to ward off the threat of the first. There are quite specific circumstances which trigger the violence, namely when he feels belittled or humiliated or disbelieved, rendered in some respect helpless. I would link this quite specifically to the nature of the 'regression therapy' he was subjected to, in which an enforced helplessness was imposed on the child specifically to provoke a tantrum. BJ described the 'locking embrace' in which the child was held while being provoked and taunted by the Director until quite helpless with fear and rage. BJ is frightened by his own temper, aware that if provoked it is not impossible that he might inadvertently kill someone. He also knows that his shouting can save both him and the other, since it often makes the other back off.

I tried to explore the extent of the paranoid state, asking BJ whether, when the whole world, even his girl-friend and probation officer, seem out to get him, a part of him could remain separate from this state, knowing that it was just that, a state; or did he become quite overwhelmed by it, completely caught up in it? He was thoughtful about this, eventually answering that he 'sort of knows, and doesn't know'. When he gets like that, the whole world becomes dangerous, he becomes panic-stricken and he has to disappear and get out of it on his own. He goes on the road for a few weeks, knocking around strange towns, finding himself in out-of-the-way places, where – because no one knows him – he can for a short while experience peace of mind. He described to me one such episode in Scotland, where he walked into the country until it grew dark, not really knowing where he was going, right to the top of a hill, where he sat for a long time shivering and soaked by the rain, but also oddly peaceful – free of his persecutors, both internal and external.

One of the features of the state, and the fierce mistrust of his important figures, is that he sits his girl-friend down at the other side of a table and 'goes to town on her mentally, to see what she knows, what she's done'. This seemed to me to link with his own crushing psychic defeats when a child in care, and to represent a defence involving an identification with the one-time aggressor (Lewis 1992). I think it represents his attempt to avoid the alternative, the persecutory breakdown. Inevitably, it means that the chances of BJ's developing a stable and trusting relationship with anyone are, without treatment, extremely small.

BJ's lack of belief in a figure who can remain stably and solidly good contributes to his self-destructive behaviour. A complex cycle is set in motion, involving an anxiety; a testing out; a failure of the person in question to relieve that anxiety for whatever reason, following by massive attacks by BJ on himself and those same figures (disappearing, heavy drinking). This cycle only seems to be able to come to an end when BJ has rendered himself unconscious, and eventually wakes to find himself still alive. He can then once again go in search of his 'good' figures, and be relieved and grateful that they have, as it were, kept him alive inside themselves, not written him off altogether.

Many attempts have been made to get BJ into some form of treatment, but he has been unable to tolerate having to stick in one place long enough for real help to begin. The fear of being trapped, the claustrophobic anxieties, become quite overwhelming. However, residential treatment in a setting where both his criminality and his history of abuse might be addressed in a constructive and experienced way, is what is needed. However, the County responsible for his treatment while in Care do not now have the funds to pay for this treatment. BJ described other attempts at counselling, and in-patient treatment, all of which had broken down. It may be that a real facing of his traumatic past feels intolerable without the containment of a trusted and stable setting, which has so far not been available. Whether or not any consistent setting can be tolerated by a man whose primary defences against states of acute persecution involve aggression and drinking himself into oblivion, and who can feel trapped by the single fact of being in a room with one other person, is open to question.

At the end of our lengthy first interview I said to him that I thought the basis of the sort of paranoid state he was describing was something that by now was so entrenched inside him that it was pretty unchangeable; but I also thought that a considerable part of it came from the actual experiences he had suffered, and the lessons he had learned from those experiences. This part of it could be alleviated by allowing himself to have rather different sorts of experiences, in which he could begin to find out the real meaning of care and concern. In other words, I thought that treatment could certainly make a difference to him, and could help soften his tendency to develop paranoid states, and their precursors, the fighting and the drinking. BJ was silent for a while, and thoughtful. He said he knows he needs treatment.

In the three years that have followed this meeting, and the subsequent court report, I have continued to see BJ on a holding basis whenever his presence in London and his general state have allowed for it. Often requests for appointments are made from phone boxes in out-of-the-way places, or by a third party – sometimes his girl-friend. Sometimes these appointments are kept, sometimes they are not: a pub-brawl may intervene if the wait is too long, and sometimes too long can be less than 24 hours, since holding on to the knowledge that he wants and needs help is deeply painful. The fact is that the legacy of incarceration and abuse from his early 'carers' have left him a profoundly damaged man: he knows this, and he is often in despair about his situation. He is consequently driven to attack his own mental faculties with whatever means he can devise (drink, drugs, violence, flight) in order to escape this unbearable knowledge.

Gradually, however, BJ has become attached to the Clinic and more confident of my continued presence and willingness to see him, and gradually – with many stops and starts – we are trying to work towards the possibility of his being able to tolerate some in-patient treatment.

CONCLUSION

Current research has made clear links between persistent childhood abuse and borderline personality disorder (Herman 1987) and anti-social or delinquent behaviour (Lewis 1992). This case would seem to exemplify these findings. BJ is a classic Borderline Personality, showing the affective instability, the chronic anger and irritability, the identity disturbance and the impulsiveness that characterize this difficult disorder. He also suffers from intermittent paranoid states which at times can become frankly delusional, involving him and the others in his life in the risk of violence. As well, he shows many of the symptoms of a chronic Post-Traumatic Stress Disorder: extreme avoidance of trauma-related situations or settings; extreme vigilance; a tendency to relive the traumatic situation; irritability, and deteriorating relationship with family or friends.

In all cases we have seen from the Director's régime, issues concerning the nature of reality and the capacity to trust are central to the difficulties. There is a chronic inability to trust others, particularly those in any position of authority, or on whom there may develop a sense of dependence. Intimately related to the inability to trust, and by now very entrenched, is the underlying paranoid personality disorder, which may well – in the absence of treatment – come to encroach further on the personality with time.

It is difficult to say how these men would have developed had there been no experience of prolonged homosexual abuse in an atmosphere of physical and/or emotional violence, coming as they all did from disrupted and sometimes violent family backgrounds.

However, all these boys were taken into a setting which was in theory designed to provide protection against the violence and disruption each had already experienced; in that new setting, they were subjected in the name of 'treatment' to prolonged severe sexual abuse and threatened with further rejection, loss or violence if they did not comply. There is no reason to suppose that had they been provided with an experience of 'care' worth the name, they would not have been able to develop both emotionally and intellectually, and pursue lives which did justice to their (in some cases considerable) potential. BJ himself is of good intelligence, and demonstrates a hunger for affectionate contact with trustworthy figures, even if that hunger is matched by an even greater fear.

An interesting feature of a chronic inability to trust other people, particularly those in any position of authority, is the way it is often demonstrated as a chronic untrustworthiness. Effectively, this reversal obliges the 'other' to be the one who is disappointed, abandoned, let down, hurt and betrayed, the one who is in a state of chronic apprehensiveness. Broken appointments, promises, hearts, unmet debts, may all be frequent. Alcohol, or other addictive substances, may seem a more reliable and controllable object than another person, in that it remains in one's pocket, under one's own control. This makes the treatment of this man, and those like him, very difficult. Yet BJ is quick to understand interpretations, and I have often seen how his states of tension can be relieved by feeling them to be understood, rather than by having them controlled by 'techniques', which is all too reminiscent of the abuse he suffered as an adolescent.

It is crucial to go on offering help to this man and those like him, and to try to understand and manage its repeated breakdown. This is not only because in general we might believe in trying to contribute to the repair of severe damage inflicted on any one human being by another; but also because in particular if we are to keep alive in BJ and in others like him a fragile belief in the possibility of hope, or of progress, or in goodness itself, we have to keep it alive in ourselves in the face of repeated rejection. This does not mean putting up with being abused, but it does mean engaging in the very hard work of tolerating, understanding, containing and interpreting the nature and significance of what goes on between us and our patients until they can begin to take in and make use of this process as their own. In that work, a psychoanalytic way of understanding psychic development offers a structure, a depth and a power that is profoundly valuable to both patient and therapist.

8

Understanding Murderous Young People

Sue Bailey and Lynn Aulich

A key issue emerging from our own work with 40 child and adolescent murderers (Bailey 1996) and 121 child and adolescent sex offenders (Dolan, Hollaway and Bailey 1996) centres on long-standing cumulative risk factors reaching a crescendo as they enter the physical stage of puberty. Critically, over a short period of weeks, social interactions prior to the sadistic act deteriorate, in other words, issues of trust, emerging patterns of verbal, physical aggression, feelings of hostility and paranoid reactions towards peers and adults reach a climax. Even where the child has gained a sense of power and pleasure from organized behavioural try outs, accompanied by the sadistic fantasies, they still, at the eleventh hour, expect an adult intervention positive or negative to occur. If the cues presented to the outside world of both adults and peers go unheeded rage explodes onto a fragile victim in a chaotic, disorganized sadistic act.

Adult sadists often report an absence of positive fantasies in their early life; whether never present or lost in very early negative experiences is unclear, but what emerges is the overwhelming importance of the secret reality of the fantasies to the individual in adolescence. The early aggressive behaviours serve to displace anger onto the victim but clinically, as fantasies elaborate, the displayed aggression (whether still in play or against an individual) occurs with diminishing fear or anxiety about adult disapproval. Each subsequent act serves to allow increasingly intense emotions to be incorporated into their imaginations, in turn allowing the intensity of violent thoughts to escalate.

For the last five years, working within the multi-disciplinary setting of the Adolescent Forensic Service the authors, an adolescent forensic psychiatrist and an art therapist, have found that a combination of verbal and non verbal therapies have most to offer those young people who have committed sadistic and murderous acts. Art therapy has enabled the children and adolescents to face the most violent and sadistic elements of their offence. This is particularly so in those cases where the legal process, pre and during trial, endured by these young people means that the spoken word has become a painful and often destructive experience.

Realistically, therapy with young people who have committed murderous acts of violence has to be tailored to the demands of the external environment and has to be approached cautiously. Motivational dynamics are complex and the monitoring of ongoing level of risk critical especially if the young person remains within the community and their family. Given the frequent distortion of perception of self and others, the emergence of a true sense of guilt and shame can and often is a slow, difficult, painful and angry process.

THE PARALLEL PROCESS OF CARE AND EDUCATION

Detention itself can provide time for further neurodevelopmental cognitive and emotional growth allowing the adolescent to gain a better grip on his or her internal and external worlds, thus possibly leading to better control of his or her emotional and aggressive impulses. Irrespective of the available, if any, treatment model provided by the care or custody institution, this parallel process is best facilitated in a milieu characterized by warmth and harmony. Clear organization, practicality and high expectations promote the establishment of positive staff–adolescent, staff–staff and adolescent–adolescent relations (Harris, Cole and Vipond 1987).

VERBAL THERAPIES

The majority of murderous adolescents dissociate themselves from the reality of their act, but gradually experience a similar progression of reactions and feelings akin to a grief reaction (Hambridge 1990). Their grief is initially about their own loss of freedom and enforced separation from family, only finally leading to a possibility of grieving for their victim. The effect on the young person's family can be as devastating as on the victim's family (Macleod 1982). Against the inevitable waxing and waning of outside pressure the child has to move safely through the process of disbelief, denial, loss, grief, anger and blame. In addition, it is being increasingly recognized that post traumatic stress disorder can occur arising from the participation in the sadistic act either directly or observing the action of their partners in the act of violence or arising from past abusive acts perpetrated against the young person in earlier years.

Qualities such as previous frequent and severe aggression, low intelligence and a poor capacity for insight, weigh against a positive safe outcome. The clinician also has to remain alert to the possibility of emerging formal mental illness, in particular depression (Stewart, Myers and Burnet 1990), what this means in therapy and what risks it poses.

In understanding the role of violence in the youngster's life it is necessary to understand the depth of their sensitivity and reaction to a perceived threat or ridicule in many day-to-day events. As the youngsters start to discuss their murderous act, they have to face past loss, trauma, abuse, fears of being vulnerable and the fact that therapy many bring about changes they do not like and, above all, cannot control.

From the outset, there has to be a clear understanding of the patient–therapist dyad and the boundaries of confidentiality. A forensic psychiatrist may well have to comment on the level of responsibility a child or adolescent can hold for the offence, as well as predict future risk, particularly when the individual reaches the stage in their sentence when they become eligible for parole and supervised return to the community. This can lead to testing of a trusting relationship between the adolescent and clinician when the clinician is asked to offer opinion on the central issue of 'time served' and/or timing of movement on from secure care to a prison sentence.

The tools available to the therapist are first and foremost the empowerment from statutory agencies, placement, family and the individual to carry out the work. Then there is the baggage of history accompanying each adolescent, the depositions (police evidence regarding the offence); and the therapist physically retracing the events prior to the offence (the adolescent often having a distorted memory of time, size and geography). All have been used effectively in offence-specific work.

Each component has to be visited and revisited as, and when, the adolescent can developmentally cope with the relevant issues. At a later stage in therapy it is important that the adolescent understands the degree and level of public opinion arising from the offence (via newspaper and media coverage). As the adolescent approaches a return to the community he or she needs to reach a safe resolution which must include a mechanism for explaining the gap in their life to the outside world and in particular to any future partner.

Addressing victim empathy, saying sorry and reattributing blame can, and does, lead to expression of anger and distress with sessions often sexualized in both form and content. When the emotion this engenders spills outside sessions it leads to disruptive behaviour within the institution. This is difficult for the child and carers and can in turn lead to both becoming collusively rejecting and dismissive of the therapists. However, disclosure and understanding is essential if safe resolution is to be achieved. In the stage of investment the youngster can assume far more responsibility for the content of sessions, honesty is enhanced, acting out diminishes and, critically, the youngster starts consciously to link murderous behaviour to conflict, loss and trauma in the past whilst coping with feelings in the present.

NON VERBAL THERAPIES

In art therapy the visual image – a drawing, a painting or a sculpture, and the process through which the image is achieved – provides the focus of attention and the primary means of communication between the patient and the therapist. The image contributes towards the externalization of thoughts and feelings which might otherwise remain unexpressed. The patient and therapist work together to search for, and reach, an understanding of the process and the products which emerge within the structure of sessions. These products of the art therapy session provide a physical and tangible record and, as such, contain valuable information about the young person's perceptions of the self, the family, other people and life events. Art work also encapsulates the emotional quality of these perceptions.

The art therapist closely observes all the choices made by the patient in the structuring of the image: the fluidity or thickness of paint; the density of a pencil line; the composition; the attention to, or lack of detail: relative scale of components or figures; the handling of clay. All are of equal importance to the content or narrative. The aim of the examination is to elicit what information the image contains. Play often accompanies art making and can be explored in terms of symbol, metaphor and quality of emotion in the same way as the artwork. The therapist is there to receive, interpret, and offer feedback on the communications when appropriate.

Art therapy is informed by the principles of psychotherapy. The relationship between the patient and therapist becomes triangular with the inclusion of the art object, and countertransference is an important tool. The art product acts as a 'third party' to hold and contain projected feelings. It is often easier for distressed, traumatized young people to work through an inanimate third party in order to relieve them of the fear that they may destroy the therapist or that the therapist may retaliate and destroy them. The most fearsome of these feelings can be safely projected and discharged into the art object.

Young people who murder, or attempt murder, respond to art therapy more readily if it is offered as soon as possible after the offence. There are problems with this in relation to the judicial system, but it avoids the young person's desire to forget all about it once the judicial process is completed.

It is made clear to the young person that art therapy is offered as an opportunity to express feelings and thoughts which concern them. Once a relationship of trust is developed the question 'what brought you here' can begin to be explored. There are no rules and limits are set as the need arises.

During the course of therapy narratives emerge which are mapped by significant life events. They are often traumatic experiences made manifest in the play and visual imagery. These may begin as ephemeral, obscure, disguised forms but because they are repeated they gradually gain in clarity. The process of evolving the narrative is painful and accompanied by feelings of anger, rage and sorrow. Traumatic experiences are relived through use of symbol and metaphor. On reflection this symbolic re-enactment of trauma reveals the same dynamics which motivate the offence. The central re-enactment is that of the offence itself.

The therapist needs knowledge of the depositions and access to a family history to assist in verifying the analysis and interpretation of the material in therapy sessions. This is especially important when the young person has not yet reached the point where they can make connections between their images, and their feelings and life experiences.

It is important to stress that this symbolic re-enactment does not occur in response to a request from the therapist but gradually emerges piecemeal in a series of images when the patient is ready. It is a process which cannot be hurried if it is to be a beneficial healing experience and not an added or repeated trauma. The events before, during and after the offence are revisited in different forms, with more information about what happened and most important, what was felt.

Clinical Vignette 1

A girl of eleven was responsible for a house fire in which the friend she was staying with died. During her sessions she performed a symbolic re-enactment of her experience of the fire and her friend's death. She had been making a picture with powder paints, became impatient with mixing water and powder and began dipping her wet brush directly onto the powder and then scattered the powder onto wet paper straight from the pot. Some powder escaped, flying up into her face. She coughed and spluttered, fanning the powder with her hand. Then she deliberately banged the pot onto the table making more fly up and shook her paper making clouds of silver powder 'It's like smoke, I'm choking'. Then she talked about the fire. In the next session she painted black inside her nostrils and mouth, and said. 'This is what X looked like when she was dead'. At the end of the session she whispered to me that *she* should have died in the fire and not X. It was decided by the court that she had not intended the death of her friend in the fire.

Clinical Vignette 2

Another girl came to art therapy for eighteen months aged between 11 and 13. She used her sessions to play out and symbolize her distress, having suffered extreme instability, neglect, physical and sexual abuse since birth.

One of the many complex themes which emerged during her sessions was that of working through denial of her offences; she had made three known attempts to seriously harm younger children. The last and the most serious was attempted murder when her victim was seriously injured around her head and neck. Gradually, during the course of therapy, came a more realistic re-enactment of this offence, the final one after eighteen months of therapy and two years after the attack. Most of her paintings, clay models, play and games expressed her sadistic feelings and working with her was often very frightening for both of us. Mess was spread over tables, chairs, our clothes, the floor and ceiling, and she frequently attacked me with paint and clay. A turning point occurred when she smeared red paint over her arms and hands, while making a painting, then put her hands around my neck leaving a red mess under my chin and over my throat, echoing the experience of herself and her victim. It was clear from many other sessions that she identified with the people who abused her, and tried to rid herself of her feelings of total helplessness by rendering her victims helpless, so that she could feel more powerful. The re-enactment of her offence symbolically appeared to be a safe way to show to herself what she had done and what she was capable of doing, in a move to acknowledge and assimilate the experience and try to understand what led her to it.

Her perception of me was of someone big, strong and resilient. I was a person in whose presence it was safe to reveal some of her hidden feelings. Her need to be sadistic and cruel could be demonstrated without harming anyone or being harmed or hated back. Subsequent sessions saw more sorrow and anger and a gradual change; a consequence both of natural maturation and the benefits of being able to work through the pain she suffered and the pain she caused.

The gradual emergence of the symbolic re-enactment of traumatic experiences runs concurrently with other themes relating to the offence. This includes grief for the loss of freedom, and being removed from family, friends and familiar environment. Grief for the victim and feelings of remorse follow much later.

Committing murder or attempted murder necessitates a harsh reappraisal of the idea a young person has about him or herself. This change of identity is a loss in itself; for example, being a bad person may be the feeling a person has already and the act confirms this. One patient demonstrated this in making a 'self box'. He was given a box and asked to think about himself with an inside and an outside – that is, the person he is to the outside world and his private self. The box disintegrated completely under the weight of black and brown paint which could not be held but burst out over the furniture. Part of the session was used to clean up the mess, although the box was kept as it was and looked after by the therapist. The cleaning up process is important in assisting the patient to take some responsibility for the mess and the art work, in whatever state of dissolution or formlessness is kept. In this way bad, murderous feelings and feelings of self hate are acknowledged as being real and valid, not discarded or discharged into the therapist.

In a later session this patient smeared his arms and face in clay, asking to being covered in earth or buried. This referred to the death of the victim by obliterating the self, symbolically dying and merging with the victim. Murderous young people often pretend to be dead, or actually sleep during sessions in this phase of therapy in an attempt to change places with the victim. To understand the motivation to kill, the young person needs to identify with the victim and revisit their own experiences of helplessness and extreme passivity which engendered such extreme feelings of rage and hate.

Another theme in therapy is the fear that the victim will return to haunt them and seek retribution. The return of the victim, or their magical restoration can also be seen as an attempt to repair the wrong done to that person, to put them back together again so that they will be whole. The appearance of the restored, repaired victim, followed by the realization that the attack cannot really be undone, is a move towards making reparation and the onset of grief for the victim.

These themes are repeated many times in different visual forms. It seems that the more often the trauma is revisited and re-enacted, the closer the young person moves towards reaching a stage where they can grieve for the life of the person they killed or injured. In art, as in verbal therapies, the emergence of grief for the victim appears long after grief for the self and the working through of the experiences they had which motivated them to kill. When the person is able to accept the reality of their actions and assimilates them, the task of rebuilding their own lives as a person who is safe to return to the community begins.

As psychiatrist and art therapist working in tandem we have striven to gain a fuller understanding of the altitributional process of young people who murder. We have sought to support each other as therapists in maintaining and sustaining the motivation of children and adolescents placed in secure settings for a period of time that at present in this country can be a 'life sentence'.

9

Murderousness

Anne Zachary

All psychotherapists are familiar with murderousness. It is probably a universal neurotic phenomenon: at best, as part of a successful analysis, a meaningful symptom; at worst, unconscious and perhaps more apparent to others, not least the object of it. However, things become more complicated and serious within the other diagnostic categories – namely, perversion and psychosis – when murderousness can be acted out. It is probably not controversial to generalize that, at the moment of killing another, or even planning a death whilst emotionally disturbed, neurotic becomes psychotic,[1] and that if the victim in a perverse situation dies, the perversion has broken down into psychosis.

When such a case comes to trial, the court decides whether the act is one of murder and using experts decides whether there is a psychiatric diagnosis to be made. Often, in these circumstances, the verdict is that the act has been one of less than murder, namely manslaughter, for reasons of diminished responsibility, usually due to psychiatric disturbance.

The focus of this chapter is on diagnosis and treatability where there has been killing and particularly on the effect the killing has in the countertransference in assessment and treatment.

It is beyond the the scope of this chapter to incorporate a discussion of evil or 'cold-blooded' killing whilst of sound mind, or whether group processes come into play in circumstances such as war. Suffice it to say that in the direction of the former that the usefulness of the legal diagnostic term 'psychopathy' is now being questioned. There is a recognition that an aetiology

---

1 I am using psychotic in the psychodynamic sense to mean a primitive mode of functioning rather than in the strict psychiatric sense. It has been referred to as psychotic with a small 'p'.

of deprivation and neglect leads to a lack of concern and it has been suggested that psychopathy be replaced by the term 'personality disorder' which might inspire more interest in the provision of treatment resources.

ASSESSMENT

When assessing a patient, the impact and significance of (an) actual killing is starkly and immediately apparent in the countertransference. Whether it is empathic feeling about the fate of the victim(s), or concern that if the boundary has been crossed before, it can be crossed again, or a mixture of both, the countertransference experience has a different quality from that with other patients. Another powerful element is often empathic feeling for the patient who usually has plenty of historical mitigating circumstances, universally deprivation, possibly provocation and abuse. How do these affect the assessment and the decision about treatment?

A first caution is not to remain isolated with a patient who has killed. The reason for this becomes very clear as soon as the assessment is shared with colleagues in a case presentation. It is likely that any empathic feeling for the patient will be lodged with the clinician who has seen him or her, whilst the negative countertransference will become immediately palpable among the listeners. This is an important reality base from which the truth can materialize. What has to be determined is how much of the positive countertransference is the result of a seduction on the part of the patient, particularly when the diagnosis is perversion. But equally important is how much it can form the basis for a therapeutic alliance.

We do not yet know enough about the relationships between fantasy and enactment. As professionals we worry about risk, but there is no absolute evident in advance about who will kill – when, and why then. Much work has been done in this area at the Portman Clinic under the leadership of Dr Mervin Glasser. To distinguish between perversion and psychosis where violence is concerned it is helpful to think in terms of sado-masochistic and self-preservative forms. There may be a sophisticated and stable sado-masochistic mode of relating which protects against psychosis and which enables a sense of security and identity. There may be violence or suffering inflicted upon the victim, but the objective will not be death. Indeed, it is imperative that the object remain alive in order for the sado-masochistic relationship to continue. In these circumstances death may occur accidentally or as an end result before another victim is sought. There is an argument, yet to be proven, that by the time death is an entity the defences have been broken down, the perpetrator is psychotic and the situation has switched into self-preservative mode. Now the victim has become a threat to the aggressor's existence and to kill is the means of psychic survival.[2]

This pattern was well described by Dennis Nilsen, who killed a series of young men. At first he befriended them for mutual company. Part of the bizarre rituals to which he subjected them were 'loving' but eventually each victim provided another short-lived opportunity for him to feel that, because they died, he lived. This has been very clearly understood in terms of projective identification by Dr Arthur Hyatt-Williams.

TREATMENT

In the exciting current climate of rapid development in the field of forensic psychotherapy we are presented with increasingly difficult decisions about whether the offer of treatment is appropriate. It has been appreciated for a long time that psychoanalytic principles and techniques are valuable in the understanding and management of offenders, often serious offenders. Concurrent with the expansion of actual treatment resources for this group of patients is the increasingly worrying lack of enough custodial and inpatient placements. Outpatient facilities are now realizing a considerable increase in the number of referrals at the more serious end of the spectrum in terms of dangerousness, risk, and past history giving cause for concern.

Clinical vignette

The patient is in his forties and many years ago when he was in his teens, he killed a young child. Sadly, having been assessed shortly before the killing he had not disclosed that already he had developed a regular practice of seducing and abusing young children. Instead, this early assessment had concentrated on his minor theft offences. Here is an illustration of the divide between assessor and audience in a case presentation. The new assessor questions the thoroughness of the previous assessment, whilst the audience notes the patient's ability to deceive. This new assessment took place whilst the patient was being rehabilitated, having been in custody for many years. Whilst he is pleased to be free, considerable anxieties remain in him and much more so in his carers about the future. He prefers to call this 'Wanting to sort out certain things from the past.' He has also suffered long bouts of depression.

The patient is ageing. He is slightly overweight with thinning hair and he makes rather old-fashioned attempts to preserve an air of youth. His manner is nonchalant. This is an immediate concern, for our business is serious.

---

2 Though self-preservative violence seeks annihilation of the object it does not by definition always necessarily end in death.

He responds to the psychoanalytic model. He is browned off by constant questioning about his fantasies, his motives and his future prognosis. He says angrily, 'If they don't stop it I'll feel they are driving me to it, putting ideas into my head. It happened years ago and I have certainly served my time.' He becomes very serious and acknowledges that he needs to sort out what it was all about, why it happened. He can see that the free association method offers the space and the chance to explore feelings, memories and experiences.

Here is the dilemma again. Is he saying things to make a therapist feel valued and effective? It does lead to evocative thoughts about the past, when as a boy about the age of his victim, his mother died and he wasn't told. Instead he was sent to live with relatives and told that his mother was ill. Years later, he found out that his mother had hanged herself. In our first meeting we reached the conclusion that in killing the child (at the time almost unaware of what he was doing, borne out later by the judge's decision that it was manslaughter and not murder), he was expressing his own sense of having died when his mother did. Unconsciously he had died; in killing the child he identified with it, enabling himself to live.

The judge's decision had been influenced by his remorse when he realized what he had done. He had killed the child by strangling it. This was a representative of what he had found out about his mother, a further identification with her. Another person might have committed suicide as she did; this man found a way to live by killing himself in another. Here is the self-preservation form of violence. For some time before this single event he had been able to avoid feelings, not by becoming psychotic but by sexualizing his aggression and abusing a series of young children by enticing them to engage in mutual masturbation. This had felt too shameful to disclose at the earlier assessment.

There is plenty of scope for treatment. The patient seems motivated. But there are tell-tale signs that he is far more anxious about opening up old wounds than he cares to admit. He is wary of travelling alone to the Clinic. He forgets to come. He confuses the arrangement and thinks that each appointment is to be booked separately. He sheepishly confesses to having got himself into trouble on the eve of his transfer from hostel to flat by being caught with a weapon. Each of these details sends an audience into a wave of concern that he will re-offend and anxiety that he is not admitting that he, too, is concerned that he will re-offend.

Finally, whilst an interpretation suggesting this anxiety to him glides across his nonchalance without touching, the further interpretation that treatment at this stage is not a sensible plan is received with relief. It is a way of saving face, of postponing further exploration until he is more confident in his independence. Meanwhile, the supportive forensic services which have brought him this far will continue their vigilance and perhaps in the future, possibly if depression recurs, psychotherapy can be reconsidered. In both forensic and psychotherapeutic decision-making, sensitive timing is crucial.

CONCLUSION

Forensic psychotherapy is a most important development but it cannot be regarded as a panacea. The psychopathology of these patients is immensely complex and needs to be viewed very seriously. What has careful assessment of this patient yielded?

(1)   That he is afraid of re-offending, too afraid to admit it and that this would be the focus of treatment.

(2)   That a relationship based on trust may be possible in time.

(3)   That he wants not only to protect himself and other potential child victims but perhaps also and more immediately the therapist.

This last point raises the real dilemma with such patients. To treat them opens up the essential re-enactment, one hopes symbolic, which is transference. The therapist can become the dangerous person who risks uncovering the fact that he could kill again and who is therefore at some risk. By not engaging in treatment the patient has symbolically killed off the therapist in the transference, whether it is a representation of himself, his mother or another child, at whichever level it is considered. Had he been able to engage in treatment, with the dangerousness at first projected into the therapist in this way, the task would have been to contain the anxiety until he could come to terms with, and own, this frightening part of himself, his internal persecutor, without having to retaliate against those who initially abused him (his mother and the conspiracy to silence in his family).

The psychoanalytic setting is ideal in that its stability, security and opportunity for trust to grow, helps contain such anxieties. Were there more facilities and resources, that is, trained psychoanalytic psychotherapists during the custodial stage, the fact that actual killing had occurred would be represented in the more secure setting. However, the advantage at the rehabilitation stage is that the patient's current life experience, including taking responsibility for his commitment to the treatment arrangements, becomes an essential focus during treatment. Assessment includes an appraisal of the optimum training for a treatment plan and long-term follow up in order to reappraise this over time.

10

Women Who Murder Their Children

Jane Knowles

Of female homicide it has been written 'usually the victim is not only a member of the patient's family but the one who has apparently been the most loved' (Kolb 1977, p.454). The largest group of people murdered by women consists of children aged under sixteen years – 45 per cent of all female homicides (by comparison with homicide of spouses at 33%) (d'Orban 1990). Of these filicides 45 per cent of those killed within the first year of life are killed within 24 hours of birth (Green and Manohar 1990). A study from Quebec found that 33 per cent of all child deaths under ten years were the result of maternal filicide (Marleau 1995).

There is general agreement both that this is probably an under-recognition of filicide, and that the women who are charged with this offence form a heterogeneous group, psychologically and socially, with a range of illnesses, with the deaths having different meanings for them. Various attempts at classification tend to reflect this heterogeneity, for example Resnick's (1969) motivation classification, Scott's (1973) 'impulse to kill' classification or d'Orban's (1990) classification.

Social stress is an important precipitating factor, compounding psychiatric illness, personality problems and low intelligence. Ten per cent seem motivated by revenge against spouse (d'Orban 1990) and there is evidence that daughters are the victims more often than sons (Marleau 1995).

Psychodynamically, each woman presents her own unique picture but there is a common tone of presentation in which she appears to have 'middle knowledge' (Weisman 1972) of the filicide. This is a detached, rather abstract knowledge that does not penetrate to the affective level. Thus one patient (Amy) could say on a rainy day 'look' (pointing out of the window) 'my baby is crying in heaven' as a part of a factual confession to the filicide of her two-year-old daughter without any apparent emotional connection with the words. So lacking in emotion was this session that as a therapist I felt suspended in unreality. This demonstrated itself externally in the coroner having classified the child's death as accidental and the staff who came into contact with Amy as being divided into two groups – one believing her innocent and the other guilty.

Amy appeared to have made little or no intrapsychic reorganization in the process of becoming a mother. Her daughter (Jade) was perceived by Amy as a part of herself. 'It's like I've lost a leg' she commented one day 'now I'll limp through life'. Her descriptions of loss were entirely physical rather than psychological. At times I worried that therapy might push her into the emotional experience but her capacity for denial, rationalization and false interpretation was infinite. She demonstrated what has been described else-where as a 'fluid transition between coping strategies and unconscious defence mechanisms' (Brezinka *et al.* 1994, p. 1). The boundaries between consciousness and unconsciousness seemed at times non-existent, so that Amy's external sense of reality came mostly from her internal world. External confrontation seemed to puzzle rather than anger her and I often experienced the same sense of confusion in the countertransference. Whether or not the staff believed Amy guilty of filicide they all reported how easy it was to like her socially and that they only experienced unease when they tried to talk at any length with her. Her family seem to have only known her at that superficial social level and as such found her warm and fun and 'the perfect mother'. Her assumption of motherhood had also been at a superficial level. Amy's mother reported with pride how obsessional Amy had been about Jade always having clean clothes. No-one in the family had questioned Amy changing Jade many times a day in order to keep her clean – this had been accepted in line with Amy's false interpretation of this being good mothering.

Being a one hundred per cent good mother was important to Amy. Therapy revealed the extent to which Jade had become the bad part of Amy, the dirty shameful aspects of herself to be kept clean, or when this failed, to be annihilated. In many ways it felt as if Jade's death was a partial suicide of Amy. Thus my fears that Amy might suddenly be confronted with the reality of what she had done proved unfounded. Instead she appeared consistently calm in her belief that the badness in herself had been destroyed for ever.

With evidence that it is more common for mothers to kill daughters rather than sons (Marleau 1995) this dynamic may be common to many filicides. Lack of family or social appreciation for the birth of a daughter might also make a female child less valuable in the inner world of these mothers.

Susanah killed her son Thomas, aged six months, as an act of revenge on her father because Thomas was so very welcome in the family and in particular by his grandparents. She revealed a history of prolonged sexual abuse of a sadomasochistic form from the age of four by the father who would say things like 'I'm hurting you because I love you' whilst abusing her. Susanah said that she dreaded having a son throughout the pregnancy and felt revulsion at his birth. 'Another man hurting me' was her description. Changing Thomas's nappies was repulsive to her: 'every time I saw his penis I wanted to chop it off'. Unlike Amy, who still saw Jade as a physical aspect of herself when aged two, Susanah experienced Thomas as 'appallingly different to me' and felt it was 'impossible to believe he was a part of me' from birth.

Like Amy, Susanah switched into a superficial and obsessive mothering of Thomas to hide her feelings from herself and others. This defence was not as complete in Susanah, however, and her feeling would 'break through', particularly when she was tired. On the day she decided to kill him Susanah described 'sliding into the knowledge that it was him or me'. It was only after Thomas' death that Susanah made the link of Thomas' likeness, physically to her father. 'I've killed my father's reincarnation' was her first words to her husband when he returned home that evening.

In therapy Susanah could speak with insight into the motivations behind the murder, initially with a form of 'belle indifference' as if the insights justified the murder as well as explaining it. Gradually a sense of the wrongfulness of what she had done began to wash over her. She would weigh evidence about whether sexual abuse or murder was the worst crime. She believed that her father had murdered part of her and that this was more painful than being completely murdered. Although she was eventually able to start to grieve for Thomas it was for the Thomas her husband had loved, photographed and spoke of. For Susanah, Thomas hardly existed as her lost child. Throughout therapy she declared herself glad of the pain she had caused her parents and believed that they deserved what had happened, had even caused it.

Attempts at therapy are limited by these women's versions of reality in which the child, even when loved, is object rather than person to the mother. The countertransference I have experienced as a reaction to this has been of anger on behalf of the infant which makes it hard to maintain a neutral caring of the mother. This was particularly true with Mary, who described giving her daughter, Louise, a 'wonderful birthday with all the things she loved most' before smothering her. Mary had been depressed since Louise's birth and had antidepressants for six months and regular visits by a community psychiatric nurse (CPN). The CPN noted some weeks before Louise's first birthday that Mary's mood had brightened. In retrospect Mary agreed that that was the point at which she had decided to kill Louise, but wanted to wait until after she had given her a 'treat' for her birthday. This experience of mood lifting once the decision is made reinforces the view that the killing represents a partial suicide of the mother. It became clear in working with Mary that she had killed off a part of herself and she talked about grieving for the part of her that was able to cry and scream. As the months passed she became increasingly tense and sometimes mute. When she did talk it was to bemoan her inability to do anything about her aggression that was 'building up inside'. She would talk of aggression in a 'small child' voice incongruous to the topic. Mary committed suicide on the fourth anniversary of Louise's death at a time when she had found new love and was recently engaged. Unusually, none of the staff who knew her felt grieved or surprised. In a staff sensitivity meeting one commented that Mary had made it all seem like destiny to which we, the staff, could be no more than observers.

I think we culturally underestimate the enormity of the normal intrapsychic reorganization that goes on within women as they become mothers. There was little or no evidence that these women had made that reorganization, rather that they had sustained the child as a part of their own inner worlds. When those inner worlds contain rage, abuse and despair the child becomes a container for whatever feelings the women cannot contain comfortably. The external pressures of the infant on the mother are then added to internal pressures of the infant perceived as persecuting the mother with disavowed aspects of herself. Any additional stress in this situation appears to precipitate the thought that these infants as persecutory objects must be killed. Such thoughts seem to set these mothers onto a course that culminates in premeditated murder but in a robotic unemotional state, in which they have, at best, 'middle knowledge' of the nature and wrongfulness of the act.

Any therapy undertaken with mothers who kill their children needs to be conservative in its aims. The goals of therapy need to be clear to the women and to others involved in her care. It is not unusual, for instance, for women who batter children to death (probably around 40% of filicides (d'Orban 1990)) to be already pregnant again – this represents part of the external stress. Therapy should not be seen as a means of making the women into a safe mother. It can however allow the women a space to explore the act and its meaning for her even if some of those meanings leave the therapist with uncomfortable feelings in the countertransference.

11

Munchausen Syndrome by Proxy

Kerry Bluglass

INTRODUCTION

The condition known as Munchausen by Proxy (MSBP), an unsatisfactory and rather misleading term, consists of 'the deliberate production or feigning of physical or psychological signs or symptoms in a person who is under the individual's care. Typically the victim is a young child and the perpetrator is the victim's mother. The motivation for the perpetrator's behaviour is presumed to be a psychological need to assume the sick role by proxy. External incentives such as economic gain are absent' (DSM IV).

The origin of the use of the name derives from the description by the physician Richard Asher of the bizarre behaviour of some patients he encountered who persistently fabricated or manufactured their symptoms (often resulting in hospital admissions, operations or investigations), until the false nature of their complaints was discovered.

Asher drew on the story of the fictional and fantastic adventures of the Baron von Munchausen as described by the German author Raspe (1944). The positive result of his identifying such a clinically perplexing form of what is now better described as a form of 'illness behaviour' was to make clinicians more likely to include the condition in their differential diagnosis. This can save the patient unnecessary investigation or surgery, and sometimes the child's life – limiting the resources spent on fruitless treatment of these patients.

A variation of such deception where the fabricated illness involves a child, usually presented by the parent or caregiver, has been known and described for many years, but was principally brought to the attention of the medical press by Meadow in 1977.

Whilst the importance of alerting paediatricians and others to the existence of such parental behaviour was great, Meadow (1995) himself has recently pointed out that the term has become misused. He is correctly critical of the increasing use of the term to describe the perpetrator as 'suffering from MSBP' rather than the abuse for, indeed, it is a form of physical and psychological abuse of the child and the parental relationship. It is now preferable to encourage the wording and terminology of DSM IV as above; in other words, referring to factitious (fabricated) illness, and classifying it further by a description of the behaviour involved – for example, attempted suffocation, administering of unauthorized medication, adding foreign substances to intravenous drips, and so on.

Table 11.1 Manifestations of MSBP

Fictitious symptoms	*Deliberate harm*
• Alleged epileptic fits. • Alleged recurrent abdominal pain. • The use of menstrual blood or blood from meat to suggest that the child is passing blood in the urine or stool. • False allegations of sexual or physical abuse. • Altering blood pressure charts, temperature charts or interfering with urine testing (e.g. adding blood, glucose, stones or faeces to the urine sample before it is tested by the staff).	• Starvation (or interfering with parental nutrition or withdrawing stomach contents through a naso-gastric tube). • Administration of salt solutions, laxatives, diuretics, sedative drugs, warfarin or anti-epileptic drugs. • Injection of drugs such as insulin or potassium chloride or the intravenous injection of faecal material to cause infection. • Causing bleeding from the mouth, anus, urethra, vagina, skin or from a birthmark. • Causing a rash by applying irritant substances to the skin. • Repeated suffocation.

Source: This table and the others in this chapter are reproduced from 'Munchausen syndrome by proxy: an overview' by Dr T. Stephenson in J. Howarth and B. Lawson (eds) (1995) *Trust Betrayed? Munchausen Syndrome by Proxy, Inter-Agency Child Protection and Partnership with Families.* London: National Children's Bureau Enterprises.

Table 11.1 (extracted from 'Trust Betrayed', see references) shows the range of acts which have been perpetrated on children. It should be emphasized that while not all parents are involved in actual physical assaults of their children, those who suggest or report non existent symptoms are often responsible for ultimately painful, invasive and potentially serious or dangerous investigations, so that the risks are still significant.

Furthermore a parent who tries, and fails, to convince a paediatrician of the seriousness of her concerns may eventually proceed to actual fabrication or production of symptoms and signs, thus escalating the risks to the child. Children unfortunately do die at the hands of their parents, although – while there may well be unconscious motives (to 'rid' themselves of a child) – the normal surface intent is not murderous. These parents are often genuinely extremely shocked and bereaved if the child dies. A helpful general classification from which to start to understand the possible motivations of such parents has been proposed by Libow and Schreier (1986), dividing perpetrators into three groups.

(1)   Help seekers

(2)   Active inducers

(3)   Doctor addicts

HELP SEEKERS

These families often present with factitious or maternally induced illnesses which superficially look like MSBP. The key factors differentiating them are symptom frequency and maternal motivation. These children are likely to be seen less persistently over time, or for a single episode of factitious complaint. This is because the mother's medical attention-seeking represents different needs. A medical confrontation with these parents often helps a mother to communicate her anxiety, exhaustion or depression. Unlike more typical MSBP parents, when help seeking parents were offered psychotherapeutic services or immediate placing of the child out of the immediate family by protective services the interventions were usually were usually met with co-operation. Indignant denial and flight from treatment are more characteristic of the true MSBP parent.

ACTIVE INDUCERS

Active inducers are the most commonly described and sensational of the MSBP cases – the prototype. These involve active and direct efforts by the parent to induce dramatic symptoms of illness in a young child. They are felt to be notoriously resistant to therapeutic intervention, and typically flee from contact.

In a few instances, described, where they had been engaged in therapy, it was usually because the courts had made it a condition of home placement of the child. The most consistent picture was of an anxious and depressed mother who used an extreme degree of denial, dissociation of feeling and paranoid projection, displacing on to others the feelings which represented her own suspiciousness and aggression. These cases often represented a worrying failure of differentiation between mother and child.

DOCTOR ADDICTS

These have been described (Woollcott *et al.* 1982) as mothers who are obsessed with the goal of obtaining medical treatment for non-existent illness in their children.

Table 11.2 Features commonly found in perpetrators

- Usually the child's birth mother.
- Previous paramedical training.
- May suffer from Munchausen syndrome (15–20%).
- Previous contact with a psychiatrist.
- Physical or sexual abuse as a child (25%).
- In local authority care during childhood (children's homes or foster care).
- History of conduct disorder (faecal smearing, petty crime, running away from home, teenage prostitution, arson) of previous criminal record.
- Previous overdoses or episodes of self-harm.
- Eating/weight disorders.
- The mother is more articulate, intelligent or dominant than the father and is the child's exclusive carer.

NB The absence of these features does not disprove the diagnoses.
Source: Reproduced with permission from Howarth and Lawson (1995).

DIAGNOSIS

The literature is accumulating on single and small studies but a true epidemiological approach is difficult. There is a great need to plan collaborative research using agreed diagnostic criteria, based on a multi-centre approach. For example, national referral centres such as Great Ormond Street Children's Hospital may receive tertiary cases from elsewhere in the United Kingdom.

Their accumulated experience together with a team liaison approach leads to a high degree of diagnostic awareness and expertise.

A district general hospital paediatrician may suspect the diagnosis (or not) but can experience the difficulty, frequently described in the literature, of 'splitting' of the team provoked by the parent's personality. This describes a tendency to divide the staff into those who have serious concerns and those who believe the mother to be unjustly accused, misjudged and victimized. Other centres, by the nature of their specialized interests, may attract a cohort of cases involving a particular sub-group of the factitious disorder – for example, the special interest of the team in North-Staffordshire in monitoring breathing problems attracts patients for investigation so that many of their proven cases fall into this category.

Although not yet universally agreed, with ethical debate ranging for and against, their use of covert video surveillance (CVS) with a locally agreed protocol, has demonstrated not only 'imposed upper airway obstruction' (attempted suffocation) but also other dangerous acts such as feeding the child unauthorized medication, interference with intravenous lines, and so on, by video observation of parent and child in a designated cubicle. For a more detailed description together with an exploration of the ethical and other issues

Table 11.3 Confirming the diagnosis

- Obtain eye witness accounts of the illness episodes from observers rather than the suspected perpetrator.
- Ascertain whether any episodes have started in the absence of the suspected perpetrator.
- Check on personal, family and social details with relatives, the GP and social services. The perpetrator is often an inveterate liar. Obtain all existing hospital records of the child from other hospitals. Check with the police.
- Retain blood, vomit, stool and urine for analysis.
- Determine whether blood is human and whether it is from the child.
- Ensure that the suspected perpetrator cannot alter nursing charts and records.
- Undertake careful surveillance of the suspected perpetrator and child by one-to-one nursing.
- Perform covert video surveillance.
- Exclude the suspected perpetrator.

Source: Reproduced with permission from Howarth and Lawson (1995)

involved see Howarth and Lawson (1995). For a serious critique of the potential over-use of such techniques see Morley (1995) and a review of 'What is and what is not Munchausen by Proxy' (Meadow 1995) in the 'Controversy' section of *Archives of Disease in Childhood.*

The most difficult task confronting paediatricians and family doctors, health visitors and other professionals is to remember to consider the possibility of MSBP whenever a puzzling illness in a child or children cannot be explained. This must be alongside a sensible and objective approach, avoiding the risk of missionary zeal and over-diagnosis and the scapegoating of anxious or dependent help-seeking parents. The potential morbidity and mortality to children and siblings is high, with some authors suggesting in excess of 10 per cent. Meadow (1977) and others have rightly highlighted the importance of detailed, consistent, long-term follow-up, especially where rehabilitation has occurred, since not only recurrences in illness behaviour (mother or child) are common, but significant physical consequences such as epilepsy or brain damage may follow previous injury, and psychological damage also occurs.

LEGAL OUTCOMES: CHILD PROTECTION OR PROSECUTION?

In cases of factitious or imposed illness (MSBP), not all end in criminal proceedings. Most commonly child protection procedures are invoked and prosecution reserved for the most serious and dangerous cases where significant injury has occurred or the child has died, as opposed to those where the parent has made factitious or false claims of fits or breathing problems which she claims to have witnessed.

On occasion both child protection and prosecution are indicated. Since the level of proof required to protect the child is less than that for a conviction in the criminal courts, and as the family may have different legal advisers acting for them in the different proceedings, the provision of appropriate reports can be complex, difficult and time consuming.

As always, good communication with, and between, experts is vital. Recently, with the rising costs of litigation, especially where legal aid limits must be set, and also where due regard to the needs of children is hindered by lengthy reporting times, the courts are increasingly asking for the instruction of a single (psychiatric) evaluation on the child or parents' mental state. Not only does this avoid an artificially adversarial contest in court, although the need for objectivity and impartiality is as great as ever, but it ensures and encourages the sharing of information and the working together with other experts namely paediatricians, social workers, Guardians ad Litem, families and the legal representatives of all these parties in a much more productive way.

Table 11.4 Factors that suggest significant danger to the child

- Abuse involving suffocation or poisoning.
- Child less than five years old.
- Previous 'cot deaths' or unexplained deaths of siblings.
- The mother has Munchausen syndrome herself.
- Denial by the mother, with lack of insight and remorse and a failure to accept responsibility for her actions.
- Fabrication by the mother persists after confrontation.
- The mother has a history of psychiatric illness, drug dependency, alcoholism or violence.

Source: Reproduced with permission from Howarth and Lawson (1995)

TREATMENT, THERAPY AND 'INTERVENTION'

What of the parents who perpetrate these acts? Are they treatable according to our current understanding of available methods? If treatment is proposed, should it be linked to conditions of rehabilitation of the victim(s) to the home, however supervised and gradual, or as a Probation condition (where prosecution has occurred)? Should it be offered even where the return of the child is not an option, or where the child has died? Welldon (1994) clearly summarizes the difficulties inherent in specifically forensic psychotherapy, where treatment may be viewed by society as inappropriate (since the public expectation is of some degree of retribution or punishment for an offence or delinquent act, rather than understanding or a search for underlying meaning).

Yet the attempt to undertake that search will be crucial in assessing risks and calculating the likelihood of re-offending or recurring maladaptive behaviour.

Since the actions, personalities and motivations of parents involved in such aberrant 'illness behaviour' towards their child or children are so diverse, it follows that the decision about treatment is inevitably going to depend on many factors. As a rule, although not always, the expert providing the original assessment for the court may not be the treating professional. Where this is the case the conflicts between forensic impartiality and the client's expectation of confidentiality must be explicitly discussed. The utmost objectivity must be maintained in dealing with personalities where serious problems of countertransference are likely and the support of the team together with access to appropriate consultation/supervision is essential.

It is now generally felt that continued denial, with or without dissociation, is a poor prognostic sign and some experts (or courts) would not expect intervention in these circumstances. Yet in a recent series of assessments of twenty such parents, I have not only encountered mothers whose personalities or intellectual abilities rendered them unlikely or unwilling to respond to conventional intervention, but others where initial denial could be approached and modified. Rarely, of course, as Cordess (1994) points out, is this task achievable through direct confrontation. Where CVS (Samuels *et al.* 1992) has been used and has resulted in a decision to protect the child or to prosecute, I have on occasions, with agreement from all the parties concerned, used the resulting videotape in work with the parent(s). Sometimes they can proceed from indignant denial towards partial and eventually complete recognition, distressed acceptance and remorse. Clearly such a situation, where possible, may pave the way towards working together therapeutically. Such material, too, may help a denying spouse to accept that such behaviour is possible before proceeding towards exploration of the reasons underlying such actions, indeed often acknowledging their own part in their partner's stress, depression or isolation.

It is worthwhile to discuss with all parties whether the court will allow, and the local authority support, the notion of several exploratory, semi-therapeutic sessions, not only for better understanding of the perpetrator's behaviour and motives, but also to assess their suitability for the likely compliance with treatment.

In one recent case I was allotted four fortnightly sessions with the mother who was epileptic and of not much more than borderline intelligence, who strongly denied giving her two-year-old anticonvulsants in hospital. Using the relevant videotape as outlined above it was possible to help her to move to a point where realistic intervention with her and exploration of her own, and her family's problems, was possible. It was agreed that she was able, with appropriate intervention, to work towards rehabilitation with her children. Sadly, however, the elder child presented difficulties which made this ultimately impossible. The mother, as do all those who 'lose' their children, whether through care proceedings or by the actual death of the child, would require skilled psychotherapeutic work to deal with the loss and grief involved (Bluglass 1990).

In another case where a child had died and the next child was suffocated but survived (the videotape was later to prove useful with the mother who had been imprisoned) the maternal grandmother wished to adopt him. With a relatively brief assessment of the grandparents' mental state and personalities for the family court (bearing in mind the frequency of dysfunctional relationships and abuse in the antecedents of some of these mothers) I was concerned about an emerging feeling that her strong wish to adopt this child was driven more by her own needs than an awareness of those of her grandson.

An outright negative recommendation would have been seen as punitive and ill-understood by these grandparents who were temporarily fostering the child and took a 'blood is thicker than water' stance – indeed the current Children Act promotes the biological family as a resource wherever possible.

Sharing these concerns with the parties involved resulted in the court granting an adjournment of six months during which the child remained with the grandparents and the relevant parties agreed to a number of sessions in which I worked with them to explore the underlying psychodynamics and to test out the grandmother's suitability for therapeutic intervention. It emerged that, although in the end the court viewed the application as based on the strong needs of the grandmother which could not meet the longer term and wider ones of the child, an extended semi-therapeutic assessment of this kind was a more appropriate and humane use of resources than an outright refusal.

In the end, however, a balance has to be struck between the circumstances of the child, possible rehabilitation and continuing protection, and the likelihood of the parent's behaviour to change. Every one of these extremely complex situations must be evaluated in the greatest possible depth, and because of the fundamental need to protect the child, risks cannot be taken.

Many of these parents have poor child-rearing skills (which may or may not be susceptible to improvement) and local authorities vary in the availability of the resources they can contribute to supporting such families. Even indications of acceptance of their actions, helpful as a starting point for therapeutic work, may not in the longer term, with or without intervention, be a predictor of successful outcome. Using every therapeutic skill available, including psychotherapeutic, behaviour and educational methods, it may be possible to work with many of these parents, preferably as early as possible after disclosure, and with the expectation of very long term follow-up.

As Schreier and Libow (1993) comment, the parent's skill 'at imposturing and in fabricating believable stories can be utilised to consistently deny their actual harming behaviour and/or falsely convince therapists of their motivation for change and it is very difficult if not impossible for a therapist to gauge the patient's sincerity and truthfulness and to successfully challenge her defensive structure when she is an involuntary or reluctant patient.'

'Given those constraints, as well as the fact that personality disorders are notoriously difficult to treat – as they represent long-standing defects in character that may not create much anxiety or discomfort in the patient – we must set realistic goals. We believe that psychotherapy with MSBP patients is more likely to be successful if focused on the goal of altering the symptom of medical attention-seeking behaviour rather than attempting deeper, long-term change in personality structure.' And 'success in therapy will ultimately depend on the individual dynamics of the patient, her willingness to acknowledge her fabricating behaviour and its destructiveness, the responsiveness of other family members to the need for change in the family system, and the therapist's ability to work supportively with the patient without being deceived by her cheerful surface presentation. With the majority of MSBP mothers, this is a highly challenging task for even the most experienced therapist.'

Table 11.5 Clues to the diagnosis of MSBP

- An illness which is very unusual and persistent or recurrent.
- The history of clinical findings does not make sense, inconsistent histories from different observers.
- The features of the illness are only apparent when the mother is present.
- The mother is very attentive and will not leave the child but, paradoxically, is less concerned about the child's illness than the professionals caring for the child.
- The mother is happy to be in hospital and forms close relationships with the ward staff.
- The mother is unusually knowledgeable about medical problems and treatments.
- Treatment is ineffective.
- Unusual or unexplained illness or death in previous children.

Source: Reproduced with permission from Howarth and Lawson (1995)

12

The Female Arsonist

Christine Foy

INTRODUCTION

Ms T was a 30-year-old lady who referred herself for therapy because she was becoming frightened by her increasing need to start fires. She was not known to have offended, but admitted to setting fire to at least two residential institutions in the past. The youngest of eight children, there was a catalogue of childhood trauma, including physical and sexual abuse at the hands of her father; the death of her mother from cancer when she was 12 and being taken into care at the age of 14 when her family rejected her. The psychiatric services became involved while she was in care due to her repeated self-mutilation and threats to kill her father. She had been unable at this stage to disclose the abuse and was misunderstood by carers. At the time of referral, she was living apart from her partner and struggling to cope with three young children. She was grossly overweight and heavily into self-mutilation.

THE COURSE OF THERAPY

The treatment was once-weekly psychoanalytical psychotherapy and initially trust was the main issue. Her early life experiences made this a particularly difficult issue for her. It took time for her to be able to talk of the guilt and shame she felt due to the abuse at the hands of her father. Her sense of powerlessness, which was compounded by the slow, lingering death of her mother and the fact that she was put into care by her family, was also difficult for her to talk about. Cumulatively, these experiences had left her feeling dangerously angry and had given rise to her need to keep a stash of emotionally charged petrol bombs in her wardrobe, which were both sexually symbolic and symbolic of power. She also described a need to keep instruments of self-harm readily available in the same way that her alcoholic friend needed to keep drink. She appeared to be desperately seeking containment while trying to resolve her inner turmoil.

In the early transference she responded to me as an idealized mother figure by whom she wanted to be loved and looked after. Normally strong and coping, in sessions she became childlike and dependent, wanting to please me. She conveyed a fear of rejection for who or what she was. She evoked a protective and caring response in me and made me feel special to her. I also felt angry and appalled at the deprivation and abuse to which she had been subjected.

Because of the serious nature of the presentation, I sought risk assessment and regional cover from a nearby medium secure unit. This was Ms T's first contact with a forensic psychiatrist and she reports feeling 'safe' at her outpatient appointment in the medium secure unit with all the locked doors. The forensic psychiatrist, on the other hand, felt alarmed to discover she had managed to reach his office, past security, with petrol bombs on her person.

This illustrates how knowledge of her dangerousness was split off and located in certain people and feelings of empathy and identification located in others, such as her therapist.

Some months into therapy, a crisis arose when a member of the public became a focus for her anger and a potential victim for her petrol bombs. She described an extreme state of hyper-arousal when she felt she could ex-plode/lose control and 'burn' her neighbour. She explained that she felt the need to do something to match the way she felt. She had stood on this lady's lawn in the early hours, petrol bombs in hand, relishing the thought of watching her neighbour suffer the terror of being engulfed in flames. She was aware there were also children in the house but she was prepared to sacrifice them to 'get' the neighbour. Her lurid description of the pleasure she would have derived from this experience had she not managed to restrain herself shocked and scared me. I could now feel some of the murderousness and dangerousness in the counter-transference.

For some time work centred on her murderous rage, its origins and how she might deal with it more appropriately. Shortly after this crisis she gave me a 'gift' of her stash of petrol bombs, which I understood I was to keep for her. This gift implies that the patient was willing to give up the bombs and trust me to contain her, but that she was also giving me all responsibility for her dangerousness and murderousness, literally splitting it off and 'handing' it over. A second gift followed at Christmas when she presented me with a lavish bouquet of flowers which she could ill afford, saying 'flowers are always an acceptable gift'. I understood this gift to be a reparative peace offering or an attempt to seduce me and make me 'forget' what I'd seen.

Therapy progressed at quite a pace. Ms T expanded on her childhood experiences and how she'd felt tortured by her father's abuse of her, especially that involving her beloved pet dog, and by her mother's lingering death from cancer. She had washed, fed and toileted her mother until a week before her demise. She had not cried at any time over her loss, but had slept on her grave for three weeks after the funeral, unnoticed by her uncaring family.

She felt possessed and controlled by the two of them; her mother occupying the left side of her body and her father the right. She said 'I don't know who myself is. I be or do what others want of me'. She repeatedly denigrated her father and idealized her mother and pointed out that she took care to only mutilate the right side of her body. She could not see that she was now her own torturer.

In the transference, the therapist had 'become' the idealized mother and the forensic psychiatrist and neighbour the hated father. The patient splits off the hated aspects of self and projects them onto the figures whom she then attempts to burn. Her lack of capacity to symbolize and think and thus her propensity to act concretely by splitting is demonstrated by the mutilation of one side of the body only.

Gradually her defences began to relax, her real self began to emerge and she appeared weak, helpless, inadequate and, in her eyes, worthy of scorn and rejection. She described the protective wall she has needed to construct around herself to be able to survive and warned me of the dangers of trying to remove it too quickly. 'If I remove the wall, I wouldn't have any skin. I'd die quickly…from myself…suicide. I'd need to toughen up to survive and I'd probably have to kill myself before I'd had sufficient time to do this.' I heeded the warning and respected her pace of work. Her dependence on me continued to increase as therapy progressed. She constantly tested out whether I would fail to protect her, meet her needs or abandon her, like her mother. She expressed a wish to be able to regress completely, hand over her adult responsibilities to me and come into hospital to be looked after. Her anxiety about this (which caused her great conflict) was that she would 'lose' herself and never again be able to return to care for her young family. She longed to be carefree and create the childhood she feels she never had. She says 'I was never a child, just a smaller person with no power'. She attempted to do this through her own children but failed, leading to feelings of hopelessness and despair.

As time went on Ms T appeared more and more vulnerable. There was growing evidence of clinical depression, which was compounded on the eighteenth anniversary of her mother's death when she suddenly began to experience grief at her loss for the first time. She said 'it's as though she's just died. It's funny, I always thought she was still with me, I'd find her just around the corner. Now I know she's gone and I'll never see her again.' Her deteriorating mental state led me to seek a medical opinion as to whether medication and/or hospitalization was appropriate.

Ms T was seen by a general psychiatrist who considered her to be a suicidal risk and admitted her informally (he was prepared to section her) to hospital. Here, she shored up her defences, managed to persuade junior staff that she was better after 48 hours away from her children, and discharged herself. Retrospectively, she says, that it was as well she was not detained as she would have had to kill herself to regain control. There was a positive outcome from her contact with the medical team in that she is now on an antidepressant and is less clinically depressed.

A movement into depression from a more psychotic state of mind could be thought of as progress – it is extremely painful and frightening and is what the more paranoid state has been defending against.

I found her depression very difficult counter-transferentially. She exuded such unrelenting pain, misery and despair, such hopelessness about the future and things never being better for her that I began to feel as though I was now abusing her by asking her to please me/others and carry on with life. She had compared her mental state to her mother's malignancy and said 'my mother didn't have a choice with cancer. I don't feel I've got a choice but others won't see it like that. I don't feel I can go on. I don't feel it's fair to be expected to.' I struggled to remain objective and put it to her that she was not allowing for change through therapy and/or medical intervention. In this way she was persuaded to carry on.

A year into therapy Ms T is adjusting to the loss of her mother and has begun to work towards disclosure of the actual abuse, talking of failed attempts in the past and how she has kept trying. She compares the danger of disclosing and having to 'own' the abuse with the recent experience she's had of finally accepting her mother's death. She fears being overwhelmed/destroyed by it. 'I have to push it away. I can't bear it. It's like I felt when my mother died. I had to pretend she was just around the corner. I'd find her sometime. When I realized she really was gone recently, I barely coped. It was too awful.'

Recently she appears to have escaped into a defensive manic state and talked of her arsonist self who enjoys the idea of burning people. She described the disappointment she experienced in the past when she felt the need to raise the alarm after she had set fire to a hostel because she had to rescue the other residents. She said 'it was never the same again. It's like you're looking forward to a banana split and somebody takes the banana away and you're left with the cream…it's not the same.' She is not in touch with the sadistic, murderous, arsonist self.

Ms T would like to present herself as a poor victim but fails to see her sado-masochism when she victimizes herself through horrendous self-mutilation. Her original torturers were her father and dying mother. She is now her own torturer. As the work continues (fortunately there is no time limit to her therapy) I would hope to be able to help her develop insight into how she is locked into torture, suffering and pain. She continues to be a risk to both herself and others but states that she feels safer/more contained in therapy.

13

A Case of Murder

Caecilia Taylor

INTRODUCTION

As a society, we are endlessly preoccupied by violence. This is nothing new; the peculiar paradox of our times is that as our fear of violence on a very personal level grows ever more pervasive, so does our voyeuristic appetite for bloodshed, mutilation and gore – even amongst children (Black and Newman 1995). In fact, TV and movie dramas are fast being overtaken in popularity by true-life footage from police and casualty department videos. But not even these bring us as close to the actual experience as the psychotherapist confronted with a violent patient, for the very process of therapy requires becoming intimate with not only *his* conscious and unconscious worlds, but the role of the victim. For all its growing ubiquity, the killing of a fellow human being remains the ultimate crime, and few professionals will view the prospect of accepting a murderer for assessment or treatment with anything approaching equanimity.

Working in forensic settings, one is soon struck by the uncanny power and primitive fascination that the murderer exerts over those around him: it is impossible to banish the sense that the killer has crossed a line that demarcates a profound, irrevocable, difference. In prisons, fellow offenders defer to the murderer as the more powerful, and accord him a strange respect. Women write letters, visit and fall in love; often they are strangers attracted by sensational publicity, but inexperienced professionals are not immune. Prison officers, despite the familiarity bred by long sentences and close daily proximity, talk warily of some 'unknown quantity' they instinctively feel him to possess. I have even heard doctors and lawyers, leading perfectly upstanding lives, express an envious half-wish that they had the murderer's capacity for action, as opposed to mere fantasy. Freud (1914) recognized this ability of criminals to 'compel our interest by the narcissistic consistency with which they manage to keep away from their ego anything that would diminish it. It is as if we envied them for maintaining a blissful state of mind – an unassailable libidinal position which we ourselves have since abandoned.'

The therapist, too, will be susceptible to many of these responses. The extreme nature of some of the material will make treatment taxing enough, but he or she must also act as an agent of healing and change – for it is only through a re-examination of the origins of destructiveness, and reworking of its mode of expression, that this can take place. Of utmost importance will be the symbolic meaning of the killing: who in the patient's early relationships does the victim represent, what experiences within those relationship were being re-enacted, and what particular circumstances provoked such a fatal repetition at the exact time that they did? In this chapter, the role of the therapist in elucidating these themes will be examined with reference to case material. In particular, the part he or she has to play in the overall management and treatment of the patient charged with murder and subject to the criminal justice process will be discussed.

THE REMANDED OFFENDER

Assessment

Murder is naturally viewed as an extremely serious charge, and even individuals with an extensive psychiatric history will usually be remanded into custody. It is common practice for the offender to be placed in the prison health care centre, at least initially, in recognition that he (or occasionally, she) will be in an extremely vulnerable state. Here he will undergo full psychiatric assessment, to find out whether he is suffering from some serious mental disorder such as psychosis or organic conditions. Even at this early stage, the therapist may have a valuable role to play, especially if the initial impression is that psychodynamic treatment might be appropriate at a later stage. In this country, it is a statutory requirement for all those charged with murder that a psychiatric report be prepared for the court, and if the recommendation is for a health care disposal, the details, including the name of any therapist, must be stipulated.

For the purposes of assessment, it will be advisable to negotiate a fixed number of sessions with the patient, having fully explained their purpose so as to avoid arousing false expectations. An appropriate room must be identified which is sufficiently private to prevent interruptions or conversations being overheard, but allows staff to be near at hand should assistance be required. While the need for it is rare (see below), an alarm button is essential. By general agreement with the rest of the multi-disciplinary team, the therapist should be free from responsibility for other aspects of the patient's care, such as his physical health or social welfare. It is generally possible to maintain confidentiality if another professional undertakes to prepare any reports, but all 'forensic' patients should be told right from the beginning that information that seriously endangers others may be exempt from this promise. This lack of a cast-iron guarantee may sit uncomfortably with some therapists, but legal precedent, at least in the United States (reviewed by Dyer 1988) and most professional bodies (eg: General Medical Council 1995; Royal College of Psychiatrists 1985) acknowledge its necessity.

Forgetting and Remembering

Assessment frequently contains elements of treatment too, at least in containing the immediate distress and turmoil of finding oneself in prison, faced with such a charge. Strange as the idea may seem, killing is an act that traumatizes the perpetrator too, the more so if the task was particularly gory: in the following hours, days and weeks many murderers suffer from partial or total amnesia for their crime. This is often falsely interpreted as malingering, but in fact in this phenomenon we see the defence mechanism of repression in operation. It has a protective function in that the horror and guilt of the act can be so insupportable that the offender literally cannot allow himself to know about it. As Symington has pointed out (1996), at this stage the public may be far better informed, via the media, than the killer. The loss of memory was particularly striking in the case with which I shall illustrate this chapter.

Clinical vignette

One morning a young man wearing a balaclava and armed with two kitchen knives went back to his old school and entered one of the classrooms, where the youngest pupils, aged eleven and twelve, were having a lesson. Brandishing his knives, he threatened the teacher and forced the pupils to line up against a wall. Starting at the top of the line, he attacked three girls and a boy; one girl he succeeded in stabbing to death, but the teacher managed to summon help, and he was restrained and taken outside before he could do any further injury. The police were called and he was arrested without difficulty. In prison, a few days later, he could remember nothing beyond sitting in his flat drinking the night before these events. He described 'coming to' to find himself surrounded by police and having to ask *them* what he had done. During the first session he came across as almost abnormally calm and undistressed, with little apparent concern about either his own predicament or the fact that he had taken someone's life.

It is important to note that nearly half of all murderers consume alcohol before their offence, which can contribute to forgetting (Zacune and Hensman 1971). This man had been drinking for several hours the previous evening while he wrote a long suicide letter – up until the eleventh hour, his only intention had been to kill himself, and the alcohol was intended to give him 'Dutch courage'. As his memory gradually returned, so did the depth and responsiveness of his emotions, and he was faced with the true enormity of what he had done. The return of full recall is the potential starting point for recovery, but some are unable to live with the guilt that now also returns to their consciousness. That there is a high risk of suicide among those remanded on a murder charge (Liebling 1992) will be important for the therapist to know, since thoughts of hopelessness and worthlessness may dominate sessions for a while. The sense of being supported by an empathic 'other' during sessions can usually avert a crisis, but the development of a serious depressive illness, or evidence of suicidal intent, must be dealt with by a medical member of the clinical team, preferably by urgent transfer to hospital.

Treatment

The patient went on to give the following account of his life:

> He and his elder sister were brought up in an unhappy household, dominated by the shrill complaints of his mother about his father's failings. She regretted having children and made no secret to them of the fact that she would have left long before if not for their existence. It was difficult for my patient to avoid blaming himself, not only for the complete disappearance of affection in his parents' marriage, but for his mother's loss of freedom to look for happiness elsewhere. Towards him, she alternated between indulgence and irritated dismissiveness, such that he never knew what to expect.

> The father passively withstood his wife's onslaught; a pedantic, gloomy man, he made little attempt to get to know his children or to refute the way she discredited him. As a younger child, my patient waited for him to assert himself, but as time went by he lost his faith that this would ever happen, and so in the man himself. The father did, however, exert his authority over the children by way of severe beatings. The ultimate act of contempt by his mother was uncovered when he was eleven and in the first year of his new secondary school. Abruptly, she ran away from home to live with another man, and his father belatedly discovered that she had for some time been acting as a virtual unpaid prostitute to various of his business colleagues. The children stayed with their father, but their mother's behaviour was never spoken of.

> My patient remained close to his elder sister, who trained as a teacher, married and settled some distance away. He and his father lived together as virtual strangers until he found himself a small flat where he lived alone. He had had no friends since primary school, and after a year's college course in computer studies never worked. Instead, he became more and more absorbed in his own writings, and took to wandering the streets at night,

preoccupied with depression and increasingly violent fantasies. It was his fear that he would eventually carry them out that led him to contemplate suicide the night before his offence.

Early sessions, in prison, were characterized by his self-tormenting remorse at what he had done. He also feared considerably for his own welfare, not without justification: one day he woke to found a newspaper cutting which had been pushed under the door of his cell. It contained an article about his offence, which included a picture of the little girl who had died. Scribbled in the margins was an anonymous threat on his life. A fellow-inmate was probably responsible – prisons being places of severe, and hierarchical, moral judgement – but my patient felt instinctively that he also could not rely on the protection of the officers. Some institutions have made great efforts to tackle bullying and intimidation, but they still occur, particularly in connection with the seemingly endemic trading in illegal drugs. There were some difficulties in getting him escorted to sessions on time, the feeling being that psychotherapy was too 'soft' a response to such a heinous crime. My patient would, I was assured, pull the wool over my eyes in order to manipulate me and the system to get the least severe sentence. Hinshelwood (1993) has written most informatively about the expectations within the institution that everyone will engage in the 'universal prison game of conning'.

As the transference developed, my patient was clearly waiting to see what was 'available' from me in each session before making what he saw as demands, by talking about himself – as though perhaps I would not be in the mood, or preoccupied by my own concerns, and so nothing would be forthcoming. It was as if, even in treatment, he needed to assure himself that my needs had been met first. A deeper hesitation about becoming dependent on me was the fear that *I* was conning *him* – and that what I so tantalisingly offered, I would whisk away just at the moment when he most relied upon it. Many forensic patients have experienced similar chaotic and intermittent parenting to this patient, and the experience of having someone make – and keep – a regular commitment is both totally new and containing. This patient admitted his pervasive sense of guilt that he was taking up my time, which was undoubtedly linked to his infantile rage at his mother's unpredictability, and the predominance in her mind of her own wishes. His compulsive fantasies of violence, which he had been at a loss to understand, began after she had made such a mockery of *his* wishes by abandoning him altogether.

Guilt and the Importance of Punishment

The theme of guilt is an important one, for the murderer often feels he has much more than just the killing for which to blame himself: it is the enormous culpability for some 'prior, inner situation' that 'impels him to dramatize it in the outer world' (Symington 1996). This situation, argues de Zulueta (1993), arises from the disruption to attachment processes in infancy caused by abusive and traumatic experiences at the hands of parents or other care-givers. Several studies record the frequency of such experiences in the early years of those who, like this patient, grow up to be violent, implicating them especially in the development of antisocial and borderline personality disorders (reviewed by Widiger and Trull 1994). The child, however, would rather see *himself* as 'bad' – rejecting and destructive – in order to be able to sustain the illusion of his parents as 'good' (the moral defence of Fairbairn 1952). The criminal justice process, especially the trial and the passing of a sentence, plays an interesting role in assuaging this sense of guilt, by meting out the punishment the offender *feels* he deserves: some admit that they become more and more careless in the committing of their crimes, half hoping to be caught, while others are made profoundly uncomfortable if, in their judgement, the punishment is not severe enough to fit the crime.

In order to gain a sense of mastery and control over overwhelming feelings of pain and loss of control during childhood trauma, the adult continually re-enacts it, either as victim or as victimizer (de Zulueta 1993). The acting out is literal and physical, because of an associated failure to develop sufficiently the use of symbol and fantasy. My patient knew that his ability to keep his violent impulses within the realm of his imagination was wearing thin – hence the development of an idea related to the flip-side of the coin of being victimizer; that of becoming victim of his own suicide, as a solution. What finally triggered action was the seemingly trivial event of coming across an old school report dating back to his first year in secondary school. The feelings associated with his mother's departure, the 'Pathogenic Secret' (Ellenberger 1966) which he had long since split off from consciousness and repressed as too painful to be aware of, were suddenly reawoken. Re-enactment ensued, with himself as perpetrator, *and* with the children as symbols of himself as victim.

Therapy with a murderer can at times feel like one is treading on egg-shells: the relationship the patient developed towards me was often heavily loaded with the feelings he had had, albeit mostly unconsciously, towards his mother and father. At times, I was frankly afraid that by saying the wrong thing, I might trigger re-enactment right there and then, and I myself might be the victim of his murderous rage. In practice, the work we had already done provided him with the new experience of a safe and reliable attachment, strong enough to withstand anger. The relief that simply uncovering, talking about and defusing painful emotions can bring should not be under-estimated. Nor, however, should the importance of adequate supervision in containing the therapist's – and therefore the patient's – fear of violent acting out.

Deciding what to plead at his trial was hard for my patient. In the early stages of therapy he did not think of himself as responsible for his crime, simply because he could not remember committing it: at the core of his being, he did not feel as though he had. Later, when his lawyers advised a plea of diminished responsibility due to mental disorder, he instinctively shrank from seeing himself as 'mad'. To do so meant acknowledging a source of aggression within himself of which he had little knowledge and therefore, terrifyingly, little control. In the end, the same awareness of 'needing help' that had led him to agree to therapy in prison, enabled him to agree to treatment in hospital instead of a conventional prison sentence.

The Hospital Setting

Psychotherapy with a murderer in a secure hospital setting contains few essential differences from that within a prison. While some patients will respond well to treatment, it has to be acknowledged that for others, too disturbed or traumatized, expectations for change must remain limited – or the hopelessness of 'therapeutic nihilism' will ensue. Even in these cases, an important contribution can be made to risk assessments of future violence, and the patient can be helped to contain his aggression and live a relatively settled life, even though it is behind locked doors (Cox 1986). Some patients experience the suggestion that they undergo therapy as coercive – the consultant psychiatrist or mental health review tribunal will interpret refusal as a black mark against future discharge. In practice, many start with these issues in mind, but continue for their own reasons. Finally, Cox (1986) has pointed out the importance of the psychotherapist's ability to 'hold' staff, who are always in danger of being engulfed by the murderer's projections of hostility and anger, leading to rejecting and judgmental attitudes that inevitably render therapy ineffective.

14

'Written on the Body'
Deliberate Self-Harm and Violence

Gwen Adshead

Clinical Vignette

Miss A is a 26-year-old woman, currently detained in Holloway prison, charged with threats to kill. She was arrested outside a psychiatric hospital, from which she had recently been discharged. She had several inpatient admissions following overdoses which seemed to indicate serious suicidal intent. While an inpatient, she secreted tablets and swallowed them, cut herself with any sharp implement available and tried to abscond from the ward in order to run under a car. She rarely hid her self-harming behaviour, and the clinical team felt that she was being 'manipulative'. They had discharged her on Friday afternoon, and advised her to return to her flat, where she lived alone. The next day, after drinking a large amount of spirits, she went up to the hospital, and threatened a female member of staff with a knife. She then went home and took an overdose. The nurse was frightened and shocked; she was the patient's key worker, and thought their relationship was good.

DISCUSSION

Miss A's case is an amalgam of many similar cases, which cause problems for clinical teams. I will focus on three clinical issues for forensic psychotherapy:

1. Diagnosis

Deliberate self harm (DSH) is a symptom of internal distress, which has both a private and a public message (Kroll 1993). DSH is common in human societies; usually there is a continuum of self-harming activities, some of which are tolerated by society, or even encouraged. However, Miss A's behaviour is not so acceptable, perhaps because of the involvement with professional carers – an involvement which reflects how Miss A's relationships are regulated by the self-harming behaviour. Diagnosis may be less important than recognizing and understanding such relationships.

Borderline personality disorder (BPD) is perhaps the most common diagnosis because of the often chronic nature of the problem. The other diagnostic feature of BPD is the presence of intermittent psychosis, which is relevant to DSH for three reasons. First, patients will often say that they harm themselves in response to 'voices'. Such voices are usually pseudo-hallucinations, which represent a part of the patient, or a significant person from the patient's past. They can be distressing and intrusive but are rarely evidence of mental illnesses such as schizophrenia.

Second, psychotic states imply a distortion, or denial, of reality: things are other than they seem, and only the psychotic knows the 'truth'. There is denial of the degree of hurt and alarm caused by the DSH, and knowledge of other's thoughts, for example 'I knew she didn't want to see me'. Finally, psychotic states are a form of altered consciousness. When self-harming, patients often do not experience pain, and may experience a sense of relief from intolerable internal tension. Such reduction of consciousness is also called 'dissociation'. This may help to explain why rational argument, or emphasis on thinking alone, does not help patients to stop.

2. Formulation

A psychodynamic formulation needs to accompany behavioural description and psychiatric diagnosis. DSH is a cruel attack on the body; a form of self-murder (Campbell and Hale 1991). Such attacks are usually a bodily reenactment of a previous trauma, where the traumatic response is somatized either because the situation is so overwhelming that the patient cannot 'think', or because the patient is traumatized at a developmental stage before full thinking skills are developed. Patients hope that the perfect carer will come and make it all right, and take their awful feelings away. When carers fail to do this, then more rage and pain are felt, and the cycle of despair, arousal and tension begins again, leading to repetition (Pierce 1986).

Splitting of experience into 'good' and 'bad' is an important way for patients to protect themselves against intolerable feelings of anxiety or loss. The patient internalizes the source of the original trauma, and acts sadistically towards her own body. However, such behaviour is also a sadistic assault on those who claim to be caring for the patient. The masochistic role can be taken equally by the patient, the patient's family or the clinical team. Alternatively, patients can recruit others to act sadistically towards them; sadly, this can be seen in the often brutal treatment that is given in casualty departments, or the rejection of such patients by psychiatric staff (Platt and Salter 1987).

In Miss A's case, the team were angry with her for not getting better, and letting them be 'good' carers. They felt (accurately) that they were being bullied or manipulated, and responded angrily by discharging the patient. This confirmed Miss A's internal view that no carers can be trusted, and she felt victimized. In terms of her victimization, she then felt justified in acting aggressively towards 'her' nurse.

The relationship with professional carers is of crucial importance. It must be emphasized that many people like Miss A experience 'care' almost as a provocation. They yearn for an idealized soothing carer, but, in reality, no care can be good enough, and attempts to provide care are denigrated. This is often enacted within the ward setting. Typically, a close relationship with a junior member of staff develops. It is often a female member of staff, but it may also be a staff member who is rather isolated from the rest of the team; the male chaplain, or social worker. The patient idealizes this carer, who is gratified, and responds with more care. Sometimes, the care becomes 'special' (Main 1957) or 'co-conspiratorial' (Grunebaum and Klerman 1967) and therapeutic boundaries may be distorted. Distortions range from failure to maintain an appropriate distance, either mentally or physically, to active physical violations, such as sexual relationships. It is important not to underestimate the unconscious attraction of vulnerability, which can make even the most inadequate carer feel good.

In this dynamic, the patient's past tragic story is rewritten unconsciously by the patient and the carer. It is clear that DSH is associated with a childhood history of poor parenting (Roy 1978; Robinson and Duffy 1989; Martin and Waite 1994). Over 50 per cent of patients who exhibit repeated DSH have been sexually abused by one of their primary caretakers (Briere and Zaidi 1989; van der Kolk, Perry and Herman 1991). In one sample of women who both self-harmed and were dangerous to others, 80 per cent had been either physically or sexually abused, or both (Adshead 1994).

In these patients, rage is felt towards not only the abuser/carer, but also the carer who failed to protect. A combination of real threat and failed care leaves the developing child with enormous anxiety, and no means of containing it. Young children have increased tendencies to somatize distress, and also to dissociate at times of trauma. These developmentally normal responses to anxiety are internalized into the developing mind and find their mental equivalents in primitive mental phenomena of splitting, projection and projective identification (Milton 1994).

Two key questions are vital for the child: 'Who will take care of my feelings?' and 'Whose body is it, anyway?'. It is these questions which are played out consciously and unconsciously with health care professionals. The patient presents with mental or physical distress. The health care professional begins to 'care'. But by accepting the caring role, the health care professional unconsciously engages in a traumatic reenactment, playing the part of both the abusing carer and the carer who fails.

3. Management

The symptom of self-harm is not usually taken seriously until it has become either highly repetitive and/or anxiety-provoking to others. It is important to take such behaviour seriously; even if the wish to die is fluctuating in strength and intensity, the message which is written on the body is basically a violent one. Although the majority of those who harm themselves are not dangerous to others, a minority are; especially those who have been subjected to particularly invasive and severe abuse. DSH and somatization disorders have been found in women who abuse their children medically (Livingston 1987; Bools, Neale and Meadow 1994); it seems plausible to argue, as Estela Welldon has done (1988) that for some women, children are simply an extension of their own bodies, and harm to children can be a substitute for DSH.

By taking DSH seriously, a message is given to the patient that their distress is heard, and not minimized or denied. This is an important first therapeutic step. The next is to attempt to construct some sort of therapeutic alliance with the patient, which may take many weeks, months or even years, and is often painful for both the patient and the team (Stone 1987).

It is during this phase that there is often great uncertainty about the use of the Mental Health Act for forcible detention and treatment. It is here that the counter-transferential acting out is most likely. A cruel dilemma presents itself to clinical teams; a dilemma presumably also experienced by the patient in the past. By imposing care involuntarily, the self-harm is stopped, but the care is experienced as punitive and can be rejected as abuse. Failure to impose care results in the patient feeling abandoned or let down by the useless, helpless carer, who sees the abuse but can (? will) do nothing to stop it. Added to this is the current political climate which makes medical teams responsible for all actions taken by the mentally ill, and thus encourages both defensive and paternalistic therapy. In this regard, of course, the word 'paternalism' is singularly appropriate.

There is no single or simple right answer. Sometimes the anxiety will be such that involuntary detention is the only answer. Medication (either anti-depressants or sedatives) can have a place, and can be experienced as a concrete type of soothing. Physical therapies should probably be avoided until the patient can experience their own or other's touch more comfortably. It goes without saying that ongoing psychological care is needed and should never be abruptly withdrawn; not an easy task when there is institutional rejection of those with chronic neurotic disorders, so that beds and psychotherapy are unavailable, and it is suggested that psychiatry should only concern itself with 'serious' mental illnesses such as schizophrenia.

Probably the most important therapeutic task, however, is the proper attention to the counter-transference (Tantam and Whittaker 1992). The clinical team may not be able to deal with the patient's feelings, but they can (and must) make an attempt to deal with their own. This includes not only discussion of negative feelings but also positive ones. This is particularly relevant for victims of childhood sexual abuse, who are often offered special 'counselling', which is carried out by relatively junior staff, and is seen as separate from the rest of the therapeutic programme. Supervision of all staff involved with the patient will help to prevent the formation of 'special' relationships, and the enacting of split off feelings and objects. 'All staff' includes the casualty and medical teams, and GPs; even if they cannot come to supervision, regular meetings to discuss the patient's management are a way of providing care for the patient.

Providing good-enough care for the patient is ultimately the most achievable goal. The patient yearns for perfect care, and experiences less than perfect care as abuse. But imperfect or failed care is not abuse. To the patient, however, it is a catastrophic disappointment, and patients need to be helped to grieve for and rage at the lost carer, and lost sense of containment; as well as acknowledging attachment to and rage at their abusers. It must be said that for some patients, the losses are too great, and they will bring about their own deaths, despite the best possible care. But for many patients, like Miss A, there is within a will to survive as well as a will to self-destruct.

15

Psychotherapy in a Special Hospital
Learning Difficulty and Violence

Jo-anne Carlyle

'All words make a life sentence'

from *Prison Poetry Reading* by Valerie Sinason (1995)

INTRODUCTION

This chapter has two themes: 'what it takes' and 'the experience of being kicked'. I shall describe the psychotherapy of a woman with learning difficulties who was violent in the sessions. I will illustrate some of the tensions of doing psychotherapy at the interface of mental handicap, violence and large institutions. The interface issues include: the function of violence as a distance regulator; the role of the psychotherapist in a secure psychiatric institution; what does it mean to be *therapeutic*? In retrospect my work with this patient involved the Group Analytic idea of 'dynamic administration' (Foulkes 1975) and the psychoanalytic idea of understanding difficulties in thinking in the presence of pain, both related to abuse and to deprivation (Sinason 1986; Tustin 1987).

THE INSTITUTIONAL CONTEXT

The ward that 'Susan' lived on catered for approximately 20 women with learning difficulties – all of whom were considered to present a significant risk to themselves or others. Many had additional diagnoses of personality disorder or mental illness and many were maintained on high levels of neuroleptic medication. The building was supposed to provide a home-like atmosphere: there was a kitchen and dining room downstairs and two lounges. Upstairs there was a series of individual bedrooms. There was also a staff room, a further lounge that was often closed and kept for meetings; a clinic room and a bathroom. The communal areas continued to have an institutional feel. At the time of the therapy, the patients were locked in their rooms at night.

The nursing staff and rest of the clinical team were often disillusioned, feeling pressurized and unsupported. Looking for scapegoats was endemic and Susan was a prime scapegoat, having always been considered amongst the 'worst' of the patients.

This was the context for the psychotherapy. External consultation to institutions caught in repetitive 'pathological' processes is well described (e.g. Jacques 1955; Menzies Lyth 1959; Main 1975; Obholzer and Zagier Roberts 1994), but as a member of staff this consultative role was not mine. Hinshelwood (1994) describes the function of a psychotherapist in a secure, closed institution as 'to keep going and to sustain ordinary relations with colleagues and patients'. He describes how containing the anxiety of being on the 'margins' and living with the 'conscious denigration' and the 'unconscious respect' is essential to the work of a psychotherapist within a psychiatric institution.

It also important to pay attention to the Group Analytic notion of *dynamic administration* if one is to try and achieve some success in this sphere. Dynamic administration refers to the attention given by the therapist to the setting in which therapy takes place and the careful attempts to provide a safe enough and predictable environment. Foulkes (1975) provides a helpful introduction to this concept.

THE PATIENT

Susan was in her early thirties when we started work together. She had been held in the hospital since she was 14. She had not been convicted of an offence but was held in conditions of maximum security because of the threat her behaviour posed to herself and others. In fact some of her actions would have led to prosecution in other settings (specifically, if she had been in the community). According to the minimal clinical notes available her behaviour had apparently changed little in the time since she was admitted. A couple of attempts to measure her IQ had been unsuccessful, but it was generally agreed that she functioned at a 'profound' level of learning difficulty (below 50 IQ points). Behavioural programmes had been tried and failed – usually breaking down when Susan was violent to the interviewer.

Susan had a history of painful separations and traumas. In particular she had sustained a serious injury to her hip from a drop from a second storey window. This had resulted in shortening one of her legs and the wound had never healed properly because she picked at it daily. Her language largely consisted of what were described in the notes as 'stock phrases' describing her experiences – or rather, that concretized her experiences into a series of autistic objects. 'Blood red needles', 'jump out of the window', 'fall down stairs', 'enemas', 'poke baby in the eye'. Frances Tustin (1987) suggests that patients may use certain objects/sensations in a manner symbolic of a 'dynamic autistic state' that arises because of early failures of attachment or trauma. The autistic quality of Susan's phrases was clear; they seemed to preserve some aspect of her experience whilst at the same time stripping it of its meaning. I think the constant opening of the wound on her hip was, like her phrases, another way of keeping something exposed – in the public sphere – while stripping it of its pain and meaning. In slightly Messianic mode I initially saw therapy as an opportunity to restore some meaning to these statements; an attempt to breathe life back into the concretized experiences. It has been suggested that to do this kind of work one must be naive or very experienced – I was naive and without a real understanding of what was being undertaken by either of us. I had, however, given the questions of whether I should start the therapy and whether the patient had given consent, a great deal of thought. This was a prime focus of the supervision that I had throughout the case. There are no easy or right answers.

THE THERAPY

I met with Susan on a weekly basis for a little over eighteen months. The therapy ended when I left the hospital to take up another post. We initially met in my office in a building away from the ward where she lived. This necessitated Susan being 'escorted' to my room by two members of nursing staff from her unit. The staff were largely consistent in bringing her to the therapy. The second half of the therapy was carried out on the ward because of difficulties of containing her violence in my office. The interpretations were based on my perceptions of what she said, how she looked, what I judged that she was feeling, or what she seemed to attend to in my office. What she said was sometimes prompted by occasional questions of mine.

Initially Susan spoke only in the stock phrases that I have described. As the weeks went by, she began to comment, in a kind of telegraphic speech, on things in my room – boxes and tins of differing sizes. She would point to a series of objects and say 'tiny, little, large'. She would then point to other objects, for example teapots, and apply the same comments. Later she began to speak about things to do with the two of us – the type of clothes we were wearing ('trousers, skirt' etc.) and their colours. This developed into comments about our physical appearance (hair, eye colour). She would, in her telegraphese, describe each of us and make comparisons in a steady development of identification: 'Jo-anne blue eyes, Susan blue eyes'. In response to questions she would tell me something of what she, and others had done in the week. Slowly this was extended to other experiences. I think I fostered this by careful attention to what she said, particularly what was new and by my guesses about how things related to each other. It seemed that relevant connections with her thoughts or her experiences would be rewarded with a little more information. At other times she would go quiet for some weeks. I understood this as occurring when I got too close.

In conjunction with the meetings with Susan I met with the staff. I tried to provide a context in which her violent and destructive behaviour could be understood. More helpful than my fine theories was a television programme about a young autistic boy, who had also experienced multiple deprivations and separations. I came to respect this and in time I tried to be more progressive. I arranged a workshop in the hospital, inviting well known and talented clinicians. As well as their presentations we talked about Susan's clinical material. Susan was my inspiration for inviting the speakers and they were my inspiration for continuing to work with her. Although organized for the staff on her ward, none of them turned up. However, the workshop was very gratefully received by other members of staff.

BOUNDARIES AND DISTANCE

The work continued, and hopeful moments were interspersed with distressing and disabling ones, as I questioned the value of my naive hopes. Susan began to refer to herself in the first person, as 'I' or 'me', rather than by her first name. She strengthened her commitment to comparing and identifying herself with me. However, as this developed, Susan began to kick me, and I understood this both as an angry response to my invasion of her safe autistic world and also as a communication of the pain and victimization that made up her experience. Weintrobe (1995) discusses the relationship of violence to 'mental space'. Essentially she describes violence as breaching of a body boundary thus differentiating it from aggression, sadism, and so on. She describes how mental space arises from an ability to see ones internalized objects moving independently. To do this requires acknowledgement of their difference from the self. Violence collapses this mental space and preserves the illusion that the object has no independent movement. Weintrobe suggests that this can occur when the person is overwhelmed by an extreme. This can be 'too much' evidence of independence and difference or the inverse – 'too much' absence of sameness. The violence defends against such overwhelming and flooding feelings. Perhaps it can be understood as an infantile demand, as well as a defence, a wish for the subject and object to be subsumed within each other.

I tried a number of ways to avoid being kicked in the sessions whilst maintaining communication in the room. Eventually, I decided to move the session to her ward and to spend the time sitting side-by-side at a round table. This did not occur without a great deal of heart searching. Was the kicking a genuine and volitional demand to stop the therapy? Was it a legitimate form of expression of her feelings that demanded attention and understanding rather than dismissal? Were the session experienced by her as abusive? Were they abusive? Were they helpful? Was this one of the times she experienced herself as being listened to? Was the violence an attempt to establish whether I were able to bear something of her pain? Was it an attempt to demonstrate in concrete terms something of the pain? If this were so, then could I, encouraging her to engage with me, really complain? or was I allowing myself to be victimized and colluding in an identification with *her*? These questions and many more were continually in my mind.

In the end I was moved to continue the sessions because I was clear that I was not the only one to experience or have experienced this violence from her, and I was aware that it had in the past usually led to withdrawal of the intervention she had been offered. I deliberated about 'informed consent' but I decided to continue. I also continued because I believed that Susan was regularly the scapegoat for the area where she lived. In theoretical terms I could provide myself with rationalizations for the intense pressure and hopelessness that the staff felt.

After the move to the ward, we met in a room sometimes used by the staff. There were many copies of the *Nursing Times*. Susan would wander around the room and pick up these magazines and flick through them with me. She was fascinated by pictures of babies and of gruesome gaping wounds. She knew the names of various types of apparatus far better than I did, and I came to appreciate her ability to communicate some of her experience of these things to me through the pictures. She responded to my interpretations about these painful things, whilst I felt silently guilty, imagining the disapproval of other staff for encouraging her pre-occupation with trauma and disability. In fact, Susan's behaviour did improve. Staff attitudes changed towards her somewhat and she was subsequently discharged to conditions of lower security.

CONCLUSION

It goes without saying that I believe Susan's IQ to be far above that of an arbitrary 50 points. Working with her provided a day-to-day experience of the reality of secondary handicap as described by Sinason (1986).

In time, in conjunction with my intervention, I got the help of a psychology assistant to institute behavioural changes in Susan's life. Quality of Life was the vogue and Susan got quality of life interventions without the requirement for good behaviour that had always been there before (and had never been forthcoming from her). I was criticized for devoting so much of my limited resources to one patient (occasionally stated to be 'non deserving'). I justified this by saying that there were parallel benefits for the ward and other patients. The behavioural and dynamic theories that I used to describe and justify the interventions with Susan were carefully described to nursing staff and the clinical team. I hoped that these would contribute to the matrix of knowledge and experience on the ward.

Susan had been in the institution for nearly twenty years. Little had apparently changed in this time and she was seen as a hopeless case – a constant reminder of the terribly difficult task of rehabilitating some patients. Brown *et al.* (1989) comment on the reluctance to admit children to institutions, particularly psychiatric ones. The taking of such action therefore, says a lot about the deprivation and neediness of the child and the inability of some other context to provide for these limitations. This is starkly true for Susan, who was admitted to one of the securest hospitals in the country when she was only 14. It also brings into sharp focus what the institution has to offer such people. *Whatever* is supplied, can it possibly make up for massive earlier deprivation? This doubt leads to an enormous pressure on staff. Brown *et al.* also talk about the state of being in 'limbo' that arises when people are kept in an institution for too long. Susan had not been particularly helped and had come to exist in such a state of limbo. She became a constant reminder of failure to staff which may, in part, explain the scapegoating that occurred. In retrospect, one of my actions in Susan's care becomes more understandable in this context; I suggested that her receiving authority be involved in her care (that is, the Local Health Authority that would have responsibility for her if she were ever to leave the hospital). This suggestion generated the *conscious* denigration of the clinical team in that they allowed me to go ahead, provided only that *I* made the contact (and thus risked the derision of the authority for asking them to consider such an unmanageable woman). However, that I was given the authority to do so, implied some *unconscious* respect. My application paid off and some considerable movement occurred. In some ways the therapeutic input with me may also be seen as providing something of a holding environment and a temporary respite in the limbo.

Acknowledgement
I would like to thank Dr Chris Evans for helpful comments on an earlier draft of this paper.

16

Music Therapy and Psychotic Violence

Ann Sloboda

INTRODUCTION

This chapter is based on my experience of working as a music therapist with in-patients in a Regional Secure Unit (RSU) for mentally disordered offenders, most of whom have a diagnosis of a psychotic illness such as schizophrenia. As music therapy is still relatively rare in forensic units, I will start with some basic information, and discuss my experience of introducing a new service. The main focus will be on clinical material, through which I will illustrate and discuss the particular contribution of music therapy to the treatment of patients.

The premise I work from is that music therapy can be used as a form of psychotherapy, whereby the relationship between client and therapist is developed through active music-making. Although some people might expect music therapists to teach or perform music to patients, in Britain this is not the case. The professional training of music therapists stresses the role of improvisation in allowing individuals to express their emotional state, and to enter into an interactive dialogue with the therapist.

Music therapists work on the basis that:

- music-making is essentially a social and communicative activity
- the response to sound is innate, and predates birth
- the use of sound as an expressive medium pre-dates the acquisition of language skill.

This implies that:

(1) Sound can be used to help people without verbal skills to express themselves, but also

(2) It can also help people who *can* speak to experience or express emotions
     for which they have not yet found words.

The therapist needs to be a highly trained musician in order to facilitate this,
and to provide musical support on their own instrument, but no prior musical
training or skill is needed in the patient (indeed, many music therapists work
with profoundly disabled people).

The RSU is a 50-bedded, purpose built secure unit in the grounds of a
general hospital and it was part of an expansion of the service that enabled my
post to be created.

As my previous experience had been in general psychiatry where resources
are spread more thinly, I was initially struck by the number of highly qualified
staff of all disciplines offering intensive input to the patients. In seeking
appropriate referrals it was therefore particularly important to explain the
philosophy of music therapy and what it could offer mentally disordered
offenders as a therapeutic tool. This is outlined below:

- The forensic patient tends to concretize his experience and act out
  rather than think. Estela Welldon (1994) writes of such patients
  'compulsion, impulsivity, inability to intersperse thought before
  action, and…a total inability to understand it'.

- Music can be at the same time both concrete (in the act of hitting a
  percussion instrument, for example) and symbolic (in that it can arouse
  many imaginative associations) but what is being 'said' in music can
  never be exactly translated.

- The act of making sounds on musical instruments gives the patient a
  medium for expression. It can also give even the most inarticulate
  person a means of relating directly to another person, thereby serving
  as a link between the inner and outer world of the patient, and
  between the patient and the therapist.

- Some patients may be able to make connections between the way they
  play and aspects of the way they behave or relate.

- In cases where such insight is not present the therapist may be able to
  analyze or reflect on the musical interaction. Even if the patient is
  unable to think or speak about the music, the experience of being
  contained and supported in an interactive duet can still be of
  therapeutic value.

In the RSU I offer two types of music therapy input:

(1) Assessment
- to help demonstrate aspects of the patient's state and patterns of
  communicating

o to see what they might reveal of their internal world when offered another medium.

This may be interesting or useful to the rest of the team, in confirming the view they had already, or showing another side of the patient not normally revealed.

The assessment can consist of only one or two sessions, after which a report is provided, or can proceed to:

(2) Treatment

This is longer term, ongoing work, part of the rehabilitation process and is aimed at helping the patients develop a stronger sense of themselves and greater insight into their difficulties.

It has been a struggle at times to establish myself, and to gain appropriate referrals without an existing tradition of music therapy in the unit. Many colleagues had a vague idea that a music therapist's main aim with forensic patients would be to give them an opportunity to 'get all their aggression out on the drums'. Others have been wary because they feel, understandably, concerned that this is what music therapists will be attempting to do. So far my experience has, in fact, been that many patients are extremely reluctant to make noises which might be construed as violent or aggressive, and are more concerned with controlling the sounds they do make. For example, one patient was worried that he might damage the instruments, and another man enjoyed playing loudly but stopped every few seconds, asking: 'am I doing your head in?'

Clinical vignette

Alan (a long-term patient in his late thirties) was referred during a ward round by the consultant, initially for assessment, and then for treatment.

Alan's parents had separated when he was a child, and his mother (who suffered from schizophrenia) brought him up alone. He developed paranoid schizophrenia himself as an adult, and his index offence was the killing of a woman he had been living with. He had been acutely psychotic at the time of his offence, believing that his girlfriend was involved in a plot to kill him.

Once in the RSU, he continued to suffer from fears that he would be killed, and at times held delusional beliefs that staff or other patients were his persecutors. He also made several suicide attempts which led to his being under constant close observation by nursing staff. He aroused a sense both of hopelessness and affection in the staff team. The reason for the music therapy referral was exploratory, namely to see whether it might be a way of helping him in his relationships with others.

Alan was quite willing to come for an assessment session although he said he was anxious. When he did play some of the percussion instruments, his response was very emotional and tearful, saying it brought back memories. He was shaking, but insisted the tears were good tears, and was also anxious about trying to follow my rhythm.

My countertransference was one of anxiety and concern. Had I unsettled him? Was the medium and the contact too powerful for him? Would it put him in touch with all sorts of emotions he couldn't cope with, and thus increase the risk of suicide?

I also experienced omnipotent fantasies, namely that through music I would be able to get through where others hadn't, and be a containing, supportive 'mother' with my music. Williams-Saunders (1996) points out that creative arts therapists (often in a marginal position in their workplace) are particularly susceptible to this kind of Messianic fantasy. As Welldon (1994) emphasizes, it is essential to work as a team with forensic patients, and I was in danger of forgetting the contribution of nursing staff and other therapists. Any improvement on the part of a patient is the result of a combined team effort.

After discussion with the team, the general view was that music therapy could be valuable for Alan as he had been 'stuck' for so long and it was suggested that I should offer an initial trial period of six sessions, which gave him a 'get-out clause' if he found the contact too difficult, but would also be enough to see the beginnings of a process and a relationship.

ASSESSMENT PERIOD

As the very nature of music-making involves therapist and patient in a concrete activity together, the music therapist often takes a more active role than in verbal analytical psychotherapy, particularly when the patient is very anxious. In his early sessions Alan was generally anxious and fearful, and said that he couldn't play any of the instruments, though he wished he could play the piano. I made suggestions to get him started: for example, a piano duet, where we both improvised using only the black notes, to restrict the choice so that it did not seem too overwhelming for Alan, and also to reduce the possibility of discordant sounds that might discourage him.

Alan began to play, tentatively at first, and then with more confidence, shaping the notes into clearly defined phrases that were quite easy for me to accompany.

These initial sessions seemed to arouse some hope and optimism in Alan knowing that he had been able to use the piano with me, and it had not sounded as bad as he feared.

In the last session of the six, he arrived in a very different state of mind, and produced music of a markedly different quality.

Nursing staff reported that he had been unsure whether to attend; he had had nightmares the previous night about people trying to kill him, and looked very subdued and anxious. He sat down at the xylophone and began to play without saying anything, and after a few moments I began to accompany him on piano. He played more slowly than usual, and very quietly. The rhythmic pulse seemed to get slower until it almost disappeared. While Alan's playing was still organized into sequential patterns, he left so

many erratic gaps between the notes that I found it much more difficult to accompany or anticipate. It felt as if he was keeping a certain distance from me in our musical interaction.

It is common practice for music therapists to make tape recordings of their improvisations with patients. I did this with Alan, and played them to him so as to give him an opportunity to comment on the sounds he had made, his own role in the interaction between us, and any other thoughts that occurred to him whilst listening. At first Alan did not comment on the recordings, but towards the end of the trial period he began to remark on certain features of his playing. For example in the session described above, he commented 'All my tunes go downwards. That's like me: I start off with a flourish, and then deteriorate'.

This rather pessimistic view fitted with his mood before the session.

However, it was significant that he linked qualities of the music with his own personality, and so might be able to use it to reflect further on his patterns of relating. Alan decided to continue with regular weekly therapy and this was then discussed, and agreed, with the team.

PROGRESS OF THERAPY

Once ongoing therapy was under way, I noticed some developments in Alan's use of the medium. Although his playing generally fell into predictable and repetitive patterns, there were occasions when he would make more dramatic and unexpected sounds. He began to choose a wider variety of instruments, including the drum, which he had avoided until now, because 'it might be too loud'.

To me there did seem to be some aggression in his drumming, certainly more than he had expressed verbally. In view of his worries that this might be too much for me, I felt it important to produce an appropriate musical response – one that was solid and strong, but not retaliatory. I did this by using the whole range of the piano keyboard to play chords that were loud, but also slow and steady.

After one such improvisation he spoke at some length about how he felt optimistic; the experience of improvising had reminded him of a time in his youth when he was well, and able to do things quite freely.

We commented that he had lost some of his fear of breaking rules or playing 'wrong' notes.

ALAN: Now I'm not worried about that. Partly because your music
          doesn't necessarily tie in with what I play... I'm not criticising!

(I linked this with his experience of his mother, where he felt he could never speak his mind with confidence for fear of retaliation. Even this observation about our musical interaction aroused a fear that I would perceive this as an insult.)

ALAN: I do notice though, that if I play a melody on the xylophone, you
          play a tune on the piano, and that does tie in, and also if I play
          the drum you go deep on the piano.

          I set the pace, you follow. You don't tell me what to play, I just
          play anything I think it's a good idea to let me do that, because
          I've got no idea how to play these instruments anyway, so, short
          of having strict instructions on one instrument at a time, which is
          impossible, the only thing to do is let me go free.

This led to a discussion about feeling freer in his mind, and how this linked with the length of time he had been constantly observed by staff, which was now beginning to be reduced. Alan said he didn't need such monitoring any more, especially with women staff. 'You see I don't like women being with me too much. I was maltreated by a woman.'

It seemed that music therapy could be a way to experience closeness, but also allow him a way to defend himself, and remain at a distance. His remarks about our musical roles showed an interest in thinking about our relationship. The fact that he saw my role in terms of 'letting him go free' as opposed to giving him impossibly strict instructions, and the fact that he linked a feeling of optimism and freedom with my keeping a certain distance in our musical interaction all seemed to make sense.

We continued with regular weekly sessions in the hope that music therapy could help him to reflect on the experience of a relationship, and particularly one with a woman.

During this period there were some small but significant changes in his condition: as said above, the level of staff observation was reduced and music therapy was the first thing he came to alone without a nurse. In addition, whilst he still suffered from paranoid ideas, fewer thoughts of suicide were recorded by staff, and the team began to discuss the possibility of his moving to a ward with more freedom and fewer staff.

In sessions I encouraged him to play, or say, whatever he felt like. He would usually begin by improvising on the instruments, and would intersperse the playing with periods of talking. He spoke much about his mother and a little about his girlfriend.

He experienced his mother as persecutory and unpredictable, always critical of him and often angry. He described his girlfriend as someone who 'never spoke at all': he had no idea what she was thinking and became suspicious of her, imagining that she was plotting against him.

Alan said of his relationship with his mother: 'I was never allowed to influence anything. I never knew how she was going to respond.' The idea of influence and response between us became a feature of our discussions and musical improvisation seemed a useful way to approach it.

Orton (1992) writes: 'Improvisation demands total involvement...one must be free to initiate ideas, to hear and respond to the ideas of others... An accident or error can be turned around and made musically meaningful'.

In Alan's case, (as with so many forensic patients), a past 'error' had had tragic results. Risk-taking had therefore been suppressed and improvisation was like free association, a frightening thing to be asked to do – 'a leap in the dark'.

Music therapy is an arena where exploration and mutual influence are essential. For one person to remain uninfluenced by the other would defeat the object. In attempting to predict my response to him, he was considering the idea that I might respond to him in a certain way – that is, that he might influence me.

He noted, with considerable pleasure, that he could rely on my response when he played a certain instrument, and said

'I can almost guarantee that you'll play like this if I do that.'

Alan continued to explore the idea of how he might influence me in the musical interaction. One session, seven months into his therapy, Alan took more initiative than usual and suggested that, rather than playing the piano as I usually did, I played the xylophone while he played the metallophone. These are pitched percussion instruments (one wooden, one metal) which look similar but sound different. He placed them facing each other. This was the first time this had happened, as we usually played positioned in such a way that we were not looking directly at each other. He said: 'You whack it, I'll respond'.

In this interaction there was more obvious turn-taking in his playing and much more direct communication.

Later, after a year of therapy, he suggested the same activity, but said 'Let's have a conversation: I'll start.' This was noticeably more reciprocal in expectation.

DISCUSSION

The role of the musical instruments was important in this work. The room is set up to ensure that the same instruments are available each week. They are concrete objects, and, for someone whose thinking is so concrete, can be comforting. In one of the very few articles so far published on this subject, Loth (1994) describes how forensic patients in a music therapy group saw the instruments as precious toys that they did not wish to relinquish.

Patients can take refuge in involvement with the instrument rather than the therapist, because an inanimate object might seem safer and more reliable than another person. I have noticed that at times when Alan seems to find direct communication with me particularly difficult, he will focus all his attention on one of the musical instruments, making empirical observations about its physical properties, that is, the names of the notes, the vibrations of the different tones, what the instrument is made of, and where it was made. I have come to recognize this as a communication from Alan that he needs to defend himself from close or emotional interaction with me. There have been several examples of this: once when Alan was angry with me but avoided saying so; another occasion when he was feeling paranoid and suspicious of me, and had misinterpreted something I had said.

CONCLUSION

At the time of writing the work is still ongoing. I am often affected by the contact with Alan and, at times, inhibited by thoughts of his crime. For example, on one occasion I noticed, as he sat at the keyboard, how large his hands were, and that he could stretch nine white keys with ease. I was about to comment on this when I remembered that he had killed someone, and, suddenly, felt afraid to mention it.

I found it essential to preserve links, and discuss experiences, with other professionals in order to balance the directness of the contact with Alan.

At other times I find the sessions extremely monotonous and frustrating. As Alan plays the same descending scale on the xylophone week after week, I think with irony of comments made to me such as 'It must be wonderful to be doing a *creative* job like music therapy!' The 'unchangingness' of his musical expression makes it hard at times for me to think or play creatively. I found the words of Nina Coltart (1996) a great help in approaching this task: 'As we listen to a patient, for the first or the 500th time, we observe with our inner, image-making eye that he is laying out pieces of his personal jigsaw puzzle for us to ponder over'. Alan's repetitive musical 'jigsaw pieces' remind me of his fear of opening himself up to new or different ways of thinking. However, the fact that he has sustained this one-to-one relationship for over a year, and has managed to voice difficult thoughts to me, occasionally a criticism, once some sexual thoughts (of which he was very ashamed), indicate a certain if fragile and fluctuating level of trust. It can be seen, perhaps, as a barometer indicating what he might be capable of and also what his limitations are. He has also on occasions revealed his psychopathology, namely paranoia; for example he recently volunteered the information that he had been using the interest in the instrument as a way of keeping me at a distance, because 'I didn't want to let you in'.

I consider the developing ability to discuss what is going on in our musical interaction as indicating that he can sometimes use the medium as a way of experiencing and thinking about a relationship. Recently, he used the word 'relationship' for the first time in a session: 'It seemed more co-ordinated today, what you were playing – or maybe it was the relationship between what I was playing and your piano playing'.

I think that the musical component has been very useful here. As outlined in a recent article (Robarts and Sloboda 1994) 'creating music and interacting musically provided the experience of a sense of self and of self-in-relationship to another'. The actual music itself is very simple in nature, but appears to help Alan experience support from me. It is equally important to be aware of how threatening it is if he feels I have got too close. The musical medium is useful here in providing him with a very concrete way of maintaining his defences and keeping me at a safe distance.

17

The Treatment of Alcohol Dependency in Groups

Barbara Elliott

INTRODUCTION

In addition to the 600,000 convictions for drink driving offences in England and Wales during 1994 (Home Office 1994) between 50 per cent and 70 per cent of all homicides, stabbings, beatings and fights in the home are alcohol related (BMA 1989) and 25 per cent of all cases of child sexual abuse (NSPCC 1992) are similarly precipitated by or closely connected with alcohol abuse. Yet, apart from the most obvious cases, the majority of individuals who abuse alcohol go undetected by most professionals who work with them. And some go undetected for many years. Eventually, certain patterns will develop which make the diagnosis of alcohol dependency (as opposed to a one off instance of alcohol abuse) glaringly obvious.

Once a problem drinker has been identified a number of possibilities present themselves. For some individuals, identification is closely followed by the acknowledgement that their alcohol consumption is damaging, and this is sufficient to effect change. It is one of the great mysteries within the addiction field that there are individuals with serious dependency problems who simply stop drinking without either medical or non-medical specialist help. Others chose a long-term, if not a life-long affiliation to Alcoholics Anonymous (AA). Another group, with less serious dependency problems may respond well to controlled drinking programmes (Robertson and Heather 1986).

However, for many problem drinkers the evidence of damage to health, income and relationships, or conflict with the law, is not enough to facilitate or maintain change. These individuals are characteristically resistant to acknowledging their alcohol dependency and highly ambivalent about undertaking treatment. They are prone to repetitions of problem behaviour once the crisis precipitating their change in drinking patterns has passed or other stresses threaten to overwhelm them. In these cases the professional has a fundamental job in helping the patient work through an understandable ambivalence about abstaining from alcohol (which is necessary in the majority of cases) and accepting treatment. Solution Focused Therapy (Berg and Miller 1992) and Motivational Interviewing (Miller and Rolnick 1991) are two techniques which have proven to be particularly effective in helping individuals acknowledge their problem and work through their ambivalence sufficiently to enable a meaningful treatment process to begin.

TREATMENT

Those alcohol dependent individuals unable to stop on their own or with the help of Alcoholics Anonymous (AA) or brief intervention specialist services, require formal, specialized and on-going treatment. I want to suggest that while may useful interventions can take place in a one-to-one setting, alcohol dependency *can only* effectively be treated in groups. This must seem a bold statement to those who fund, or make use of the many specialist counsellors and counselling services which are to be found throughout the UK. In order to support this statement, I want to look at some of the characteristics common to most dependent drinkers who approach services for help, as I have experienced them, and to place this within the context of some of the literature on group psychotherapy.

CHARACTERISTICS OF DEPENDENT DRINKERS

Within both psychiatry and psychoanalysis, individuals severely dependent on alcohol and other drugs are often classified as borderline personalities. While not wanting to suggest that psychoanalysis is the treatment of choice for these individuals, even if it were affordable on a large scale, the psychoanalytic literature does have some very important things to teach us descriptively about problem drinkers.

The concept of borderline personality disorder has been a controversial and confusing one but over recent years, largely due to the work of Otto Kernberg (1975), there has been considerable agreement about definitions. Borderline patients have aspects to their personalities that are consistent with certain elements found in both neuroses and in psychoses but borderline personality disorder is conceptualized as structurally different and separate from both. The fundamental agreed characteristic (Jackson and Pines 1986) is that a stable, integrated, consistent and cohesive ego structure has not been developed and this creates a severe disturbance in the processes of individuation and separation. Because the ego structure is not in place, the individual cannot effectively use the normal range of defense mechanisms such as repression, sublimation or displacement, and must therefore rely heavily on the more primitive defence mechanisms of projection, introjection and projective identification.

Borderline patients, time and time again, resort to primitive splitting mechanisms in their attempts to defend themselves against psychic pain which feels both unmanageable and unbearable. Not only is the world experienced as a series of fragmented extremes (populated by heroes and villains) but the individuals themselves, in resorting to these defences, also suffer from the fragmentation of their own egos and identities. This accounts for the severe mood swings which are such a predominant feature in this group.

These patients suffer intensely from a sense of insecurity and lack of self-esteem which strangely runs in parallel with a grandiosity, superiority and sense of omnipotence. As a group they have a very low tolerance for emotional pain (frustration, anger, depression, boredom) and are extremely sensitive to criticism and feelings of rejection. Their relationships are one sided rather than mutual. In working with them, one often has the sense of not being recognized as being separate and independent but rather as an extension of the patient and used accordingly in various ways to support a precariously weakened sense of self.

As a result of the persistent threat of unmanageable pain – a fear of falling apart, of literally being shattered into pieces – these individuals' lives become more and more centered around pain avoidance. Repeated, dependent use of alcohol as a form of psychic anaesthetic provides us with the conceptual link between borderline states and drug dependency.

In working with individuals who have a history of serious alcohol abuse, I have come to recognize four fundamental characteristics which reliably emerge when contact goes beyond a brief intervention stage and these do indeed resonate with much of the description of patients with borderline personalities.

(1) The speed and intensity with which dependency is formed
This is not surprising if one remembers that patients in abstinence-based treatment have abruptly stopped using a substance which had previously provided them with a reasonably affective defence system; offering a partial sense of identity, safety, fusion, cohesion and an on-tap psychic anesthetic. It seems reasonable therefore, with the termination of drinking, that the dependency will become firmly established elsewhere such as with a doctor, counsellor or AA activity.

(2) A tendency towards extreme forms of splitting through Projective Identification

This is a feature that is in evidence throughout the problem drinker's life but is often seen in the treatment setting in the form of an overt enthusiasm and idealization for the 'recovery process' (the programme is wonderful, the counsellors are wonderful, the patient feels good, never felt better, so glad s/he got some help at last). The other extreme – the hostility and contempt – are sometimes observed in the treatment setting as when a patient is particularly disruptive, critical or rebellious. But more often than not, this side of the split is invisible. The patient simply disappears and drops out of treatment following an experience of anger or disappointment, often never to return unless compelled to, and in many cases quickly returns to abusive levels of consumption.

(3) A pre-occupation with boundaries, structures, limits and authority which often brings a rather adolescent feel to the relationship

The effect of this pre-occupation on therapists and other professionals is that they often get caught up with rules and the implementation of policies around relapse and attendance. Patients get caught up with similar issues – can they argue their way back onto a programme or into the counselling room? Or can they avoid getting caught altogether? Either way, professionals become pushed into authoritarian stances and patients are not enabled to focus properly and meaningfully on issues of responsibility and choice.

(4) A generally low self-esteem and a below average tolerance to emotional pain and discomfort

This means that even moderate amounts of frustration, boredom or anger can trigger a relapse and is precisely why relationships at work and at home have often gone so disastrously wrong in the past. Patients who seek treatment with the hope that they will learn how to handle outside relationships better, often find themselves confronted with the very same problems and feelings that trigger the desire to drink in the first place.

INDIVIDUAL AND GROUP THERAPY

It is not altogether surprising that with this range of presenting characteristics, most psychoanalysts and individual analytic psychotherapists have turned away from working with addiction problems (see Arroyave 1986; Hopper 1996; Limentani 1986 for some exceptions) and it does seem that the addiction field is influenced predominantly by practitioners of cognitive and behavioural methods or else treatment programmes based firmly around the principles of Alcoholics Anonymous.

Individual analytic psychotherapy is certainly hard to establish and harder to maintain with these patients. To begin with, most of them are not able to establish a firm therapeutic alliance based on a consistent understanding of the 'as if' aspect in transference interpretations. In fact, interpretations are usually experienced as criticisms or attacks. Patients are very easily wounded and the stresses inherent in meaningful psychotherapy (including depression) cannot be tolerated and often in themselves trigger relapse. Because of the over-use of projective identification, the view of the therapist often moves quickly from a highly idealized image to one of a hated and dangerous persecutor, which in turn precipitates relapse, abrupt termination of therapy, and usually both.

The way to move beyond the many problems of working analytically with a range of borderline patients seems to be by working exclusively with them in groups (Welldon 1994). Groups suit very dependent problem drinkers far better than one-to-one interventions for a number of reasons. Some of them have been described (Yalom 1985) as curative or therapeutic factors and include: installation of hope, universality, imparting of information, altruism, development of socializing techniques and interpersonal learning. Group life provides endless opportunities for mutual identification, support and sharing, all of which can contribute to a sense of increased self-esteem and containment within the individual.

As well as providing intensely profound intrapersonal and interpersonal experiences, there also occur more relaxed, neutral experiences where clients can gain a sense of being in relationship with others in ways which feel expressive of, without feeling hazardous to, the self.

But the most important reason why groups should be the treatment of choice for this client group is that relationships with therapists (and others) are much easier to manage over time; and recovery from dependency problems takes time. For example, when the inevitable intense, negative feelings are experienced towards the therapist, other group members can be taken up as allies. This in turn makes the negativity more bearable and thus, the therapy process itself is much less likely to turn sour. By surviving the crisis of negative feelings in combination with more neutral or positive feelings, problem drinkers can begin to slowly integrate diverse parts of themselves and others. As ambivalence becomes possible and tolerable, an acceptance of the good and bad in the self and in others becomes stronger and more stable. If patients can be held in a group programme over time, they have repeated opportunities for building up and internalizing new psychological structures which in turn fosters an increased ability to manage emotional pain and hence, stability.

Considerable success has been reported (Pines 1978) in treating one or two borderline patients at a time in heterogeneous out-patient groups. However, a strong case can be made for treating certain categories of borderline patients in homogeneous groups such as those dependent on alcohol and other drugs

(Arroyave 1986; Stevenson and Ruscombe-King 1993; Vanicelli 1988; Matano and Yalom 1991).

Problem drinkers do not need to be treated together because they are difficult or because they require particular restrictions. As I have already suggested, these patients are characteristically (in the beginning, at least) cooperative, polite and highly motivated. They need to be treated together because it is the only way that the necessary underlying culture can become firmly established.

The culture is in response to the strong pull towards a narcissistic, regressed state which is re-created through alcohol consumption. The culture in itself represents the understanding by all therapists and patients that the first and most important aim of the therapy is to enable the patient to survive another day without drinking. Analyzing behaviour, emotions and relationships is invaluable in the recovery process but is always secondary to the primary aim of abstinence. This has important implications and leads to specific adaptations in the traditional group analytic approach. Problem drinkers who are treated in heterogeneous rather than in homogeneous groups are rarely held by their therapy and often cause disruption in their groups.

CONCLUSION

I want to emphasize that the ideal setting for serious alcohol dependency problems at the commencement of treatment is not weekly out-patient groups, but rather a day centre or non-residential clinic operating loosely along therapeutic community lines. This kind of environment provides sufficient structure and containment to hold clients through the fragile and often volatile period of early abstinence, while simultaneously providing opportunities to explore issues around dependency, separation, boundary, authority and responsibility.

It is beyond the scope of the present chapter to describe the theoretical perspective and the detailed structures required of a specialist programme which would enable patients to make the shift from severe dependency to separation and integration, and from day attendance to out-patient evening groups (see Elliott 1995). For the majority of non-specialist counsellors, probation officers, social workers or psychotherapists, early and accurate assessment and the vital work of motivating patients genuinely to seek and use help for their dependency problems, can take place within the individual encounter. However, for most patients with serious alcohol dependency problems, it is in groups where the work of treatment and recovery is made possible.

18

Violence and Alcohol

Maggie Hilton

INTRODUCTION

This chapter is based on a man, in his late twenties, who was referred for problems of alcohol abuse and aggression. He reported a ten year history of alcohol dependence resulting in frequent blackouts and acting out of aggressive, revengeful and envious feelings towards others. He felt a great sense of excitement at 'living on the edge' and would recount how he would first charm and then persistently provoke others to a point where his behaviour became intolerable to them. He enjoyed the sense of being in control of others' emotions and manipulating their feelings by his behaviour. At times this would provoke physical aggression and he was occasionally badly beaten up while drunk. He would often physically attack his wife and would further act out his aggressive and omnipotent impulses by driving whilst drunk, occasionally deliberately driving other people off the road. He talked about enjoying a sense of danger and recounted fantasies of doing dramatic things, including robbing banks. Particularly worrying were fantasies about sexually assaulting women because he believed that they were all enjoying happy lives and rejecting him. Underlying this was a belief that he was unacceptable to others, both socially and sexually, and that the only way he could get what he wanted was to grab it. In fact, he was intelligent, creative, humorous and physically attractive. He believed himself to a good judge of character, but his judgements reflected nihilistic negative projections of his own greed, manipulativeness and hostility.

BACKGROUND

The patient was the second born of three children brought up in a middle class family. His father was described as strict, cold and unavailable to the patient, who felt that he could never please him. He was expected by his father to have a stoical ability to cope with difficulties in life, any sign of weakness or vulnerability being unacceptable. His mother was alcoholic and described as destructive, sadistic and aggressive when drunk. Distressing tirades against family members were common. The patient, in a desperate attempt to get close to his mother and receive some evidence that she cared for him, identified with her a great deal. This was expressed by his alcohol abuse and aggression in adulthood and, in his youth, by an inability to condemn her verbal and physical attacks on his father and sister. There was no acknowledging or facing of the mother's alcoholism within the family.

The patient was sent to boarding school from the age of six which deepened his sense that there was no-one available to care for him. There was a great deal of bullying and teasing at school and he was unable to remember any positive relationships experienced whilst growing up, except with his grandmother who sometimes cared for him during school holidays. The patient's sense of alienation and of being different from others intensified when, at the age of ten, he was brutally sexually abused by older boys at the school. He told no-one about this abuse but continued to experience extreme distress and anger when remembering it. The patient increasingly began to isolate himself from others, believing that they were rejecting him, although there was no evidence that this was so. Despite these difficulties he did well at school, though he dropped out of college after a year, primarily as a result of increasingly drinking alcohol to cope with social anxiety.

Infrequent contact with women during his early life, particularly with those who offered a positive experience, resulted in a great deal of anxiety and insecurity about heterosocial and sexual relationships. In his early relationships he was unassertive and easily hurt but later became dominating and cruel. He viewed women as depriving, sadistic and untrustworthy. In his relationship with his wife he acted out his need to control others omnipotently, using aggression when necessary. He also felt misused and manipulated by the men in his life. His lack of assertiveness in social relationships led to situations in which he felt that others abused him and did not consider his needs, leading to retaliatory fantasies and impulses towards them. He believed himself to be innately unattractive to others, leading them to despise and reject him. His behaviour towards others regularly triggered responses which reinforced his irrational beliefs and expectations, which were extremely rigid and uncompromising.

THE FIRST PHASE OF TREATMENT

My view of treatment was that, while no progress would be possible until the patient's dependence on alcohol had been tackled, the core therapeutic task was to facilitate changes in the patient's object and self-representations.

Therapy began with a standard cognitive-behavioural approach to alcohol abuse, identifying abstinence as the goal of treatment. We examined the roles that alcohol played in the patient's life, discussed the physiological, psychological and social repercussions of alcohol abuse and used relapse prevention techniques (Marlatt and Gordon 1985) to increase his awareness of factors triggering an urge to drink. Ways of avoiding relapses as well as managing any relapses that occurred were formulated. A decision matrix helped to identify the advantages and disadvantages of both continuing to drink and of total abstinence. Anxiety management techniques were used to reduce the level of tension experienced and reading matter was given on cognitive approaches. While responsive to these ways of working, the need to abstain from alcohol completely was frequently tested. Even when the dangerousness of alcohol was repeatedly identified in his diaries, the patient continued to use alcohol destructively at times, particularly when feeling emotionally vulnerable. The excitement and sense of power over others experienced while drunk made abstinence extremely difficult, particularly as, when not drinking, the patient felt himself to be alienated from others and in an emotional void which at times led to depression, including suicidal feelings.

THE MIDDLE PHASE OF TREATMENT

After four months, when the initial cognitive-behavioural work on alcohol abuse had been completed, therapy focused upon my patient's difficulties in relating to others and his low self-esteem. The content of sessions was guided increasingly by what the patient brought. Experiences in early life had resulted in extremely damaged object relations such that his beliefs and expectations about others fuelled envy, a sense of entitlement and an urge to seek revenge through aggression and theft.

Problematic situations were dealt with by drawing links between the present and past experiences to clarify the part my patient played in creating situations in which he believed others were abusing him. These links also facilitated a greater understanding of factors driving his abusive behaviour towards others. Distortions in the way he was perceiving events were tackled using cognitive techniques. We examined the split in the way he presented himself, either as a charming, intelligent, caring and sensitive person or a loutish thug. By examining his perceptions of the positive and negative aspects of these two 'identities' it was possible to have a dialogue about their effects on his self-image and relationships. A trainee clinical psychologist also carried out an

IQ and vocational guidance assessment with him, which was used to discuss his potential to be successful and the type of work situation that would suit him best. At the beginning of treatment he was encouraged to involve himself in social events, such as evening classes, but it was only after four years of therapy that he felt able to join a club and use this to work at his difficulties in relating to others. It was also suggested that he involve himself in a much wider range of activities, particularly those which might provide him with a sense of danger and excitement that prior to treatment he had sought in drinking. Social and assertiveness skills were encouraged and his key relationships were discussed in terms of their effect on him. In particular the relationship with his parents was examined, including his continuing hope that he might eventually receive the recognition and care that he had longed for.

The Therapeutic Relationship

Although not working with an explicitly psychodynamic model, psychodynamic theory was used to inform my thinking. Transference and counter-transference phenomena were inevitably experienced and worked with. Initially I was idealized, possibly because I provided a space where my patient could be listened to, taken seriously and attempts made to understand the distress driving his behaviour. However, this inevitably put the patient in touch with his neediness and desire to be cared for which made him feel very vulnerable during breaks in treatment and sometimes between sessions. He often invited me to reject him for his failure to abstain from alcohol. At times drinking relapses appeared to be fuelled by an attempt to reassert his control over his life when he felt manipulated by therapy to change. Breaks also triggered acting out in the form of seeking sexual relationships with women, including prostitutes, in order to be physically comforted. Although at times such approaches were made with the intention of physically attacking the women, these feelings were not acted upon.

His growing recognition of feeling dependent on me was accompanied by urges to hurt and attack me as well as fears that, following sessions in which we had talked about his difficulties in socializing, I would sneer at his vulnerability. He felt that I was humiliating him when he became tearful in sessions and experienced me as playing with his emotions and taunting him with unrealistic expectations of how his life could be. He expressed fears that I might tell the police about him or might wire the room up in order to get evidence against him. I was also felt to be a threat to his masculinity by encouraging him to be more in touch with his emotions and vulnerability.

There were surprisingly few attempts to denigrate the therapy directly, either verbally or by physically acting out in sessions. He would, however, describe aggressive acts to me in a self-justifying manner, inviting me to concur with an omnipotent, heroic view of himself. Also, he would describe fantasies of sexually or physically assaulting women, believing that I would find such descriptions very unpleasant and potentially threatening. Rarely, he would describe fantasies of acting aggressively towards me and dare me to say something that would make him feel entitled to attack me. At times he felt very angry with me but was unable to explain what lay behind this.

I rarely felt that there was a real risk that he would act upon his aggressive impulses and attack me. However, there was a period during the middle phase when his distress and confusion about therapy and the therapeutic relationship was so great that it seemed as if he might feel that attacking me was the only way he could leave therapy, which was becoming increasingly uncomfortable for him. During this period I paid special attention to security in the clinical setting and discussed with him ways in which he could contain his anxiety and work with it. For instance, we discussed other services that he could make use of in a crisis, and I suggested that he telephone me between sessions if he was feeling out of control. Techniques for dealing with excessive emotion were also discussed, including distracting himself by activities such as running, noting down his thoughts and feelings for later discussion within sessions, or deliberately focusing on his emotions, and at their height trying to get in touch with situations in which he had experienced similar feelings as a child.

TERMINATION OF TREATMENT AND PROGRESS MADE

Therapy continued for six years, and termination occurred over a planned 18-month period. The patient was able to express his feelings of abandonment and sadness at the loss of his relationship with me, while remaining positive about the effects of treatment on his life. Although there continued to be occasional periods of acting out in the form of drinking relapses these were brief and far less destructive than previously. Despite many years on social security, after two years in treatment he started his own business and demonstrated very quickly his ability to be successful in this. Initially, he often threatened this success by acting destructively in relation to his work, but by the end of treatment was working very successfully and had built up a good reputation for the quality of his work. He was proud of his business and the skill evident in his work.

During treatment my patient's relationship with his father improved considerably. He was able to express feelings more openly and confront his father about his mother's drinking and how this had affected, and was continuing to affect, him. His father was eventually able to admit to the severity of his wife's drinking and the destructiveness of it. However, he remained unable to act in a way that would truly acknowledge the unacceptability of her behaviour and the pain that this caused. My patient also wrote a letter to his mother in which he expressed his feelings about her drinking and the effect of this on him.

While her response fell far short of what he would have wished for, and she continued to drink in an extremely destructive way, she did at times manage to control her drinking at family gatherings.

Early in treatment my patient's violence to his wife was a focus for discussion. This led to a recognition of his desire to feel in control, which was achieved when he saw his wife terrified. His aggression towards his wife and others ceased during treatment. For the first time in his life he began to build up positive friendships, although these remained tenuous. Experiences on holiday and at the social club reinforced his discovery that it was primarily his own behaviour that determined how others treated him. He discovered, too, that others enjoyed his company and would seek him out to confide in him.

CONCLUSIONS

I have outlined six years of once-weekly therapy with a patient suffering from alcohol abuse and aggression. Cognitive-behavioural techniques were used to provide a concrete external holding and containing structure to increase the patient's sense of self-control, self-efficacy and self-confidence. Working in this way allows some of the expertise residing in the therapist to be directly handed over to the patient in the form of specific techniques and educational reading materials.

However, when working with complex cases, my experience suggests that cognitive-behavioural approaches need to be underpinned by a working knowledge of psychodynamic theory, particularly that relating to object relations and to transference and counter-transference phenomena. Without this, patients often fail to engage in treatment or, if they do, may fail to benefit, or may even experience therapy as a further abuse. An overly rigid, inflexible approach can also result in denigrating the patient. For instance, patients may be labelled as untreatable with no recognition that it is the limits of our knowledge and ways of working which results in failure.

In my view, such work requires an ability to stay with very difficult experiences and material and struggle to foster an understanding and working through of very complex damaged aspects of the personality. It also requires an ability to struggle to maintain a dialogue with those who may long since have lost any belief that they can be understood or that their lives can be different.

19

Addiction
Loving and Hating

Jessica Williams-Saunders

Icarus...intoxicated with the power of flight, flew too high and lost his life...the myth of Icarus symbolises the course of addiction – from its desire to flee an imprisoning situation, to the heights of euphoric escape and freedom, to the consequent fall – and the burning and the drowning that ensue. (Schierse Leonard 1989, p.10)

DISCUSSION
Addiction and Violence
In her book *Creativity and the Veil of Addiction*, Schierse Leonard (1989) describes addiction as the killer.

Addiction – The Killer – kills love and creativity within the addict. It devours the heart of creativity with its insatiable hunger and drains it of vitality like the vampire that lives off the life blood of its victims. (p.165)

It is undoubtedly the case that drug addiction can and does kill people. Addiction is also a killer in the sense that the addict attempts to kill off the internal world and life; anything creative and good internally and externally is savagely attacked by the destructive force that is inherent in it. Lurking behind the veil of an addiction is a violent and murderous rage that emerges when the drug of choice, the desired love object is denied the addict.

The following vignette highlights this destructive force and the homicidal and suicidal component of drug addiction which can present serious risks when working with this patient group.

Clinical vignette

Miss A, a 35-year-old woman, was in prison for supplying drugs, her forensic and addiction history dating back to when she was an adolescent. I saw her five days a week for group therapy as part of the addiction treatment programme and the following is taken from a Monday morning session. I use my initials to signify when I am speaking.

MISS A: I'm really pissed off man, I asked to see the nurse twice over the weekend to get the dressings on my legs changed and she didn't come. It's not right – I'm fuming, I feel completely powerless locked up in my room, I can't do anything to get help.

JWS: Last time you were fuming it triggered an inferno inside of you resulting in you setting fire to your curtains. I wonder how you managed your rage this weekend? (*I am wondering if she used drugs.*)

MISS A: I know what I wanted to do. (*Starts to get worked up and aggressive in her speech.*) I wanted to get a dirty great needle, fill it full of gear (*heroin*), and stab the fucker right into my vein. No-one bloody cares what you do here, I wouldn't have cared if I'd gone over (*overdosed*).

The murderous and violent drives that are part of the addict's psychological make-up are clearly presented here. In this instance I believe the words 'dirty needle' were referring to an unconscious suicidal drive, dirty needles being synonymous with HIV and AIDS, although I think the patient was using it as a manner of speech. Her use of the word 'stab' was an indication of the murderous feelings that rise up when her needs aren't met, which later led us into making links to her mother's alcoholism and her own childhood deprivation. When her request for the nurse was not met, the violent feelings about being deprived are projected into the dirty needle and the wish to stab herself. She seeks to annihilate through the heroin the outside punitive authority figure (the withholding mother), the prison, and her internalized persecutory objects.

The masochistic component in addiction, as with Miss A's wanting to stab herself, is also related to a defence against the sadistic impulses that drive the addict to use.

> Simmel is also aware of the importance of sadism in drug addiction and he feels that because of the murderous impulses and the need for self punishment the treatment of the drug addict is fraught with danger, particularly suicide. (Rosenfeld 1982, p.224)

When working with addicts, close attention must always be paid to the unconscious communication of suicidal ideation and intent and underlying psychosis. The use of drugs is often a manic defence against feelings of despair and hopelessness and fragmentation of the ego and internal world. Miss A's words, 'dirty great needle, fill it full of gear and stab the fucker right into my vein', also bring in the theme of the needle as symbolic of a phallus and the erotic component in drug addiction.

> During analysis it becomes apparent that drugs are often identified with urine and faeces and related to a compulsion to drink something disgusting. Often the bottle or syringe represents a phallus, but in the deepest symbolic layer the phallus stands for the maternal breast which the drug addict longs to unite with. (Rosenfeld 1982, p.226)

The eroticism creates a dynamic where the addict turns the therapeutic relationship into an addiction bringing excitement into the consulting room, as opposed to forming a dependency with the anxieties attached to this, i.e. trust, attachment and loss. In Miss A's case I think the needle full of heroin also related to her mother's milk (her mother was alcoholic), poisoned with alcohol, and her own thirst, longing and compulsion 'to drink something disgusting'. In relation to this she began to explore her feelings about whether or not she could feed on the good breast / milk of the programme and how when she was able to do so she then attacked and attempted to destroy this benign mothering in her violent outbursts and drug use when she was deprived of the group at the weekends.

The case of Miss A illustrates the violent component of drug addiction, especially when the addict's needs and wishes aren't immediately met and gratified, demonstrating an incapacity to tolerate frustration and an inability to express anger verbally in a way that is safe and contained. The anger invariably taps into a primitive infantile rage and flares up like a fire, manifesting itself in physical damage to people, property and the addict themselves, as with Miss A setting fire to her curtains and her self-destructive acts against her own body. The propensity for destructive acting out with these patients cannot be underestimated.

ADDICTION AND DEPRIVATION

The use of drugs is frequently an attempt to fill a place inside that feels empty and desolate, a dead place in which nothing good can be held on to. In my experience addicts have often experienced severe childhood deprivation and trauma resulting in an enormous sense of internal depletion and emptiness. Addicts are frequently addicted to their mothers as idealized love objects, when the normal process of bonding and separation, and the development of a healthy dependency have been damaged. As a result of this, the child's capacity to grieve and mourn is also undeveloped and thus manic defences (i.e. drug abuse), are created in the face of loss and separation. The addict forms his primary relationship with his drug of choice, defending against developing a relationship to another person and ultimately remaining unable to move towards the depressive position. The world is viewed from the paranoid-schizoid position by the addict, where people and situations are seen in black and white terms, a symbolic equation of the relationship to the drug, i.e. when it is unobtainable it is the idealized answer to psychic and emotional pain. When internalized, however, it becomes a persecutory object that engulfs and takes over, rendering the addict powerless in the face of his addiction.

This dynamic and the inability to trust and to form a healthy dependency in relationships can be seen in the transference with these patients. Etchegoyen (1991) discusses addiction transference where the therapist becomes the drug of choice in relation to the addict who then attempts to control her/him as he attempted to control his internalized objects by manic defences through his drug use. These unconscious processes have, on occasion, evoked a countertransference reaction in me where I have become so engrossed and controlled by the patient's material that I have temporarily lost my capacity to be objective about what is going on in the relationship. I have been drawn into the patient's process, like an addict is drawn to his drug of choice, excited by the content of what he brings, rather than being attentive to the feelings and the unconscious communication that is being defended against by the patient. In this sense I become the addict who gets hooked on the patient's often rich and absorbing material (addicts can be very engaging people); in Etchegoyen's words I fall into 'the trap of counter transference addiction' (p.201).

ADDICTION TRANSFERENCE

The following clinical vignette with another patient, Mr. B, who also had a long forensic and addiction history, depicts how I came to be seen as the addict and the drug in the relationship. It also shows the link between this and Mr B's concern about my capacity, health and ability in being able to bear his feelings of depression (I had previously had a period of time off work due to ill health).

MR B: I didn't really want to come today – I don't think I've got much to talk about – I'm really tired – maybe I am depressed, I hate that word depressed. (*Pauses.*) Some people get depressed from working too hard, from burn-out...they use valium, all those respectable seeming professionals surviving on valium.

JWS: Maybe you're wondering whether I was off sick because I was depressed and suffering from burn-out.

MR B: (*Long pause – his eyes flick to the window sill where there is a yellow biro.*) Just checking to see that the biro is still there.

JWS: You said recently that you saw the biro as 'a works' (*needle*). I wonder what it means to you that I might have a works on my window sill?

MR B: (*Laughs.*) You'd be an addict. (*Pause.*) Smoking heroin was the closest I got to having my mother.

JWS: Perhaps you're wondering whether I am a depressed mother disguised as a respectable seeming professional, who relies on chemical substances to be able to bear her feelings of depression, or whether I have real substance in my life and in myself to bear the feelings of depression that you bring into this room.

MR B: (*Pauses, then makes a sudden head movement, his eyes widen and he says excitedly*) I just saw you as a works full of heroin.

JWS: Perhaps you hope that I hold within me a drug that can fix your depression and take it away, rather than exploring and bearing the empty feelings around it.

What struck me about this interaction was the sudden switch between Mr B seeing me as the addict and what he did with my interpretation about having real as opposed to chemical substances to sustain me and him. When he heard that I might have real substance he immediately became more animated and alert and saw me as the injection full of heroin, i.e. the breast holding the milk, linking to his reference about smoking heroin 'being the closest he got to his mother'. Mr B's fantasy is that I am the needle that can be inserted directly inside him, uniting him with his craving and longing to be one with the idealized object, the drug. His reference to intravenous drug use I believe relates to breaking the body boundary and the patient's wish to fuse with me, which we have discussed.

After making the reference to my being the injection Mr B became excited, engaged and manic; he symbolically turned me into a container full of drugs and his excitement about this defended against his depression and his despair that I may be sick and depressed myself and unable to meet his needs, being so in need myself; reflective of his relationship with his own mother. The excitement he evoked in the room also highlights the eroticism as referred to earlier. The patient's mania symbolically becomes the drug which he then seeks to inject into me when I am seen as the depressed, dead object. Interpreting the transference as an addiction and the dynamics in the therapeutic relationship that result from this as shown in the example with Mr B, is tantamount to getting hold of the control issues inherent in such patients.

The issue of control and the notion of the therapist being separate from the patient is a continual theme when working with addicts, who always like to have their drugs on tap; the end of sessions for addicts can be experienced as being thrown into 'cold turkey' withdrawal. However, if the patient can begin to grasp this dynamic and the part they play in it, and can begin to tolerate the experiences of waiting, delayed gratification and separation, they can gradually begin to internalize the therapeutic relationship without feeling engulfed and taken over by it (as with a drug). Paramount to this, however, is the addict's ability, or not, to recognize and relate to the therapist as a person separate from him and not just the object of their desire and /or hatred whom they might seek to manipulate and ultimately destroy.

The destructive impulses and drives in addicts and the extent of the damage which they will invariably have caused in their drug using lives both to themselves and to others, must be continually watched and interpreted. Addiction is an insidious process and seeps into every corner of an addict's life, whilst also reflecting the real depletion and deprivation that is experienced internally by them. The impact of these dynamics upon the therapist, especially when engaged in primary treatment (as in the case of Miss A), needs careful monitoring as the addict's 'insatiable hunger' can evoke the same sense of depletion within the therapist.

There is also, however, a richness afforded in working with these patients. If and when they can begin to move beyond the narcissistic and self-obsessed positions they have operated from, the gratitude and the love that can follow as they progress through treatment can be quite extraordinary in terms of the depth of feeling that is expressed and given on occasion like a gift both to the therapist and to fellow patients.

CONCLUSION

In working with addicts the capacity of the therapist to hold a middle position in the face of extremes is greatly tested. To watch, observe and comment, to be involved in the process without becoming lost to the content of the material, and to the passionate and intense feelings that can be evoked in the room (that I have witnessed and experienced in this work), is a continual process of learning.

Addiction is about extremes, good/bad, love/hate, life/death. Like Icarus, addicts seek to transcend the realities of what it is to be human, defying mortality as in a game of Russian roulette; they are fuelled and excited by danger and risk. Addicts are also people who live in extreme isolation, incarcerated in their impoverished lives in the despair that lies beneath their often cruel and hardened personas. The mania and the depression rise and fall like the crest of a wave soaring and crashing on the shore, and the loving and the hating can warm and chill in the same breath.

20

Rape

Sheilagh Davies

Sophia, a voluptuous and elegant woman of mid-European extraction presented for admission at a Gynaecology Clinic for a 'D and C' (Dilatation and Curettage – a common minor investigatory procedure usually performed under a general anaesthetic), charming and engaging she held court, clearly accustomed to this position in the natural order of things.

The Consultant emerged from his interview with her to state that she was insisting she could not have an anaesthetic. It emerged that she had been the victim of a gang rape by S.S. men in Nazi Germany some 30 years before, that she still suffered from constant nightmares, and stated that an anaesthetic would be an impossibly frightening experience for her. That was my first encounter as a young doctor with the shocking residual trauma of rape – and I have met many Sophias since.

In this chapter, I will touch on legal and clinical issues – and describe something of the complexity of potential collusive systems arising with the family of a victim, the society, or with the professionals who offer help.

LEGAL ISSUES

Rape is defined as the offence of forcing a person to have sexual intercourse against that person's will.

The Criminal Justice and Public Order Act of 1994 has broadened a previous definition, acknowledging men as potential victims as well as women, and including anal penetration. The law also now offers anonymity for the victim (though not yet the man accused of rape who, if unfairly accused, may stand to have his life and reputation ruined).

Considerations of the complexity of the definition of mutual consent continue apace and further changes in the law are likely. In contrast to popular belief, it is estimated that 83 per cent occur by a person known previously to the victim. Increasing and commendable attention is given to the phenomenon of 'secondary victimization' recognizing the trauma that police enquiries and the criminal justice process can impose in themselves as the 'truth' is sought from people at their most vulnerable, but these proceedings remain long drawn out and highly stressful.

Victims are often discouraged from seeking professional help, which is held to be inevitably pathologizing and stigmatizing, while many contemporary professionals concentrate on defining short-term confrontative techniques which aim at rapid 'cure' and must run the risk of becoming secondary traumatizers in themselves in the hands of the inexperienced or insensitive. To study the history of rape is to recognize a phenomenon where the victim is held to be responsible and in collusion with the rapist – hence to share the blame and sanctions.

In wartime, as recently seen in former Yugoslavia, it again becomes the norm, and rape constitutes part of the victor's spoils – the 'heroic rapist' whose act signifies victory, revenge, ownership and the most profound humiliation of the vanquished, forced to see their people ravaged and to have to accept their inability to protect them. Yet it is in our knowledge of individuals who serially rape that we learn something of the most profound and shocking facts about human development, the vicissitudes of interpersonal relationships, and the fatal impact of early childhood trauma on the individual and his/her later need to hate and to destroy through sexual assault, perverting one of the most prized of human activities.

THE RANGE OF RAPE

(1)   'Date rape' with the difficulties of defining consent and responsibility.

(2)   Rape occurring in the context of an established partnership – which may involve a long standing sadomasochistic relationship.

(3)   'Stranger Rape' – to include serial rape where the act is central to the rapist's psychic functioning.

(4)   Rape sanctioned by warfare or political unrest. It is a fact of life all must live with; recognizing age is no protector, and superior physical strength is ignored at peril.

This recognition must be involved in developing and taking responsibility for an adult sexual body – a major task of adolescence.

RESPONSES

Rape trauma syndrome is generally considered as a variant of post traumatic stress disorder with many symptoms shared by others who experience overwhelming and life threatening trauma.

However some quite specific sequelae are associated with the aftermath of rape, which epitomizes dehumanization – the ultimate invasion of one's body and psyche – and the privacy and safety of the environment.

(1) Identification with the Aggressor

The victim at the point of trauma identifies with the aggressor – hence is liable to feel responsible, guilty, ashamed, and deserving of punishment – and to be vulnerable to secondary victimization, to future abuse, or to self-destructive activities aimed at his/her own body.

(2) Contamination

The experience of having been dirtied and polluted – often manifested in the need to wash and clean compulsively.

Repeated bathing and scrubbing rituals are common.

(3) Fears of Having Been Permanently and Physically Damaged Internally

Fears of damage, pregnancy or disease (e.g. AIDS) – of the destruction of one's capacity to function sexually or to conceive and bear healthy children.

(4) Disorders of Eating

Weight control, exercise and purging as if to cleanse the body and to regain control of it, or alternatively binging and vomiting, employed as physiological devices to escape memories and affects – moves to discipline the body and to combat feelings of powerlessness. Drug and/or alcohol abuse may occur.

(5) Sexual Problems

Frigidity, aversion to sex or alternatively despairing promiscuity and an increased availability to abusive encounters – the revenge of the 'damaged doll' who will allow herself to be used and then discard the male. Some males who have experienced rape report feeling they have forfeited the right to be heterosexual.

(6) Relationship Problems

Problems may arise within an established marriage or partnership – the innocent partner finding himself held responsible, and treated as if he had been the aggressor.

He may well need help in adjusting to the violation, and in coping with the responsibility assigned to him and his sex.

Clinical vignette

A woman in her mid thirties travelled to London for treatment from a far distant prosperous island community. Married with two young children she had been bound and raped at knife point by an intruder into the house at night while her husband was away at work. She remained, two years on, tortured by self-blame and remorse as if she had been guilty of adultery while driven to bathe several times each day. She remained hostile and rejecting with her husband while unable to interact with the children, one of whom had seen the assault.

It was striking how unwittingly the husband and her parents seemed to have colluded with her sense of responsibility; she had been forbidden to inform the police and vowed to secrecy in a closely-knit community – feeling then alienated from her friends by her dark secret and from professional help. The Catholic priest in whom she had eventually confided had made her feel she should 'thank God for the experience' – she said perhaps he felt she should 'send the rapist a bunch of flowers'. Eventually it had been agreed she should have 'treatment' in far away London.

She felt unable to forgive her husband for his absence when the rape occurred. She felt defiled as a sexual partner and mother, and unable to face her children in whose eyes she felt she had become a monster.

PREDICTORS OF A SEVERE REACTION TO RAPE

(1) The degree of violence involved.

(2) The experience of threat to life.

(3) Past experience of victimization especially of Childhood Sexual Abuse.

(4) The quality of the victim's existing relationships and of the social network – attitudes encountered to the rape.

(5) Previous psychological and social difficulties including eating disorders, drug and alcohol abuse.

(6) Insensitive handling and prolonged proceedings in police enquiries and the courts.

Case Study – Who is culpable?

INTRODUCTION

A male patient, Bill, presents following a breakdown coinciding with the birth of his first child.

His own history is that he was born with a physical abnormality which meant he had to spend long periods of time as a child in hospital undergoing surgical interventions and operations. His experience had been of being left alone to cope – his parents rarely visited and sounded ill equipped to offer him support. He reached his teens impossibly shy and unable to look girls in the face. At this point he committed a number of rapes, some at knife point.

After many years in institutions he had been discharged and rapidly found employment and married. The pregnancy had been welcomed and he had been excited and supportive of his wife through pregnancy, electing to attend the labour. All went well until an episiotomy was proposed – at this point the wife became hysterical, screaming 'Don't do it!' It was quickly done and the baby born. However the patient himself developed an acute anxiety state which continued over days and additionally found himself to be impotent, running off to a psychiatric hospital demanding admission and refusing to leave, to the astonishment of the staff who saw him.

Over time it became possible to understand the destabilization which had occurred, and the knife threatening the genitals which had revived old memories and instincts long put to one side. More contact with the wife revealed her own story of sexual abuse at the hands of her father, and of being raped at the age of 15.

'I understand him very well' she stated – 'I've been raped myself'. Her object choice in her partner is understandable – also her own panic at the sight of the Obstetrician with the knife.

Paternal abuse?

Years went on, a second child was born and Bill found convenient reasons not to be present at the birth. He attended interviews once more bland, sealed off and impenetrable, while his wife's pathology became clearer – alternating as she did between presenting as a protective and moralistic mother, and an alternative state of mind – where she seemed intensely excited by her husband's past, and to be quite openly exhibiting it to friends and neighbours, apparently with his assent.

Calamity struck when the older girl was five years old. The mother rushed up to a Casualty Department concerned that the child had a vaginal discharge – and simultaneously concerns were expressed at her school. She was given the Doll Test and experts concluded that sexual abuse had taken place. The children were rushed into Care, the father dismissed from the family home.

He continued to attend fortnightly for exploratory/supportive interviews, apparently distressed and puzzled. He viewed the video of the test repeatedly and agreed that an outsider would conclude the child had been abused.

He insisted he had not abused her, and ruminated endlessly about alternative explanations – could it be the effect of her having slept in the parents' bedroom for a time? I was aware of unwelcome doubts creeping into my own mind – yes, the test had been validated but had it been validated for the children of rapists? I was aware of critics of the Doll Test. What would be the effects on a child of a mother who quite openly said 'Daddy's a bad man' and 'Don't let Daddy touch your fanny'. On went the unhappy situation, the children returning to live with their mother, and the professionals involved caught up in dispute, doubts and mutual accusations, which often made meetings heated and extremely painful.

The Mother's Revenge?

Years passed until one day the mother and the two girls were away staying with her own mother and her stepfather in the country.

Their mother presented in Casualty with the younger girl this time, again concerned about a vaginal discharge, and making veiled suggestions that there had been abuse at the hands of her own stepfather. Examination revealed that the genitals of both girls were scrubbed raw – by the mother. Could this be Munchhausen by Proxy – was the truth that the mother in her search for revenge had interfered with the girls, in order to implicate men – her husband and stepfather?

The truth remains unclear. Is either of these parents culpable, or do they share the responsibility in some deadly dance involving revenge and their individual psychic survivals? How do professionals involved survive their burden of responsibility and the uncertainty placed on them – the temptation to place blame prematurely?

Man's capacity for perversion has long been accepted –it has been less easy to accept that women too can be perverse, and take their revenge characteristically on their own bodies, or on their own children.

IMPLICATIONS FOR PROFESSIONALS

(1)   The need to grapple with the complexity of issues involved, in the understanding of which Object Relations Theory must play an

essential part. Some training in psychodynamic principles is essential for those involved in the treatment of Rape Trauma Syndrome.

(2)   A recognition of the particular sequelae of rape and the need to place it in the context of an individual victim's personal history.

(3)   Hence, an acquaintance with factors which will prognosticate badly – both in the circumstances of the rape and in the victim's background so that the most vulnerable can rapidly be offered substantial help and treatment.

(4)   Awareness of the professional's own attitudes towards sexuality and rape in particular.

(5)   Access to discussion groups and/or supervision – in an atmosphere which encourages frankness and constructive introspection.

(6)   Awareness of the implications for the husband/partner and children who may need individual/couple/family work.

(7)   Patience and tolerance in relation to the seductive concept of 'Cure' – the recognition that trauma of this order may need time and patience, even that 'recovery' is a concept less appropriate than the hope that a severely traumatized person may come to some kind of integration of the episode in his/her own mind.

21

The Flasher

Ü. Elif Gürişik

INTRODUCTION

A flasher is someone who exposes his genitals to someone outside the context of the sexual act and when it serves as the major source of sexual pleasure, or is compulsive or repetitious, exhibitionism is regarded as a perversion (Rosen 1979). The erotic acting out is an attempt by the flasher to resolve his internal conflicts and to achieve tranquillity at the expense of the victim. 'In a flash' he gains sexual gratification by paralyzing his victim's senses and thinking process.

Exhibitionism is one of the most common sexual deviations and sexual offences in the UK but exhibitionists are not a homogeneous group. Some have a preference for children, either of the same or the opposite sex. The propensity to paedophilia increases in this group and there is a poor prognosis. Other exhibitionists prefer to expose themselves to older women and some attempt to communicate physically or verbally with their victims, whilst others keep their distance. Some of them make sure of arrest, while others carefully avoid detection and may never be caught. In some cases, use of force or violence might be involved.

Women's response to flashing extends from the anxious giggle, extreme fear, shock, horror, disgust, to ridicule and verbal abuse. Some pretend to be oblivious and remain totally indifferent to the act and yet others appear to be fascinated. For the flasher, any response is preferable to indifference and being ignored.

Children's reactions are as varied as adult women's. A child may run away experiencing fear and excitement. Another may feel paralyzed and frozen. He/she may even obey the exhibitionist's demand to watch him while he is urinating or masturbating.

This presentation will deal with the psychopathology of exhibitionism from a dynamic psychoanalytical point of view through a single case study.

Clinical vignette

Peter was 34 years old when he sought psychoanalytical psychotherapy. He was exposing and masturbating to orgasm daily, if not two or three times a day. Though he had never been caught, he became increasingly depressed and anxious about his 'evilness' and about being out of control. He was afraid that he might sexually assault or even rape a woman. His anxiety about being out of control was countered by a high degree of pleasure in exhibiting himself and getting away with it. He linked his obsession with sex to his internal turmoil and to his relationship with his mother whom he described as 'the biggest tart'. Apparently she was very promiscuous, sleeping with many men in front of her children, who were both emotionally and physically neglected. She seemingly showed a scant concern for their sense of confusion, shame and shock. Peter was expected to look after his younger brother and sister, while his mother had sex with her boyfriends and he was mocked about his mother's promiscuity by his friends.

Throughout his childhood Peter regarded his father as a stranger who served as a radio operator in the Air Force and was often posted abroad, and over the years he became estranged from his parents and sister. He could not stand his mother's hypocrisy; in her later years she behaved and acted like 'Mary Whitehouse'. He hated his sister – 'another tart' – as much as he hated his mother. Being sent to a children's home at the age of four, for six months, remained one of his most painful memories. He was divorced after seven years of marriage and had two children who he saw monthly.

Peter had weekly behaviour therapy at a hospital for eight months which did not help him.

With regard to his exhibitionism he was somewhat in touch with his hatred and denigration of women whose 'shocked expression turned him on' and he saw how he treated women as 'a sexual object, rather than another human being'. However, he was also very sensitive to women's perceived lack of interest and rejection.

Peter's exhibitionism related to complex defence systems, dealing with his unconscious conflicts, infantile sexuality, and object relationships. His lack of internal satisfaction and recognition intensified his need for external gratification and recognition. By exposing himself he sought to receive narcissistic confirmation and recognition about his maleness and his acceptability, as well as to overcome his castration anxiety and to restore his self-esteem. However, the sexual acting out failed to bring about this anticipated satisfaction and recognition. Furthermore, he experienced narcissistic injury instead of narcissistic confirmation when he was humiliated or rebuffed by women. Their rejection stimulated his hatred and aggression, which in turn increased his internal dissatisfaction, and thus a vicious circle was established.

Peter was not sexually abused directly by his mother but, as a captive spectator at an early age, he was forced to watch his mother's sexual activities from a distance. His passive participation in variations of the primal scene heightened his visual eroticization and he learned to use sexualization as a defence. He moved from a passive voyeur position to an active exhibitionist position. Interestingly, he exposed himself from a distance to unsuspecting women in his adolescent and adult life. By doing so he took his revenge for his passively experienced trauma and his past suffering; in other words he successfully projected his pain, shock and vulnerability on to his victims. He enjoyed his promotion from being a victim to a victimizer. In his eyes, every woman became a substitute mother who had to pay for what was done to him. His identification with the aggressor – the exhibitionist mother – was evident in his acting out.

Peter procured a double benefit by successfully projecting his confusion, paralysis and sense of outrage on to the woman and by managing to reverse the roles. A woman became his helpless captive spectator who was forced to watch and be humiliated, just as he once was as a child. However, he could not escape from being ridiculed.

There were one or two specific problems in Peter's treatment in the once weekly group analytical psychotherapy. This was due to his having been deprived throughout his childhood of individual care and recognition as well as having been overwhelmed by the responsibility to defend himself and his younger siblings. Thus at the beginning of his treatment he craved for my individual attention at the same time as he felt obliged 'to look after' his siblings – the other patients. I had to make sure that he was not unduly burdened by such responsibilities and I was also careful not to rekindle his sense of neglect. It was important to pay enough attention to his individual conflicts and needs through my interpretations, while I addressed the whole group in the here and now and in the transference.

Working with Peter, and other perpetrators in the group, made me understand how sensitive they were to any sign of rejection or slight which easily mobilized their sadism. Peter's sense of deprivation intensified especially during the breaks, in which I was perceived like his mother – 'the biggest tart' – or his absent father, both of whom were regarded as uncaring or even sadistic. At such times Peter retaliated against my apparent neglect in the only way he knew; flashing.

He sometimes attempted to paralyze me with his 'shocking' acting-out and my patience and capacity to contain his hostility were severely tested. He exposed himself whenever he felt depressed or angry; his relationships with his first, and second, wife became increasingly sado-masochistic and his job suffered. His perception of me oscillated between 'the neglectful tart' and 'the condemnatory Mary Whitehouse' and I struggled to strike a right balance and not to be pushed into either role.

However, by the end of the second year Peter had began to use the group as his external super-ego, i.e., he felt shame and guilt whenever he talked about the actual, or fantasized flashing, which was increasingly sporadic. Peter stopped flashing altogether in the fifth year but still remained sensitive to humiliation by women. To highlight this I will describe a brief vignette from a group session.

On her first day in the group, Veronica, who had been sexually abused by her sister, displayed her identification with the aggressor, by taking up an abusive role in the group. By the way she dressed; a black leather trouser suit, red lipstick and red nail polish and by the way she spoke, she gave an exhibitionistic performance. Although she was the youngest member of the group and one of the newcomers, she almost took the group over, with her sexually explicit language, and her capacity to torment and intimidate the men. Her voice rang with sexual excitement which in no time became infectious. Two other newcomers – Pauline, a lesbian with a violent criminal record and Colin, a transsexual who was physically abused by his mother – joined in Veronica's condemnation of the perpetrators when they learned that Peter, Simon, Harry were flashers and Robert and John were sexual abusers. She embarked on a vicious personal attack on each perpetrator, by demanding justice for the victims like herself and punishment for the perpetrators. The offenders, while acknowledging her 'justifiable anger and pain', appealed for her understanding for their suffering.

I took up the role reversal in the group: Veronica moved away from the tormented abused victim role to a tormenting abuser role and, conversely, the abusers behaved as if they were the victims. I suggested that the new members, especially Veronica, attempted to encounter their fear of being taken over, humiliated and abused by the existing group members, by forming an unholy alliance against the existing old members. The creation of the erotic atmosphere enabled the whole group to deny their powerful fears and conflicts over sibling rivalry, supremacy, subordination and destructive and sado-masochistic wishes. I also pointed out how they all engaged in a power struggle.

Peter, in the role of ex-offender and as the oldest member of the group, attempted to establish a dialogue with Veronica throughout the group session. He repeatedly pointed out to her that he was an offender as well as a victim of his past. However, his appeals were repulsed, and Veronica treated him with utter contempt. Peter, like the other male members felt misunderstood, humiliated, and sadistically attacked.

In the following session we found out that Peter took his revenge on Veronica after the group meeting. Over the past seven years, Peter had always meticulously observed the group rule of not meeting or socializing with other members outside the group, but on this occasion he offered a lift to Veronica while she was waiting for a bus in front of the Clinic. She was terrified of being attacked while being in his car and rejected his offer. Throughout the week she remained unsettled and enraged. Peter's acting-out had a devastating effect on her as shown by her attendance at the following session just to announce her decision to leave the group. It was obvious that she was terrified of being put in the victim role again.

The session began with four members – Veronica, Pauline, Colin and John. Veronica was furious. She turned all her fire onto John, who looked frightened and was speechless as she denounced him and the other male members. After that it was my turn to be accused of exposing her to danger and being insensitive to her fears. She then left the room in a dramatic fashion after which Peter, Simon, Robert and Harry entered.

Thus, at the previous session, Veronica successfully projected her victim's self onto the men, but when Peter turned the tables on her outside the group, her projective identification failed her. She perceived me like her mother who sided with her abusive sister and she therefore believed that I would side with the abusers and not protect her from the abuse. She ran away after dumping her hatred and her victim self into the group. On the other side Peter succeeded in getting rid of the tormenting, exhibitionist, castrating mother substitute and restored his injured self-esteem.

Over the years Peter gradually internalized the super ego control over his wishes and his sense of shame and guilt increased. He understood his need to defy authority through his flashing which was linked to his resentment against his absent father. He took up healthier sporting and social activities such as skiing and ballroom dancing, through which he gratified his exhibitionistic urges. He formed a satisfying partnership with a female partner and became a well liked and respected member of the group. Respect and acceptance led to diminishing desire and fantasies of exposure and in the fifth year he stopped flashing altogether. When I discharged Peter, seven years later, he had gained considerable maturity in every aspect of his life. His impulsiveness gave way to thoughtfulness and his exhibitionism gave way to sublimation, and he won many medals for ballroom dancing. He walked away from the sado-masochistic relationships and established a healthier relationship with women, his parents, siblings and children.

CONCLUSION

In my experience, exhibitionists are greatly helped by group therapy. At the early stages, their sadism and acting out, in and outside the sessions, may escalate. This is due to their resistance against the emerging painful memories they now confront. However, their acting-out decreases when they begin to work through their intense hatred of women and destructive wishes; they learn how to regulate their self-esteem without resorting to the flashing. It becomes more possible to tolerate depressive feelings and to obtain pleasure from the sublimated activities.

22

A Case of Voyeurism

Francesca Hume

INTRODUCTION

A Keyhole is meant to be looked through. (Sartre 1995)

This quote reminds us of how ubiquitous the urge is to peep. In one study (Storr 1964) 65 per cent of a group of males admitted to having engaged in voyeuristic activities. But where does the sexual excitement come from in looking? Stoller (1976) notes that no one is interested in nudity in societies where it is freely available, but where the child's discovery of the anatomical differences between the sexes is obscured, to look at body parts may be both forbidden and desirable.

When does voyeurism become a disorder? Freud (1953) suggested it did so when, instead of being preparatory to intercourse, it supplants it, and psychoanalytic theory links voyeurism with castration anxiety. Such a link between seeing and castration anxiety is evident in the myth of Oedipus who blinds himself as a retribution for his incestuous crimes. Freund, Scher and Hucker (1983) have regarded voyerurism as a 'courtship disorder' in which pre-copulatory behaviour cannot be accomplished because of particular anxieties.

The prevalent view is of the voyeur as a harmless nuisance rather than a criminal. The penal system abolished the charge of 'eavesdropping' in 1967 and for a voyeur to be convicted, he must be charged with another offence (e.g. breach of the peace). Yalom (1960) suggested that voyeurism and exhibitionism were occasionally associated with rape, burglary, assault and even homicide, and Bluglass and Bowden (1990) recommended prognostic caution when violent fantasies exist. However, Langevin and Lang (1987) note the paucity of empirical research.

Although there is not conclusive evidence that voyeurism is a precursor of assaultative behaviour, Stoller (1976) claims that, in voyeurism, can be traced hostility, revenge and a dehumanized object. In other perversions (e.g. rape) these features may be more apparent, but in voyeurism too, the intention may be to harm and triumph over another. For example, looking can become sexually exciting if the voyeur believes he is acting forcibly upon an unwilling woman. In so doing, he defeats her and gets revenge for past frustration. In 1930, Strachey also suggested a more sinister view of voyeurism. He said that in 'libidinal' looking, it is not the world that approaches the eye, but the person looking makes an onslaught with his eye upon the world in order to 'devour' it, and to render the object paralyzed and defenceless. (Here perhaps we see the reverse of the child 'paralyzed' by the sight of the primal scene.)

The patient I will present illustrates the depth of hostility and fear that can belie voyeurism's often benign connations. It highlights some of the practical problems in working therapeutically with a highly disturbed patient on a once weekly basis, and how issues of safety and containment are an essential part of forensic assessment. This patient terminated his treatment prematurely after one and a half years, perhaps because his disturbance had been underestimated, but through our contact we were able to reach some understanding of the conflicts underlying his fantasies and behaviour.

Clinical vignette

The patient was a single man of 29, referred by a general psychiatrist to our out-patient forensic psychiatry service after divulging acts of voyeurism and obsessive sexual thoughts about women (some violent). He was chronically anxious and harmed his hands by punching walls. His contact with psychiatric services had begun about two years previously when he was briefly admitted in an agitated state following the break-up with a girl-friend. He had subsequently attended a day centre where he was described as having an 'inadequate' personality but was generally polite, aloof and unaggressive.

He presented as intense, with poor eye contact and great difficulty in verbalizing his problems, yet eager to convey his distress and wish for help. It was unclear what level of dangerousness he posed, for whilst he confessed to rape fantasies and to stalking women to spy on them, he also admitted that he had exaggerated these problems to ensure an assessment. He seemed highly anxious and his obvious distress and motivation coupled with the excellent support he received at the day centre led to our offering him once weekly supervised psychodynamic psychotherapy.

His childhood was described as lonely and emotionally arid and his accounts of relationships seemed hollow. He had felt neglected and es-tranged from his large family and also felt he had been 'kept in the dark' by others who withheld secrets which he was obliged to discover illicitly.

He was born with cataracts in both eyes which went undetected until he started school, possibly contributing to his sense of being excluded and neglected. He felt that no-one 'saw' him and he had once truanted from school for a whole term without being detected. He had done so because he somehow felt that he was 'missing out on what was happening at home'.

The peeping had begun at 13 when he would spy through windows with other boys. However, he began preferring to gaze in solitude from his bedroom window at mundane scenes in neighbour's houses, often for hours at a time. During adolescence, he started spying on women undressing, accompanied by masturbation.

The voyeurism diminished for a while at 17 when he befriended a 14-year-old girl. He claimed her parents failed to notice when they began a sexual relationship after he had moved into her family home. She soon tired of his wish for solitude but he remained in the home and began spying on her mother and sisters, even drilling a hole between bedroom walls.

In therapy he was morose and often uncommunicative. This seemed to be his way of reversing his childhood experience and keeping me in the dark; curious and worried about his mental life and activities between sessions. He would hint at alarming incidents but it was never clear what was real and what fantasy. He would become intensely anxious after divulging anything of import, fearing my rejection and contempt. Yet his silences would leave him feeling unnoticed and neglected, almost to the point of feeling invisible. To overcome this he would make dramatic gestures like a sudden jerky movement, or he would stare at me fixedly, paralyzing me with his gaze. He would turn up wearing fingerless gloves and gradually removed them to expose a fist bruised and swollen from punching walls. He would pick at the scabs as if to show me how hurt he was, yet strategies to engage him in more useful contact rarely seemed to help. Instead, he felt objectified by me, intensely scrutinized and exposed. Yet if I averted my gaze from him he would accuse me of indifference and neglect. As a child he had fallen from trees to gain his mother's attention and I was left convinced that he had been deprived of any ordinary empathic experiences, leaving him unable to respond to my concern now.

It is hard to convey the quality of his hostile, menacing silence and just how anxious he could make me feel. Wherever interpretations were made which accurately caught something of his internal state he would experience me as overwhelmingly intrusive, as if I had quite literally drilled a hole in his head and stolen his thoughts. The result would be an increase in paranoid anxiety and anger. He would then treat me as he felt treated – the object of a sadistic, voyeuristic devouring. For example, after one interpretation he said, 'Your skirt is a few inches shorter this week – I can see more of your leg'. As his sense of vulnerability and intolerance of gaps between

between sessions increased, so did his need for control, and the voyeuristic comments gave way to more aggressive ones. After the long summer break he returned in an intensely hostile state and in mid-session said, 'I was thinking how long it would take me to bridge the gap between our chairs and do you in'.

Concern about my physical safety prompted a review with colleagues and for the next few sessions a security guard sat in an adjoining office. We had unwittingly created a bizarre reversal of the patient's past experience: it was the guard now left worried and in the dark, unable to see or know what was going on between the patient and myself. This crisis coincided with the return of his ex-girlfriend, in flight from a violent husband, and bringing what he saw as further intrusive pressures. At that point he decided to terminate treatment. Perhaps he sensed that substantial change carried too many risks. I also wondered whether he left in order to protect me from his violence. He wrote some months later to say the sessions had helped him 'to see things from a different angle' and understand his feelings more. Perhaps his letter showed that he did feel that I had kept him in mind. Feedback from the day centre did not indicate an escalation of offending.

CONCLUSION

'Seeing' for this patient seemed not to be a symbolic activity but only a concrete physical act. Bally (1931) describes a primitive mode of looking which cannot be divorced from motility but is instead a piece of active behaviour, by means of which one enters the object seen. I felt this patient experienced my interventions (my 'in-sights') as forcibly entering him. In turn, he sought to protect himself by destroying, devouring or paralyzing me with his stare. Rosen (1996) notes that in the first year of life, taking in visual impressions may be linked with the way objects are taken in via the mouth. If oral incorporative experiences are charactized by greed, hunger and persecuting anxiety, seeing may come to be experienced as devouring and compulsive too. A related question is what role the patient's cataracts played in the development of his perversion? Was their delayed removal experienced as a welcome relief or a further trauma? Was the psychotherapy symbolically equivalent to the cataract operation, forcing him to open his eyes and 'see things from a different angle'?

The challenge that an offer of therapy poses for patients seen by forensic psychiatry services is immense. Most are young men, often neither bright nor articulate and not part of a verbal, psychologically-minded culture. Macho pride and self-esteem may make the patient role feel like a submission, and the psychotherapy an arousing and provocative experience. Most have been bru-talized and few have had reason to experience authority figures as wise, non-judgemental and helpful. Gallwey (1992) also stressed the need in forensic assessments to take account of the therapist's skills, orientation and enthusiasm, and the availability of supervision and a cohesive staff group.

Sexual offenders pose particular problems. Most theorists agree that perversion is difficult to treat and, as a stable organization, functions to protect some underlying ego disturbance. Dismantling this may risk decompensation into violence or psychosis. If perversion involves a turning away from human sexual reality, Limentani (1987) warns that a psychotherapy aimed at promoting reality-testing may be experienced by the patient as an enemy to be defeated. He says, 'The patient's awareness that they are defending themselves against some unthinkable pain makes them less than communicative'.

In his favour, my patient was of normal intelligence and a voluntary patient. His unhappiness and general dissatisfaction with his life was highly evident to him, and the voyeurism and violent fantasies were a source of shame and concern. Given the limited comfort his perversion afforded him and his concern about violent loss of control, he was offered treatment in the knowledge that this was of course an ambitious task for the once weekly sessions available. Access to regular psychotherapy supervision also influenced the decision to offer treatment, and proved to be necessary. There was, however, some evidence from the outset that his wish for treatment had more to do with wanting concrete care than enhanced self-awareness and behaviour change. Also, his tendency to feel persecuted by interpretations was not immediately evident. A therapeutic community was considered first, but the patient feared this would be too intense for him. His response to an earlier attempt at focussed cognitive behavioural treatment had been to become morose and non-compliant. He seemed to recognize that such treatment could not address wider questions that his present disturbance begged of his past history.

Overall, the resources of a forensic mental health service – the professional experience with offender patients, awareness of safety issues and access to secure facilities – justified an attempt at exploratory treatment in this case. The patient agreed to a formal contract regarding ground rules and limit-setting. Treatment nonetheless broke down after one and a half years. The extent to which this might be seen as a therapeutic failure, or whether it might turn out to have been helpful contact, remains an open question.

There will always be such individuals in society and the question for forensic services is how and when to intervene as an alternative to or in conjunction with the penal system. A measure of modest therapeutic optimism, albeit tempered with realism, is perhaps required if one is to engage at all with offenders with these problems.

23

From Sado-Masochism to Shared Sadness

Marisa Dillon-Weston

INTRODUCTION

This chapter is about Mr A, a bi-sexual patient whose confusion about his sexual identity and whose perversion were part of his defenses against the violence of the primal scene, as he had experienced it, and the cruel, chaotic behaviour of his parents. Through his perversion he replayed his childhood traumas, but in a way that enabled him to feel in charge of others and himself; in other words, no longer the helpless victim. In reality he was perpetuating a sadomasochistic way of relating, denying the separateness of others and his own fears and destructiveness. However, a small part of him, the more mature part of his self, knew that the 'sexual magic' (Coen 1995) he pursued was only an illusion which masked, but did not alter, his underlying depression and sense of inadequacy. This part of him, looking for guidance, led him to ask for psychotherapy. From the beginning of our work together I knew that he would reproduce with me the sadomasochistic interaction, playing either the victim or the persecutor.

Clinical vignette
THE PRIMAL SCENE AS THE ORIGIN OF THE PERVERSION
A was the eldest of four children from a working class family in the East End of London. His father, a violent man and a womanizer, left home when A was nine, but kept returning and being violent to his wife. During the therapy A recalled an incident which took place during one of father's visits. He was nine at the time and he was playing ball outside the empty basement of their house when he suddenly felt that there was someone hiding in the

basement. He dismissed the fear but later, when trying to sleep in his bedroom on the ground floor, he heard footsteps coming from the basement and in terror asked who it was. It was father who had hidden in there and was now finding his way into mother's bedroom. Later still A heard screams and realized that violent beating was in progress. In spite of his terror he forced himself to go upstairs and open the door. His father was trying to push his mother out of the window while holding her by her throat. A stood totally transfixed and horrified. Then his memory went blank. All he remembered next was sitting on his mother's lap, alone. As a consequence of this, A said, his mother had a breakdown and was hospitalized.

This traumatic memory kept coming back in the course of our work together, either in direct form or under the disguise of dreams, and in our last session A told me that he had written it down in the form of a short story. It seemed to me that this signified his ability to begin to think about, and perhaps symbolically manage, an experience which had stunted him for so long. In order to reach this point he had first to acknowledge the extent of its power over him. It became clear that he had internalized a primal scene permeated by extreme violence leading to seemingly irreparable splitting and destruction. Mother went into hospital and A and his siblings were put into care. His whole world collapsed and he was totally powerless in the same way in which he had been an impotent spectator to his father's violence, and a sacrificial victim to his mother's needs. He had desperately tried to help his mother and to be for her the partner she lacked and yet he could not possibly begin to contain his mother's madness and could not prevent her abandonment.

Later, when mother recovered and re-established a family home for herself and the children, she was often experienced by her eldest son as either seductive, or controlling and cruelly denying his separateness and his needs. Thus the models he carried inside were of a murderous father and a castrating mother. If he tried to defend himself from the mother he might become the violent father possessed by the murderous penis.

Out of the unbearable distress of this position the perversion was born with its promise of relief. A indulged in various forms of body piercing and, when having sex with either men or women, he often asked to be tied, dominated and hurt. All this, however, paled in relation to what became the masterpiece of his perverse fantasies through which a scenario was created of extreme complexity and subtlety where 'the perversion like the pearl surrounding the grain of sand, grows by sensual pleasure, out of mastery of otherwise unbearable distress' (Stoller 1991). He conceived this master drama at the time when his wife had conceived, and later given birth to, their first child, an event which probably caused him to feel excluded and abandoned. He persuaded her, after much pleading, to act out the fantasy with him. They began to follow a ritual which started with them secretly plotting together to find a third party, a man who would then be invited to become her sexual partner during sessions which saw A in the role of the excited spectator who would watch and masturbate, although at times he might join in the action with one or the other. This behaviour continued for nine years until the day when A's wife decided to stop it, probably out of guilt. Subsequently she became very religious. It was an incredible blow for A who saw himself deprived of what seemed to give him power and control. Without the perverse behaviour he felt he had reverted to being the powerless child, terrified of being devoured by mother.

FROM SADOMASOCHISM TO SADNESS IN THE THERAPY

I saw A once a week at the Portman Clinic over a period of one year. In the first session he asked whether the offer of treatment was dependent on the kind of reasons he had for seeking therapy. He was afraid that if I knew his motives I might withdraw the offer. Then he added that he did not want to give up his sexual inclinations, but he would like to understand himself. He seemed afraid of rejection even before we had started. Later he talked at length about his marriage. He felt that his wife gave him nothing; even their sexual activities were extremely disappointing because his wife was not interested in sex. I thought that he seemed to be projecting on to his wife the cruelty he had experienced in his mother. Whatever his wife did or said to express her love for him he remained adamant about her cruelty. The only time of real closeness to her had been during the enactment of the threesome fantasy. Without that he felt useless and completely in her power.

He seemed totally identified with the role of the victim and he would come to sessions with a precise agenda on his mind containing examples of how that role had been imposed on him. As he recited the narrative of his humiliation I felt and commented on his emotional detachment from it and on the way in which he kept me at a distance by crowding me out, with his pre-planned agenda.

He talked about his hatred of his mother, whom he still saw as ready to chastize him and put him down. Unable to rebel openly he rebelled secretly, indulging in behaviours she would strongly condemn. He knew she would be horrified by his sexual preferences or by the body piercing he had done to himself. He then proceeded to give me a detailed and gruesome account of the pain he had endured when his nipples were pierced. I felt, and said, that by giving me such an account of that act of self-inflicted violence he might be trying to seduce me into a sadomasochistic kind of collusion either as a silent accomplice or as a horrified spectator.

Frequently A expressed feeling like shit after the sessions. It was as if by masochistically turning what I offered into attacks he allowed himself to be beaten by me; an experience of emotional contact between us became a trigger for denigration.

As we were approaching a Christmas break I linked his feelings to the break and my abandonment of him. This he totally denied. Soon after the Christmas break, in a session during which I had felt crowded out as usual, there was suddenly a long silence and, from feeling controlled and angry, I felt very sad and it seemed to me that I was experiencing the sadness which was concealed behind his sadistic omnipotence and it moved me deeply. I said to him, 'I sense much sadness in you, behind your words'. He seemed totally stunned and asked, like a child who can trust the adult to help him understand, 'Sadness, where?' As if speaking to a child, I said 'Where does sadness live? In one's heart, I suppose. Yes, there seems to be much sadness in your heart'. He received my words in silence. He did not stir, neither did he look at me but I felt that we had made a real contact and that he felt touched and cared for by me at that point.

In the next session he did not mention that interaction at all. A moment of intense and moving contact seemed to have vanished into thin air. He talked about his depression. He could not get out of bed in the morning. His wife had been telling him that she loved him but he had been unable to respond. I then linked what he was saying to what happened in the last session and to how difficult it seemed for him to keep alive a moment of real contact.

He then said that he had been stunned by me being able to perceive and express sad feelings in him. It had been a deep, moving and overwhelming experience and yet he found himself betraying and distorting the experience and reporting to his wife that I saw him as a 'poor sod', a 'sad case'.

So once again he had superimposed on to me the blueprint of the sadistic mother who put him down and castrated him. All he could do was wallow in the humiliation.

I found myself talking to him about how he seemed to carry inside him an 'internal saboteur' (Fairbairn 1952) ready to attack good, creative experiences. As I said this I thought of Rosenfeld's concept of the 'powerful gang'(Rosenfeld 1971).

In the next session he came in with a sense of urgency. He had thought about the words 'sabotage' and 'saboteur' that I had used. They bugged him. He could not get rid of them in his own mind and yet they were not really right. Then he realized that his phrase for it was 'self-destruct button'. He felt that he had a self-destruct button which he pushed automatically. Then a memory came to him. He must have been six or seven, his father was still living with them. His father asked him to go and buy four cones, one for each child, from the ice cream van. He gave him the money and added, 'Make sure you don't lick them'. He went off and as he crossed the road back with the cones, he licked them knowing his father was watching from the window and that he would be inevitably punished.

He now realized that what he did was to push a 'self-destruct button'. I said, 'Perhaps it was the only way in which you felt able to retaliate'. He agreed that his father's injunction had felt like an attack; he had been 'set up' and at the same time he was unable to defend himself openly. So he had attacked himself. The word 'self-destruct' entered into our vocabulary and became central to our work.

In the following weeks he talked about his misery and his fear of 'cracking up'. He remembered when his mother was in hospital and he lived in a home feeling extremely depressed and unable to trust anybody.

I commented on how devastated he must have been by the sudden abandonment he had experienced and by the terror of out of control chaos and madness that mother's condition brought up. There was nobody he could trust, then, but what about now, who could he trust now when he felt abandoned and afraid of 'cracking up'.

Could he trust me? Was I depressed and potentially mad like his mother had been or was I someone who could support him because I was myself supported by strong partners and I did not need to make inappropriate demands on him?

A's depression became worse. The sexual fantasy lost strength. He still thought of it but he now felt that it would never be enacted again. He was given antidepressants. He was also given time off work. He expected to be rebuffed and was surprised and moved by his boss's understanding and empathy. Some sort of reparative process seemed to be in motion.

With me in the sessions he was quieter and terrified that this might draw us too close. Women gave him hell in his life; his mother came to his house and caused problems and this created havoc with his wife. I commented how one woman put him in the shit with another and what he needed was a strong man at his side capable of keeping the women under control. I wondered whether, although I was a woman, he could trust me to provide that manly presence which he lacked.

As the Easter break approached he reported being better able to challenge his mother, triggering her anger. Sometimes he talked about his wish to re-enact the sexual fantasy but together with the familiar excitement he now experienced a sense of guilt. He said, 'A part of me knows that I should not have asked her to do it and that I should give it up'. Soon after the Easter break I told him that I would stop working at the clinic where I was seeing him in two months' time. When I started working with him I had warned him about this possibility. He said he had forgotten me saying that. He listened to the choices he had, to stay at the clinic and be seen by a male therapist or continue therapy with me at my private practice at a reduced fee. He said that he needed to think, he felt dazed. In the next session he talked about his sadness at my leaving. Nevertheless he had decided to stay at the clinic because he wanted to work with a man. He brought a memory of being in bed with his mother and father and how he had experienced his mother's disgust and hatred towards his father. I talked about the male therapist who would continue with him and what his fantasies about him and about my relationship with him might be. Did I resent letting go of him or did I feel that he now needed a man at his side? Did I respect the male therapist, did I have a good relationship with him or did I harbour negative feelings which would make the transition difficult?

The theme of the 'man' kept re-emerging in our final two months of therapy. A brought memories involving men who had been important in his life. On the whole they were men who had turned from being friendly to being attacking. I kept linking this with his anticipation of the male therapist. Would he provide the needed strength of the 'missing' man in order to help or in order to attack?

In the last two sessions A presented to me a picture of great depression. I linked it to our imminent ending and how difficult it must have been to trust me when I was about to leave him.

He said that he was confused. If he began to feel that I might care then he reminded himself that I was just doing a job. Once we had finished, he would be totally gone from my mind. In other words I said he felt that I had used him and now I could dispose of him.

In the last session he talked about feeling out of control. He had caught himself thinking of death, of committing suicide by throwing himself under a train. There had also been thoughts involving perverse fantasies. He found himself attracted to a very young girl whom he saw at his daughter's school. He felt excited and horrified at the same time.

I interpreted his terror at my leaving. In a way I felt that he had learned to trust me a little and that is why he could confide in me these terrifying fantasies and fears. He had learned to trust me but now I was leaving and he did not know how to cope with his destructive side which felt so out of control. Would I abandon him or would I still be alive inside him and through my alliance with his next therapist so that he could feel contained and able to contain the destructive impulses? Could the murderous primal scene begin to be modified?

Auto-Erotic Asphyxia
and Art Psychotherapy

Rein Innes

INTRODUCTION

Some people have been forced, or seduced, through circumstances when children, prematurely to relinquish their capacity to play. When faced with art materials and the possibility of exploring these imaginatively, most people I encounter appear to be self-conscious, as if they are thin skinned and this is with good reason. They have not had the full experience of the mother as a 'protective shield' and are fearful and suspicious of losing control if they allow themselves to be spontaneous in a non-directive setting. For them, appearing 'child-like' can mean humiliation, appearing not 'good enough' can mean disappointment, 'not having an idea' can evoke terror and 'becoming messy' can signify inner disintegration/contamination.

In the art therapy setting the dropping into creative engagement can lead to the usual controlling factors of resistance and expectation beginning to lose potency. Ideally, treatment is not strongly goal driven and judgement is put aside as much as is consciously possible. The objects and the pictures which emerge within the art therapeutic setting have a unique usefulness because they are outside, yet connected to the maker's inner world.

The meaning and value the picture or object comes to symbolically represent might emerge and become consciously clear. Yet, it need not be known and perhaps is never consciously comprehended. The picture can act as mediator when it is imbued with personal meaning for its creator and this meaning not only exists but can be felt. The mobilizing of the feeling sense via creative engagement holds the potential for adding to and nurturing the undeveloped or damaged ego and of integrating conflicting feelings. The experience of wholeness and cohesion might be short lived and similar to the 'islands of clarity' described by Edward Podvoll in *The Seduction of Madness* (1990, p.5). Something has happened; a shift in being and it is forgotten, stops or is lost temporarily. So a return to being 'out of the picture' whilst the picture is being formed presents a paradox. It is in this tension of tolerating opposing forces of passivity and activity through the interplay of conscious and unconscious, a person is able to play (Innes 1996).

Clinical vignette

Mr X is a 37-year-old single, high achieving man, referred to me by a consultant psychiatrist for art psychotherapy. Mr X had no previous experience of using this model of intervention with his presenting problem – auto-erotic asphyxia which he has practised with varying intensity, over 23 years.

With Mr X's agreement I have selected some clinical material from the art therapy sessions which span a period of eight months. I will include salient features from his family history and briefly attempt to offer some understanding of the precursors of his potentially life-threatening perverse behaviour.

First, it might be useful to define auto-erotic asphyxia as a paraphilia or sexual perversion, with a compulsive desire for a state of oxygen deficiency and/or strangulation to enhance sexual-erotic arousal and orgasm in a solitary auto-erotic activity. DSM IVR (American Psychiatric Association 1995) uses the term hypoxyphilia. In the literature there is little about live practitioners who, it is believed, die sooner or later due to loss of control when organized safety mechanisms fail.

Historically, the practice of auto-erotic asphyxia (AEA) has been attributed to the pre-Christian Celts in Britain and the Mayas of ancient Mexico acknowledged a female deity, Goddess Ixtab of the hanged. The Marquis De Sade describes AEA in his novel *Justine* published in 1791, the same year the Austrian composer Frantizsek Kotzwara died in London as a result of this practice. More recently, the tabloids had a field day over the death of Stephen Milligan MP, who was found dead in sexually bizarre circumstances.

The 'accidental' death of an adolescent boy Mr X had known through his work and the widely publicized death of Stephen Milligan acted as a catalyst for him to seek treatment – he said he was frightened he might die. Some time later, when he was referred to me, I considered carefully whether I felt I *could* work with him art therapeutically or, indeed, if I *wanted* to, before an assessment meeting was arranged.

Although it was impossible to answer either of these questions clearly before I met Mr X, I realised from the outset the importance of consciously monitoring my internal responses relating to such extreme perverse behaviour. I already knew he had encountered rejection during an early attempt to get help when the treatment had stopped abruptly. Apparently, the content of the sessions proved 'too much' for the person involved. I did not wish to re-enact the scenario of feeling engulfed and then rejecting, or to erect defences as a way of denying or holding any feelings of disgust or antipathy in what Mr X might disclose in the sessions relating to his AEA.

These thoughts led me to suggest a three month period of once weekly art therapy sessions. This time limit was introduced with the idea that it would symbolize a container, at the end of which we would discuss continuing. There would be a breathing space, a punctuation before the next stage was entered into. Simultaneously, I anticipated that the time limit could act as a container for my anxieties, in how I monitored my responses in the transference and countertransference dynamics.

During the assessment interview Mr X said, 'I've never been any good at painting but I'm keen to give it a go'. He seemed ambivalent but rather desperate to try anything. Mr X struck me as having a subtly seductive manner in his quality of verbal communication, choosing his words carefully with a gentle lilting tone of voice whilst maintaining strong eye/face contact. These features have remained noticeable during the treatment.

Family history

Mr X's **Mother** was 40 when he was born and, a month prior to the birth, her father had died. She developed severe post natal depression and, as a result of her unpredictable responses, she could not be left alone with baby X. A neighbour, who came to be called 'Auntie' (and is still alive), took over the mothering and house cleaning duties for many years. Subsequently, mother maintained a rigid domestic routine involving cooking vast amounts of food for Mr X and herself. She remained chronically depressed, overweight and agoraphobic throughout her life. She died after a short illness in 1983 aged 62 from cancer. Mr X said he felt nothing when she died.

Father was 50 when Mr X was born, the youngest of eight children. He worked as a manager of a factory and his income provided a modest life style for his family living in a large rambling house. When Mr X was five years old, father became bankrupt and this was followed by a serious breakdown, the treatment of which included medication and ECT. Mr X says he changed at this time – 'he wasn't the same as before, he stopped smiling'. Father died in 1970 aged 63 from a heart attack.

Mr X remembers always having to be quiet and tidy as a child – he felt continuously isolated and lonely, having no early memories of his 14-year-older sibling, a brother, who is married and works in a manual job. At about four years of age, Mr X began fantasizing imaginary friends and games where he would organize triumphant endings with himself always the victor. Insatiable book-reading fuelled his fantasies where he would live by proxy through the characters in the narratives. Up until ten years old he slept in his own bed in his parents' bedroom, moving into his own room on discharge from hospital after a seven week admission for treatment of nephritis. His persistent bed wetting stopped abruptly during this stay in hospital. During puberty he joined a church, often attending three services on a Sunday as an escape from home. Throughout his childhood only one of Mr X's peer group visited his home, a terminally ill boy of 13 who Mr X tutored for about 6 months after school. He felt no emotion when he heard in a school assembly that the boy had died, or later when he read a lesson at the funeral service.

When Mr X was 13 his father died and he began masturbating, gradually incorporating his father's clothes, particularly belts and ties into his compulsive auto-erotic activity. There is evidence of covert masochistic homosexual trends in his sexual fantasies which exclude any heterosexual elements. He says he has no experience of sexual play or relationship with another person.

The only physical contact with his mother occurred during an elaborate hair washing ritual which continued until he was 12 years old. A distinctive aspect of the ritual was of Mr X being stripped to the waist with a towel tightly pinned around his neck.

Mr X finds eligible women especially demanding, and all physical and emotional proximity he experiences as frightening and intimidating with the exception of one trusted male friend. Since leaving university, Mr X has developed a successful academic career and he uses intense involvement in his work, far beyond what is required, in an attempt to repress and control the addictiveness of the auto-erotic activity. This control works for short periods only.

SOME IDEAS OF THE PRECURSORS OF AUTO-EROTIC ASPHYXIA IN MR X

A great deal has been written on the complex subject of perverse behaviour and how it primarily functions for, and acts as, a regulator of self-esteem (Rosen 1979; Steiner 1993; Stoller 1986; Welldon 1988).

In individuals like Mr X who have experienced, consciously or unconsciously, early cumulative trauma (Khan 1986), with rejection and humiliation, overwhelming anxieties threaten the ego's capacity to contain the conflict. Through the interplay of sexual desire, hostility and the eroticizing of anxiety, temporary relief is experienced from the internal conflict which threatens engulfment of ego functioning. An attempt to achieve a state of homeostasis or psychic equilibrium could be another way of describing the function of perverse behaviour.

With the exception of unintegrated gratification through his chosen career, Mr X has described his life as being bereft of warmth, spontaneity and play, particularly during his early developmental stages. With what appears to be a total lack of empathy mother was unable to respond to his narcissistic needs, probably because she remained chronically depressed, and Mr X has said that he was perhaps an unwanted child. Mother fed herself, and Mr X, vast amounts of food as a replacement for ordinary mother–child interaction and empathic relating.

I am suggesting that, as a result of the unconscious repressing of his narcissistic needs, Mr X turned to himself early on for gratification. He discovered, and then elaborated, a substitute representation for the idealized parental image and its main function as a requirement of developing self-esteem, a cohesive self-image (Kohut 1977).

> We have discovered, especially clearly in people whose libidinal development has suffered some disturbance, such as perverts and homosexuals that in their later choice of love objects they have taken as a model not their mother but their own selves. They are plainly seeking themselves as a love object, and are exhibiting a type of object choice which must be termed 'narcissistic'. (Freud 1914, p.88)

Via the secret imaginary games and friends, Mr X acted out self-appointed triumphant roles; this continued with his intense identification with strong characters in the books he read. With his comment, 'father stopped smiling after his breakdown; he changed', Mr X, (then aged five) suggests an internal conflict from a shaken idealized parental image. Father had become a ghost of himself, he was no longer available. In an attempt to salvage a remnant of the good father, to re-establish the union representing the narcissistically invested lost object, Mr X incorporated his father's clothes, as symbolic representations, in his auto-erotic asphyxia activity.

After Mr X's father died he found himself in early puberty alone with a mother, he says, for whom he felt revulsion. He could only act in minimal dutiful ways towards her and she towards him. Through his high academic achievements at school, which led to university, Mr X invested hope that he could finally remove himself from his depressed and emotionally suffocating mother and the accompanying desolate controlling home environment.

Physically this has been practicable, but internally he has been unable to disavow himself of mother and her representations. They remain as powerful internalized forces attached to repressed rage and desolation and there is evidence of these forces in the images Mr X has painted.

That Mr X has been practising auto-erotic asphyxia for 23 years indicates the degree of splitting as a defence against narcissistic damage. The resulting conflicts he is compelled to act out literally by dangerously auto-eroticizing them in an attempt to regulate his self-esteem.

Any sense of achievement or gratification he has experienced remains unintegrated. Mr X controls his 'bad' inner reality as separate from his external reality which he attempts to maintain as 'good'.

When this control fails and there is a threat of actually feeling, his anxiety levels rise simultaneously with the auto-erotic asphyxia practice.

Course of treatment

It might be useful to begin with how the therapeutic contract changed at the initial three month period. This transition was initiated by Mr X and I will briefly comment on this. A feature in the early sessions was for Mr X to describe how he experienced the demands of his work as overwhelming and his life generally as 'joyless'. In a session leading up to the end of the three month period Mr X said with a depressed manner and tone of voice, 'I feel there is a foundation block missing in my life and this has created a fault which is difficult to correct now...I would like to have more of what

Figure 24.1

I see other people having (me?), perhaps it is impossible… I find more time is taken up thinking about the content of these sessions; sometimes I feel quite churned up thinking about things deeply afterwards'. I responded 'Perhaps you are feeling anxious about the possibility of the sessions ending'? Mr X said 'Yes, I would like these sessions to continue'. Whilst talking he began to paint, 'I do like coming here, I do want to go on with this'. At this point I said I was willing to continue working with him. Mr X chose the colours carefully and painted a long orange rectangle placing a short black line on the top edge. Then he surrounded this line with a large yellow/orange oval and the outer edges of the paper he painted black. He ended the session smiling asking me, 'what do I think it is?' I said 'it looks like a candle'. Mr X says 'yes, it's the best one yet', with a note of triumph, looking as if he had enjoyed himself. The candle seemed symbolically to represent the therapeutic relationship and the relief in it continuing with anticipation of light being thrown on his dark inner world. The quality of Mr X's image making changed markedly after this session, reflecting some development in the quality of his life generally and in his ability to make use of the treatment though he remained utterly forlorn when on his own in his house unless he was intensely occupied with work.

In a later session I had suggested to Mr X: 'perhaps home is synonymous with your mother and the accompanying desolate relationship with her'. He agreed and was curious enough with this interpretation later to begin painting a house in bright colours, becoming engaged in discovering he was able to mix the primary colours to get the shade he wanted. This mixing process seemed to allow Mr X a sense of achievement and control which became creative rather than destructive. Stage by stage, always carefully, he added to his image of the house over the following three sessions, including golden fields of corn, trees, blue sky with clouds and a green lawn. Finally, when he finished he said, 'do you know what is different about this, it hasn't got any fences'. A rhythm became established during the making of this image, where I would 'hold' the picture safely in between sessions. This process seemed similar to the containing role of the mother with her infant and the accompanying mirroring exchanges which Mr X had not experienced with his own mother, in a benign way.

The first interruption of six missed sessions happened a year into the treatment when Mr X said he was unable to attend the usual times due to work commitments. On the surface this seemed reasonable and I entered into negotiating alternative times until I realized the unconscious seductiveness in his strategy. I later experienced a forceful sense of his attempting to manipulate me as a part object to gratify his narcissistic needs, serving the function of defending against intimacy. On his return from this interruption, Mr X said he would like to see me once a fortnight. I interpreted, 'you are

Figure 24.2

wanting me to collude in your only having little bits; perhaps you are
frightened of intimacy in these sessions?' Mr X emphatically denied this
suggestion saying rather crossly, 'The reason is financial, I've just spent
£3500 on my roof so the *rain* can't get in'. I said 'You are trying to keep
me out, you seem frightened I will get inside'. In the following session Mr
X told me his house had recently been burgled. Initially he denied any
meaningful links with the therapeutic relationship until he made an extremely messy blue and white image. Despite anxious effort he was unable
to control the paint, eventually leaving me with his messy chaos to look
after.

I have kept until the end writing about whether Mr X's auto-erotic
asphyxia practice has altered. Perhaps I have needed to firmly place, for
myself, the therapeutic process as being alive enough to survive Mr X's
attacks and to meet any anxiety I have regarding working with the material
from such a patient. The second interruption 18 months into the treatment,
namely a 10-week absence of mine, Mr X could have experienced as an
attack. Currently there seems to be emerging some signs of delayed
retaliation in response to his feeling abandoned.

During the first few months I was unsure whether I would see Mr X
from week to week, realizing that auto-erotic asphyxia rituals are akin to
suicidal behaviour. Whatever antipathy I experienced early on seemed to

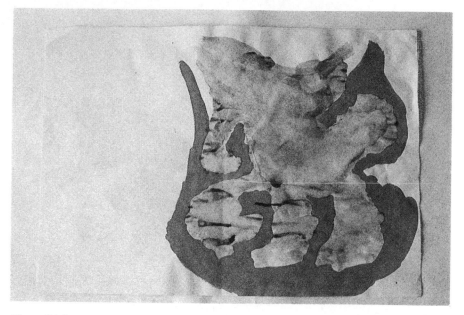

Figure 24.3

be connected to the daunting prospect of whether it was possible to engage with a part which wanted to be alive, however split off or neglected this was in Mr X. For somebody whose head and body are so disconnected and compounded by his rituals, using paint has introduced an element of the 'other' as connecting.

Mr X practices AEA less compulsively, with weeks where he says 'it is quiet', meaning non-existent. His masturbatory activity remains attached to the same homoerotic sado-masochistic fantasy, which he says is less intense. Images on TV of fighting or any sort of bondage no longer arouse him and any auto-erotic activity only happens in his home. Mr X's homosexual urges are in conflict with his religious beliefs, and he feels they have therefore to be repressed, apart from elements in his fantasy life. It was revealing when Mr X said, 'if you can hold what I tell you about my sexual activity you can hold anything. In a way it doesn't matter what happens afterwards because you have held me and it'. I believe it does matter what happens afterwards; being 'held' is a start but it is not enough to develop a cohesive self.

During the last year Mr X has begun to integrate his experiences of gratification and disillusionment through an enriched social life. He is able to interact enjoyably with a variety of people and to travel without his previous overwhelming feelings of 'being hemmed in and suffocated', which had spoiled any attempt at spontaneity. His professional work has shifted onto a rewarding level, including enhanced relationships with his colleagues. His home is now a place Mr X says he enjoys being inside, in contrast to the intense antipathy he hitherto experienced where he said he would become depressively immobilized after half an hour at home on his own unless he was occupied with a work deadline. The compulsion to act out his auto-erotic asphyxia ritual would often emerge during these times of intense anxiety at home.

25

Female Prostitution

Ü. Elif Gürişik

INTRODUCTION

In this chapter I will explore the psychopathology of female prostitution in relation to physical and sexual abuse.

It is known that sexually abused children can end up being prostitutes. Prostitution is used by these women as an antidote against depression and pain which stems from being used as a debased sex object but never being loved or valued. Unfortunately, this antidote works only briefly. When its initial anti-depressant effect wears off it becomes soul destroying in its own right. Instead of alleviating depression it exacerbates the sense of despair and hopelessness.

The abusive treatment the child has endured over the years shapes her identity and her way of coping. Her psychic strategy is that of a survivor – a complex strategy in which she comes to believe that the maintenance of her fragile ego boundaries is only possible under the constraints of the abusive situation. By transforming her hatred of her parents into identification with them as sadistic and powerful objects, she achieves a sense of power, pleasure and freedom from the fear of pain. She assumes that she will never be the victim again. The essential component of her psyche not only depends on the role reversal from the exploited victim to the exploiting victimizer, but it also depends on the reversal of the associated feelings, such as helplessness, impotence, into omnipotence, and power. Through prostitution she attempts to exact her revenge from those who damaged her. However, she unconsciously repeats her nightmarish early experiences while she tries to master the original, often overwhelming and unforgettable trauma. She yet again finds herself in the role of the abused and the denigrated object. With the collapse of her self-esteem she increasingly hates herself and her body. The initial gratification of her revengeful wishes become dissatisfying. Thus, the sadomasochistic chain remains unbroken.

Clinical vignette

Vivianna, a petite, elfin like Italian woman, sought help when she was 28 years old. She had been supporting herself through prostitution since she was aged 21 years. In recent years she had increasingly felt depressed, at times suicidal. She lived in perpetual confusion. She did not know where to go or what to do next. All she knew was that the roots of her problems were sexual and her present predicament were linked with a 'ghastly childhood'.

As far back as Vivianna could remember she always felt neglected and brutalized by her parents. Her mother – a nurse – was an alcoholic who fought endlessly with her husband. Their quarrels usually ended with violence. Vivianna was six years old when her mother died and soon after her mother's death, Vivianna had to spend some time in a sanatorium because she had caught TB from her mother. Her father re-married two years after his wife's death. Her stepmother also became an alcoholic.

Vivianna recalled that her father always related to her sexually if not violently. She and her brother were repeatedly locked up in a cupboard or, after being stripped naked and tied up to a chair, they were either whipped or photographed.

Vivianna was told that even before she was born her father – a well respected family doctor – swore on the Bible that, if he had a daughter, he would defy God by violating the most sacred commandment, that against incest. From a very early age he tried to convince Vivianna that incest between fathers and daughters was natural and normal. He read her literary and religious articles to support his claim. Her father began to have sexual intercourse with her when she was about 14 years old. He asked his second wife to watch him while he sexually abused Vivianna.

Her stepmother eventually left her father and Vivianna and her father lived alone for a further three years. Vivianna increasingly felt trapped and claustrophobic while her father became more and more possessive and controlling. Whenever Vivianna attempted to leave him, he threatened her with suicide. He eventually got involved with another woman and let Vivianna go to London when she was 21 years old. Soon after her arrival, she joined an escort agency and became a call girl. She worked in the massage parlours as well as acting in sadomasochistic films.

Her initial freedom from her father's clutches gave way to despair and despondency as she found herself being financially and sexually exploited by her 'boyfriend'/pimp. She ran into debt to support his gambling habits and she gradually gave up her hope of ever finding a 'sugar daddy' to take care of her. The more disappointed and dissatisfied she became, the more she felt unable to cope with 'the mess in her life'. At such times her hopelessness increased and she wanted to commit suicide.

Before I offered Vivianna a place in a psychoanalytic psychotherapy group, I had given serious consideration to her likely impact on the group. Since she was assessed by a colleague, I did not know if her capacity for reparation and her ability to tolerate frustration and psychic pain without resorting to gross acting out was enough. I had little idea how she would present herself to the group: a femme fatale/high class prostitute, or a wounded, exploited little girl. I had similarly little idea about how the group members would relate to her. Was she going to be too threatening for them? Was I going to be able to contain the possible sexualization of group processes, if and when Vivianna flaunted her sexuality and became seductive? However, I was very impressed with her candour and keenness to explore her emotional difficulties and often confusing life experiences which she wanted to understand fully. There was something very appealing about Vivianna. She radiated sensuality without being overtly sexy but all the same she looked like a lost anxious little girl. Maybe due to this, without knowing whether she was far too damaged to make use of group therapy, I decided to take her on.

When Vivianna joined the group, she openly talked about her long-standing sexual relationship with her father and about the prostitution. She was insightful and understanding while the other group members were very sympathetic to her predicaments.

Soon after, it became clear that the prostitution was not only financially profitable but it was also less confusing for Vivianna. She felt that as a prostitute she remained in control of her body and, more significantly, in control of her mind. Being in charge of her body, mind and time were important to her. Prostitution as she saw it kept her sane: 'my clients can fuck my body but they cannot fuck my mind'. As she learned how to fake her sexual arousal and orgasm she felt free of the guilt and confusion which had paralyzed her throughout her incestuous relationship. She saw herself as a spectator rather than a participant in the sexual activities. Shifting identification with both the victim and the victimizer enabled her to maintain the spectator role. Being a spectator to her own bodily experiences offered Vivianna a great safety. By presenting herself as an onlooker, she effectively felt free from her pain, sadistic wishes and erotic enjoyment. However, in her new role as a sadistic voyeur, she masochistically dealt with her own suffering. The gratification of sadomasochistic needs became a significant mode of relating for her.

In the group Vivianna's anxiety about being sexually exploited was played upon, often unwittingly, and at other times more blatantly.

On one occasion Paul, a homosexual with unrealistic heterosexual aspirations, asked Vivianna out. Although she 'reluctantly accepted Paul's invitation not to hurt his feelings' she insisted on going to a cafe in a very public place. While they were having tea at one of the Euston Station cafes Paul asked her to sleep with him. He hoped that sleeping with Vivianna would enable him to overcome his homosexuality. After politely declining Paul's suggestion she demanded that they should bring the matter up at the next group session, and she did exactly that. On the one hand Vivianna was pleased to be seen as a liberator but on the other, she was deeply hurt to be seen and treated as nothing but a prostitute. She sensed that not only Paul, but also other men in the group did not relate to her as a fellow patient who needed help as much as they did. She said 'yes, I am a call girl, but I am here because my life, like yours is in a mess'. She wished to be able to promote Paul's heterosexuality through working with him in the group, but not through sleeping with him. Paul apologized for hurting Vivianna's feelings 'without intending to' while the others acknowledged their sexual fantasies about her and their rivalry with one another.

Vivianna's past and present lifestyle stirred up very disturbing feelings in each member. Her incestuous relationship with her father reactivated the others' infantile incestuous wishes and merging fantasies. Heterosexual fantasies were not only mobilized to encounter these unconscious desires but also to disassociate from homosexual anxieties. They desired Vivianna but at the same time they feared to be consumed by her, though her hostility and contempt towards men were well disguised. Treating Vivianna as a prostitute, a denigrated woman, enabled them to deny their difficulty in relating to adult women and also to express the hostility they harboured towards their mothers. By ignoring Vivianna's despair and neediness, each member tried to disown their own despair and neediness.

I was inevitably experienced as a depriving as well as unreachable object. Because of this, they turned to Vivianna for emotional intimacy and close human contact but they customarily sexualized these cravings. They also maintained the split between the idealized and denigrated mother. Vivianna came to represent mother, madonna and whore (Welldon 1988).

This session was a turning point for Vivianna and the whole group. In the following weeks they grappled to understand these complex issues. They become more willing to challenge their own assumptions that they had no choice but to be a prostitute, a paedophile, an exhibitionist, and so forth. Vivianna's integration into the group as a fellow sufferer speeded up. She was accepted and seen as someone who needed consideration, respect, time and space like everybody else.

Vivianna gradually disengaged herself from prostitution. She only saw a few regular clients. However, in the second year, her progress temporarily halted when I introduced Henry to the group. When the group convened, unbeknowingly, Henry and Vivianna sat next to one another as if they were magnetically drawn together. Vivianna became listless and abject after she learned of Henry's incestuous relationship with his sister and stepdaughter. Henry's enjoyment of Vivianna's discomfort was unmistakeable. Other members behaved like fascinated but mute spectators.

I worked hard to make the group understand how rapidly the incestuous family dynamics were re-enacted within the group; Vivianna unconsciously acted as a submissive little girl to gain Henry's favour as well as to placate him, and her subservient attitude allowed Henry to regain his power. He took up the intimidating abuser role to get rid of his fear of being attacked. In the meantime the others – by becoming onlookers – gratified their sado-masochistic and voyeuristic wishes from a safe distance.

They equally put me on the spot to test whether I would be protective enough to stop 'Vivianna's mind being fucked up' or to be oblivious to her plight, by turning a blind eye to the abusive interaction between her and Henry.

This interpretation led Vivianna to recall her mother's tragic death. Following an alcoholic binge her parents began fighting on the landing while Vivianna was tied to the staircase. She saw her mother losing her balance and falling downstairs. She felt terror stricken and impotent to help her mother who was lying motionless on the floor at her feet. Vivianna also told the group how her stepmother knowingly kept quiet about the incestuous relationship. In turn, Henry talked about his parents, who remained oblivious to his sexual abuse of his sister. Peter, an exhibitionist, complained that throughout his childhood he was forced to watch sexual intercourse between his mother and her boyfriends.

Vivianna increasingly recognized that through prostitution she not only attempted to exact her revenge on her abusive father by repeatedly being unfaithful to him with other men, she also attempted to take her revenge on her mother by attacking her own body.

Vivianna was conscious of her wish to inflict pain on to her father. However, it was harder for her to acknowledge her resentment and rage against her mother. She seemingly perceived her mother's death as her ultimate destructive act 'against herself' since by dying she left Vivianna at the mercy of her father's perverse sadistic and sexual desires. In any case, while she was alive she induced a state of constant terror in Vivianna through her drunkenness and participation in violence. Furthermore, she infected Vivianna with tuberculosis. Being forced to supplant her mother sexually and to witness her death compounded Vivianna's rage, sense of helplessness, and guilt.

She understood her deception, the perversity and futility of her attempts to deal with her past suffering by putting herself into constant abusive situations and permitting men to treat her as a denigrated sex object; although she satisfied her aggressive revengeful wishes and her addiction to genital overstimulation and she gratified her need for bodily intimacy, she remained desperate for emotional closeness. While she strived to avenge the attack on her body and mind, like the others, she perpetuated and endured pain, confusion, degradation and humiliation through her acting out. As the group continued Vivianna made excellent progress in many aspects of life and gave up prostitution altogether, although her relationship with men remained problematic for her as she still let them take advantage of her emotionally or financially.

At the end of the fourth year Vivianna decided to leave the group. She was planning to open a restaurant on the channel tunnel route, having been encouraged by her success in running a souvenir shop for the past two years.

26

Technical Problems in the Psychotherapy of Perverse Female Patients

Jane Milton

INTRODUCTION

In this chapter I will discuss some issues involved in the psychotherapeutic treatment of women who act perversely or are entrenched in perverse relationships and states of mind. Such patients pose severe therapeutic challenges because of the complex and disturbing countertransference experiences they arouse. They are likely to have suffered serious abuse themselves in the past, and there is considerable potential for this to be repeated in the treatment. I will try to show the importance of rigorous boundary-keeping and supervision in such cases.

THE PSYCHOTHERAPEUTIC PROCESS AND THE PERVERSE PATIENT

In any psychotherapy, the patient's particular ways of relating to others and causing others to respond will be enacted time and again with the therapist. In psychoanalytic psychotherapy this is understood as being part of the everyday stuff of the encounter, as Joseph (1985), Sandler (1976) and others have shown. The psychoanalytic psychotherapist, as participant observer, makes it his or her business to try and understand, interpret and modify this process. This understanding is achieved by the therapist intermittently stepping back to observe his own behaviour and feelings while also observing the patient. He may find himself subtly protecting and reassuring a patient who seems at that moment childlike and unable to think; he may feel judgmental, and find himself speaking a little moralistically to a patient who seems to be wilfully uncooperative. Such patterns inevitably occur, and may provide evidence of internal relationship patterns of the patient's, projected out and enacted in the treatment relationship. The strain and difficulty of this sort of work, and the honest self-scrutiny required, are part of the reason why intensive personal psychotherapy or analysis, and good supervision, are essential.

Strongly perverse object relationships occurring in this way in the therapeutic encounter are technically particularly hard to handle. By their very nature they are strongly loaded with seductive, erotic power that can be hard to stand back from and notice. The therapist may become caught, as the patient is caught, in entrenched, repetitive patterns that feel inevitable, obvious, 'right' in some way, while at the same time indefinably uncomfortable or worrying. There is often unusually great pressure to break analytic boundaries; to offer more time, reveal personal details, even to touch or hold the patient. There often seem on the surface quite compelling reasons why *this* patient should be a special one, given special consideration and not treated harshly and unsympathetically by sticking to 'rigid rules'. On the other hand the therapist may find himself feeling and reacting uncharacteristically harshly, even cruelly. One way and another the therapist may feel himself caught up in a situation of *suffering* in the work, whether it is his patient's, his own, or perhaps both.

EXPRESSIONS OF FEMALE PERVERSION

I am focusing in this chapter on issues involving perverse *female* patients, for a number of reasons. Although the essential elements of perversion, 'the erotic form of hatred' in Stoller's (1975) words, can of course be seen in many varieties of sado-masochistic encounter, subtle or unsubtle, in any analytic situation, in both men and women, there are some special things about the ways women may present to our services that merit individual consideration. Welldon (1988) has discussed the diverse ways in which female sexuality in its broadest sense can be expressed and hence perverted. This will include the relationship to the body and to babies internal and external. A forensic service may often become involved with such a person when she injures her child in some way. It is very often the case that she in her turn will have been injured and abused by adults as a child. In order to survive psychically, she will have dealt with the experience of helpless suffering by erotization, thus structuring and achieving some control over it. Her own hatred and cruelty will be stimulated. Internally, there will become established cruel, fixed object relationship patterns that she is compelled repetitively to act out, often taking the part of either victim or aggressor interchangeably. The woman's child is often psychically to an extent a 'part-object', projected into massively. The child is thus felt as a possession of the mother, often a very persecuting one. The woman's body is frequently experienced in a dissociated way, and abused by, for example, self-mutilation or anorexia and bulimia.

Women often present to services of various sorts as victims, historical or current, of physical and sexual abuse. I think there is a general pull towards a sort of idealization of this 'victim' status, and a difficulty in looking further at the complexities of the situation, which does not occur to such an extent in male patients. Such idealization may do these women a great disservice, as it does not allow a proper look at some of the most serious aspects of their plight, including those about which they may be most ashamed and most need help with. These are the sorts of problems mentioned above, to do with the erotization of cruelty and the ways in which they have become identified with the aggressor and are maintaining the abuse on themselves and on others.

Clinical vignette – Miss A

Miss A, a single mother, put her only child, a four-year-old son, voluntarily in to foster care because she had become frightened and appalled at the way she was increasingly losing control with him. She would hit him in a rage, and, something she was even more ashamed of, lock him up and in a more deliberate way, terrify him with cruel threats; something that gave her a heady sense of power, excitement and triumph, until she recovered herself. She had been intermittently fostered as a child herself. Mother, an alcoholic, had been 'out of it', as she put it, when father had sexually abused her from the age of about eight. Her social worker referred her for psychotherapy and she saw a female trainee therapist with a nursing background.

Once psychotherapy started there was great pressure on the therapist to be gentle and non-confrontative, and to see the patient as a helpless victim. To introduce any other point of view felt cruel to the therapist, who found herself preoccupied with the patient, wanting to give her longer sessions, and see her out of hours when it would be more convenient for Miss A. She felt at first at odds with her supervisor, who seemed to carry hard and unsympathetic views of the patient. She began to wonder why she was supposed to keep such rigid boundaries for the work; after all, as a psychiatric nurse she sometimes gave her patients a hug – why not Miss A? It would help to make up for all the love she had missed out on as child. Surely as this sort of cold therapist she was *adding* to this sense of rejection rather than helping?

After a while the therapist was helped to realize that Miss A's reason for coming for psychotherapy – the cruel treatment of her child – had somehow slipped out of the mind of both her and her patient. When, struggling with herself, she started to address with the patient the collusion they had got in to, she found them suddenly catapulted into a painful situation. She, the therapist, would feel terribly reproached, and feel guiltily that she was clumsy and insensitive. She would also feel intimidated by worrying suicidal threats, often made near the ends of sessions. She would feel incompetent and at times quite frightened. She dreamt, after one session, of a courtroom scene in which she was accused by her professional body. At other times she found herself suddenly hating the patient, and wanting to say something accusatory and reproachful herself, asserting her power and authority as therapist.

On the more helpful side, the courage and honesty that had led Miss A to seek help, together with the therapist's ability, with the help of supervision, to maintain a thinking, analytic stance, enabled work to take place. Miss A was able to take her child back and mostly to start resisting the impulses to violence and cruelty, trying to talk to the child about what was happening instead, or to put some distance between them until things calmed down. This was particularly difficult in the face of the child's own evident developing perverse defences. Typically, and tragically, a child in such situations will become masochistic and subtly provocative in their turn, as Miss A had become herself, and the cycle of cruelty and violence will continue through the generations.

Many women who have been abused in their families as children will, on the surface, identify the father or other male adult as the 'bad' one and the mother as good but weak, relatively blameless, or a fellow victim. The psychic split between 'bad father/man' and 'good mother/woman', which can polarize and simplify what is often a more dire situation of collusive maternal neglect and cruelty, may be a necessary sanity-saving mechanism at first, preserving some idea of a good object. The impulse to preserve this split may mean that many such women instinctively avoid psychoanalytic psychotherapy, where their defences will be challenged, and head for varieties of supportive counselling, or 'alternative' and 'active' therapies, where the therapist sets him or herself up as a good parent substitute, encouraging further splitting and attempted banishment of the bad object. The danger in any therapy where the transference and countertransference are not understood and monitored, however, will be a re-enactment of the trauma and a treatment where there is sado-masochistic acting out, sometimes overtly sexual, or which becomes stuck and interminable.

Close supervision in such cases, especially where the therapist is inexperienced, is essential. The patient will tend unconsciously to try to re-create a close, exclusive dyadic relationship; the third member of the oedipal triad being shunned and avoided. The therapist will at times inevitably identify with the patient's view that no one else can really understand, and may herself find supervision intrusive and unwelcome. At these times it may, however, be most important to challenge collusions being set up, as in the early part of Miss A's therapy. It can be striking to find, as in the case described next, that helpful freeing of the therapist's mind by supervision can actually be experienced by the patient as neglect or betrayal, as the third member of the oedipal triad is symbolically introduced.

Clinical vignette – Miss B

Miss B sought help on the advice of her probation officer following a series of shoplifting offences. Suffering from severe bulimia, Miss B would steal food compulsively and binge and vomit as many as ten times in one day. She would also make deep cuts in her arms, then bandage them herself, without telling anyone. Severely beaten and sexually abused in childhood by father and an uncle, with, it gradually emerged, mother's collusion, Miss B lived in a lesbian community which she at first described in idealized terms as a haven from the cruel world of men. She had insisted on a female therapist, and was seen by a supervised trainee. The therapist quickly found that Miss B got 'under her skin', in a worrying way. Sessions would be filled with long, disturbing silences, in which the therapist would feel sick, or frightened, or despairing, unable to think of anything useful to say. She felt terribly responsible for Miss B's life. Words, when they were spoken by either one of the women in the room, seemed very powerful, as if they were either blows or caresses, in a charged, electric atmosphere. The therapist found it hard to think, and it was striking that when she did find space in her mind for reflection, or tried to imagine what her supervisor would say at this point, the patient would become anxious, and accuse her of being uninterested and uninvolved. The therapist's over-riding experience was one of suffering herself, or of helplessly witnessing the suffering of Miss B.

As the therapist struggled to understand what was happening and, with the help of her supervisor, to try to put something of these vivid but almost silent interactions into coherent words for the patient, more material at last began to emerge about the patient's current life. It seemed that far from living in a kind, ideal world, the patient's sexual activities involved cruel beatings, where she was either the victim or a third party observer. Although these activities gradually diminished once they had been lived through and put in to words in the psychotherapy, the patient seemed worryingly raw and vulnerable without the protection of these perverse activities. A premature ending of the treatment imposed by NHS constraints raised ethical dilemmas about the short-term treatment of such ill people in the mind of both therapist and supervisor.

CONCLUSION

I hope I have shown some of the difficulties and challenges of treating women with markedly perverse defences. Such deeply disturbed people paradoxically tend to get themselves seen by therapists with minimal training. It can be seen that their serious plight in fact requires that their therapists are of the highest integrity, with maximal training and supervisory support.

27

The Burglar

Judith Whale

INTRODUCTION

Burglary can be defined as trespass on property with intent to steal. It may also include intent to do grievous bodily harm, rape or unlawful damage to property (Faulk 1988). It is important to keep this definition in mind when assessing and treating the burglar, as trespass and theft may also pervade the psychopathology. This intrudes upon the treatment process in subtle ways which need to be addressed for successful treatment. In this chapter I intend to look at some of the issues of assessment and treatment which relate more specifically to the burglar, basing my observations on a patient I treated.

Clinical vignette

Mr A is a 54-year-old man whose initial contact with the law occurred when at the age of four he threw stones at a policeman's bike. His subsequent career took the following path of delinquent behaviours as a child, for example truancy, shoplifting sweets and damage to property. In early adolescence he became quite violent and aggressive and was frequently cautioned. When he was 17 years old an uncle suggested to him that rather than constantly getting into trouble with the police for fighting he would be better to concentrate his anger and energies on theft. Whilst he would still be at risk of prison he would get something out of it. He became involved with a gang which would carry out systematic shoplifting, armed raids and burglary. He was imprisoned on several occasions and was regarded as a troublemaker – arrogant and concerned only for himself. In later years he had worked alone, mainly shoplifting, for which he was on probation when referred for assessment for psychoanalytic psychotherapy.

During the assessment certain questions needed to be considered. Why was he presenting now? Was he motivated to change his behaviour? What had happened in his life to necessitate this way of relating to others? Could his need for burglary be understood in dynamic terms? If so, did he have the capacity to symbolize and to use psychodynamic interpretation? Why did he steal: did he get from it something more than money? In other words could we begin to understand what the burglary symbolized for him and whether treatment was an appropriate option.

As the assessment progressed it became clear that he had an ability to care for others of which he was almost ashamed. He would shoplift for other people, giving away many of his acquisitions. He now stole for the excitement of outwitting major store anti-theft devices. He considered it immoral to steal from small shops. He was asking for help now because he wanted to stop stealing. He did not want to back to prison at his age. In effect he wanted help to retire from the only career he had ever known. However, he was afraid that his addiction to the 'buzz' would prevent him unless he could begin to understand his need to be a burglar. A picture emerged of a man who could express himself symbolically through the media of paint and music. Indeed he was beginning to find an excitement from performing to match the thrill of theft. He had taken active steps to prevent himself from shoplifting by using only small shops and by working during shop opening hours, indicating an authentic wish for change.

When his early life was explored it became clear that at the age of six there was a major change in his circumstances. He was a war baby whose father had been absent in the forces for some time. One could speculate that this affected his ability to form a satisfactory three person relationship. Practically this stole from him any choice of which parent to go to. He had been allowed great licence, playing in the rubble with unexploded bombs by a mother who was having difficulty coping alone. This gave him his initial experience of the fearful excitement he later felt during burglary. As a child it was the fear of potential explosion and as a burglar of potential capture. He recalled this as an idyllic time with mother to himself. Suddenly when he was six his father returned and immediately imposed a strict regime against which he had rebelled with the inevitable resultant punishment. With father back he now had to share mother. It could be hypothesized that the loss of mother might have been felt as theft. Bad feeling and bitterness between him and his father had remained until shortly before his father's death two years previously. There seemed to be unresolved Oedipal conflicts which needed exploration and which might well be relevant to his choice of criminal career.

From this sketch of the assessment it can be seen that therapy was an appropriate option. Mr A called himself and was a professional burglar. He could be violent, arrogant, contemptuous and self-centred but he had a reason and the motivation to change. He wanted to understand why he stole and there was the beginning of a dynamic understanding of his pathology which bore exploration. He was therefore offered once weekly psychoanalytic therapy.

TREATMENT

He presented in therapy initially with a nonchalant contemptuous attitude concealing his anxiety and curiosity. He would sprawl in his chair, legs outstretched, hands behind his head and initially I felt uncomfortable in his presence. Before the second session I found myself moving the chairs farther apart than usual. On analyzing this I realized that he was actually intruding on my space in the room and stealing it. With some trepidation I shared my observation with him. He found it immediately comprehensible and was shocked to discover that he could relate it to many situations from the past. An example he gave was how when sharing a room he would spread his belongings around in order to 'take over' as much of the space as possible. As therapy progressed it became clearer that this need to intrude, steal and penetrate what is not allowed pervaded his inner world.

His timing was at first extremely erratic. On the occasions when he arrived late he would start a fascinating and relevant story just before the end of the session and it would be a struggle to end on time. He would ignore my usual end of session cues and I would have to resist both my own curiosity and his projection that a few minutes here or there did not matter. We explored this behaviour using the language of theft. His fantasy was that by being late he was stealing my time. I pointed out that it was his session therefore his time. I added that wanting extra time at the end of the session seemed related to an unconscious need to steal time from a fantasized next patient. He was unimpressed by this interpretation for some months but the timekeeping improved considerably.

Time, timing and doing time were important themes of therapy. He wished to put the exact amount of money into the parking meter even if this meant leaving the session to replenish it. He felt that the council were stealing from him if there was time remaining on the meter when he left. Once I had to miss a session unexpectedly without being able to notify him. His response was to be disproportionately angry, have violent thoughts towards me and miss the next session. Some of this anger was appropriate but, on exploration, his experience had been of me contemptuously stealing a session from him. He then had to steal it back to retain his self-respect. A fear of his own potential for violence emerged. He was convinced that he would be capable of murder in the context of a fight. He believed that the thrill he felt from theft defused his natural aggression and he therefore saw it as an acceptable option. It is of note that staff who had had to face his anger were frightened of him.

As therapy progressed I noticed that he would present in two main ways. At times he would be arrogant and contemptuous, albeit witty, with an intrusive stare which seemed designed to steal my thoughts. The material during these sessions would include grandiose stories of deceit and cleverness in outwitting authority figures. I would often become unexpectedly sleepy despite the apparently interesting material being presented. At other times the contempt and intrusion were replaced by a creative thoughtfulness. He apparently had been caring for terminally ill friends and it became clear that part of the arrogant burglar persona was a defence against experiencing the associated emotional pain. The sleepiness became a useful warning sign for me that such a defence was in action, so that we could then challenge it.

Gradually an understanding emerged of pathological mourning for a father who had suddenly died just as he began to know and love him. As we learned more about his childhood the dynamic hypothesized at the assessment of how father seemed to have stolen mother from him and of his inability to recover from that, gained substance. He also felt that his chance of a good relationship with father had been stolen from him by the war. It was pertinent that his most recent offence had occured on the anniversary of father's death.

At this point Mr A re-offended in an amateur way encouraging detection. He had experienced a thrill but this time it was as a result of being caught. We looked at how he had re-offended just as painful memories were emerging. He realized that he wanted imprisonment in order to avoid thinking about the death of his father and friends. He could not bear the psychic pain involved in the loss of psychological objects important to him. To avoid it he stole alternative physical objects. He said that the deaths left a hole inside that theft filled, albeit temporarily. To him prison was an escape where, although doing time, he did not have to confront time as he would always be told what to do and when. It was somewhere where he could avoid thinking about life outside. He had neither told the authorities that he was in treatment nor had he engaged a solicitor. In therapy we were able to look at his offence, the nonchalant way in which he had responded to it, and the wish for imprisonment as yet other defences against feeling psychic pain. As a result of this he engaged a solicitor and therapy was able to continue.

CONCLUSION

I have presented this material briefly in order to highlight some aspects of therapy and psychopathology of particular relevance to the burglar. The definition of burglary includes trespass with intent to steal. I hope I have shown how this definition in respect to property also has relevance to the state of mind. I have found Jung's concept of the Trickster archetype useful during treatment (Jung 1968). Some manifestations of this are to be manipulative, lacking in concern for others and adept and plausible in deceit. An example of the trickster at work in him occured when he started comparing the use of metal bars or guns in raids. He approved of guns as he was more likely to think carefully before using them. He thought that he would be more likely to use a bar indiscriminately. For a moment in the session I found myself thinking how reasonable that sounded until I realized that he saw nothing wrong in using either if he considered it necessary! Following this I found the trickster concept most useful to bear in mind when Mr A was at his most reasonable.

During therapy it is important to use the language of theft. It is readily understood by the patient and serves to highlight the symbolic aspect of the offences. Throughout assessment and treatment it is imperative to keep the therapeutic boundaries intact as Mr A's response to the missed session shows. It is relevant that he was able to tolerate planned breaks as he felt that the planning showed concern for him. Precise time-keeping can be seen to be crucial. It has been seen how even two minutes in either direction has dynamic implications for him in relation to theft.

So far in therapy he has become more caring of others and shows less arrogance or contempt. He has found alternative ways of achieving a thrill using his marked artistic abilities. He tends to be more direct and honest in his speech and show less manipulative behaviour. He has begun to recognize how much the concept of theft has pervaded his life and recognize the trickster in himself. Obviously I have only been able to present a little of all the work that has been done. There is still a long way to go but a beginning has been made. Even with some understanding of the meaning of his burglary there is no guarantee that it will totally cease, but he has not re-offended yet.

28

The Female Fraudster

Jenifer Anne Clarke

INTRODUCTION

'The false self sets up as real and it is this that observers tend to think is the real person' (Winnicott 1965). Winnicott goes on to describe how in friendships, working relationships and living relationships the false self begins to fail leaving those around in some confusion 'the fraudster not being the person observers thought they were'. Fraud is defined in the Oxford Dictionary as, 'criminal deception: person or thing that is not what he or it seems or pretends to be.'

Clinical vignette

Ms A was referred via the courts for treatment of her depressive illness and underlying temperamental difficulties. Over a two year period she exploited her position as a care worker in a nursing home for the elderly to obtain from patients five thousand pounds by fraud and theft, using cash point cards and cheque books.

The Responsible Medical Officer initially saw Ms A to explain the planned treatment programme which was that she'd receive psychotherapy once weekly and he would see her every six weeks to monitor her mental state. He also briefly described some of the principles of psychotherapy. The setting in which I see Ms A is a medium secure unit, in a fairly spacious office with easy chairs and a coffee table.

During our first session I explained the ground rules for psychotherapy and invited her to ask any questions she may have. During the initial assessment she described her birth as unremarkable but recalled her childhood and adolescence in very negative terms due to a poor relationship with her mother. About her mother she said:

> 'She used to beat me for no reason at all. I would pray for my father to come home, he was my saint…my protector.'

Ms A's father died suddenly from a heart attack when she was 17 years old:

> 'I couldn't believe it. All I kept thinking was why did God take the wrong one. I knew my life would be unbearable without him there to protect me and it was. I had to leave home shortly after.'

It was evident that Ms A felt cheated: robbed of a father and left to cope in isolation with her mother's physical and emotional abuse. She felt she had no choice but to leave school in order to support herself and, subsequently, discontinued her A level studies. Ms A felt that she could have achieved far more academically if it hadn't been for her mother, and resented this.

Ms A is the second child in a family of three. She has a close relationship with her older brother and a more distant one with her younger sister.

At 19 she commenced nurse training but failed to qualify, which was another major disappointment for her. Her first marriage broke down after three years when she discovered her husband was having an affair. Her second husband (with whom she had one son now 10 years old) did very little work, so that Ms A had to support the family. In addition, her second husband was violent towards her on numerous occasions, such that she needed medical attention. Ms A said that all her relationships with men involved violence towards her and required her to take financial responsibility.

With regard to her son, she has tried hard not to be like her own mother and described their relationship as good and more of a 'friendship'. Ms A's current relationship is with a 41-year-old widowed man with three children aged between 6 and 11.

During our initial sessions Ms A appeared eager to please and gain my approval and admiration. She continually spoke of her achievements and how valued she was by all who knew her. Ms A described events leading to her offence, stating that she'd been under a considerable amount of pressure. She spoke of her financial problems and the lack of support from her family. Ms A also described the humiliation she had felt when being questioned by the police and when they had come to search her home.

> 'They came into my home; it was just awful having to sit there while they went through my personal belongings. I can remember going to court, not knowing if I was going to go to prison or not. My mother wasn't speaking to me; she said it was my own fault and my boyfriend didn't want to know. I couldn't bear to go out after that, I was so afraid someone would say something to me.'

In transferential terms I had become her 'protector' – someone she could 'trust'. In the countertransference I felt sympathetic regarding her difficulty in expressing her vulnerabilities. Yet reassuring her would be to no avail as this would not enable her to gain insight into why she'd committed her offence. Soon after I was able to address this when Ms A was describing how hard she'd worked in the nursing home:

'I had to do everything. I even took them on holidays and that was really hard work. They weren't grateful, I remember Mrs B counting her coppers in her purse continuously, she had thousands in the bank. Then there was Mr C he was incontinent everywhere: and I had to send him home. After all the trouble I'd been to they were so ungrateful.'

I made the interpretation to Ms A that she may have felt that they owed her for the trouble she'd gone to and she had taken their money because she felt she had deserved it. Although Ms A initially denied this she did admit to feeling extremely angry about all the demands that had been placed upon her.

The following week when Ms A attended the session she had obviously given the interpretation further thought:

'I did think they owed me the money; they would never have noticed I had taken it if I hadn't been reported. I felt I deserved more for all the work I had done which everyone took for granted. I know now I shouldn't have taken it.'

She also acknowledged that she had felt cheated by her elderly patients in a similar way to that in which she felt cheated by her mother, who had also ignored her efforts and worth. As sessions progressed it became evident that Ms A repeated a similar pattern of behaviour in her everyday life. She often spoke of how much she was expected to do for others and how little her efforts were appreciated.

During one session after a period in which she had been caring for her mother who had been physically unwell she said:

'I don't mind looking after her, she is my mother after all but there's no pleasing some people. I stayed with her for a few days; she nearly drove me mad, she was instructing me to clean her cooker, go to the shops. I had a row with my boyfriend so I sent my son to see her but that wasn't good enough. She doesn't appreciate anything so I've decided to stay away.'

It is noticeable that Ms A assumed that her son would visit her mother in her place, thereby unconsciously repeating with her son her mother's expectations of herself although, with her boyfriend's children she found herself again assuming a subordinate, servile role. She said:

'I don't mind them trying on my clothes, playing with my jewellery. I spend all weekend entertaining them but they still resent me spending time with their father.'

I put it to Ms A that she placed conditions on what she did for others but did not make it clear to them what she expected in return and thus felt cheated, just as she had with the elderly people from whom she had stolen. Ms A had considerable difficulty in accepting such interpretations as they were suggestive of a weakness in her sense of self-worth. She was keen to express her value and worth to me, relating how she was valued by her friends and reminding me that she had been successful with her application to commence a counselling course at a local university. I felt challenged in my role as a therapist and provoked into irritation by Ms A. It became clearer that I, in the transference, had been defrauded and that up until then there had been a brittle, somewhat idealized transference with myself as the 'protector' who had to be lied to. This meant that the aggression and destructiveness was split off and located in 'old people', 'partners' and 'mother'. In other words I was the 'good father' and she was the 'good daughter', an untrue, fraudulent situation, because her father didn't protect her and was only maintained as 'good' by use of splitting. I put it to her that she wanted to become her own therapist, thereby denying her dependency, feeling more able to meet the needs of others than to address her own needs.

There followed a holiday break of two weeks during which Ms A reflected upon her failure to acknowledge her own needs. When sessions recommenced she described an argument she'd had with her boyfriend and her mother:

'I couldn't stop crying. I was walking through the streets crying, feeling I had nowhere to go.'

I put it to Ms A that she felt abandoned and suggested that she may also have felt abandoned by me as a result of our break. Ms A did not dismiss this interpretation, stating:

'I did miss coming here. It's different coming here than talking to my friends because you don't offer me advice or compare yourself with me. I actually look forward to coming here now.'

I thought the session during which I made this interpretation to be the most significant session so far. It occurred one year into therapy and I felt that Ms A was acknowledging both deep need and benefit from this therapeutic relationship. In the countertransference I again felt like the 'protective father', sympathetic to her needs and aware of a sense of satisfaction at being valued. Ms A failed to keep her appointments for the next three weeks and I recall feeling concerned about her and confused as to why this had happened, after what I had thought had been a productive session. I hypothesized that it was a negative therapeutic reaction – a reaction to the fact that contact had been made and thus need and dependency acknowledged. When she returned after the break I was surprised by her demeanour. During the session she appeared to denigrate the therapy and I was aware of feeling increasingly irritated by her. Ms A stated

'I had to go down to the probation office to sign this week, it was an awful experience. You should see the people down there, all the down and outs. It got me thinking about appealing against my sentence, especially because when I start my counselling course I won't have time for all that.'

Here she was defending against the fear of being 'broken down' and 'down and out', and she had to usurp my place as therapist, become me, in order to deny need. This confirmed my hypothesis.

In the countertransference I felt enraged by her conceited attitude and was aware of a desire to punish her and make her pay for her offence. I felt she was rubbishing the therapy she'd been receiving and I was aware that I wanted to reject her. But I also realized that she had reverted to her former defences because the insight she had gained into her feelings of anger, insecurity, distrust and hopelessness had proved too challenging. It is also possible that Ms A became afraid of the degree of trust that she had begun to invest in the therapeutic relationship, in the way Guntrip (1968) describes as characteristic of schizoid patients who fear a good relationship because of the deep needs it can arouse, needs which threaten to overwhelm the false self. Thus Ms A returned to the subject of the abusive relationships she has had with men and particularly within her current relationship.

'He demands sex, I refused the other night and he dragged me upstairs by my hair. It's easier just to give in to him. He never listens to me.'

I referred again to Ms A's need to be valued for her own sake, putting it to her that she must feel hurt by this man's failure to take her seriously or to be interested in her needs. I also reminded her that when she described difficult events during our sessions she tended to laugh. Ms A acknowledged that she would try to 'make light' of such situations, stating that to admit she was hurt would make her too vulnerable. She spoke of never allowing herself to be sensitive as this was too painful. She was actually in identification with her partner in her failure to take treatment seriously.

Ms A made significant progress over the first year in gaining insight into how she responds and copes with her day-to-day life. It was evident, however, that Ms A continued to run the risk of acting out when a sense of deprivation increased her need to gain the things she believed she deserved, as her right, her entitlement. Although Ms A was now less inclined to regard herself as the victim, I felt she required a significantly longer period in therapy, preferably on a voluntary basis rather than as a condition of a court order. This suggestion was upheld and Ms A was offered a further year of therapy on a voluntary basis.

A crisis arose eight months later when quite suddenly Ms A's sister died. She telephoned me almost immediately explaining what had happened and requesting an urgent appointment. We arranged a suitable appointment time which she subsequently failed to attend. She did, however, attend her appointment the following week. During the session she spoke of how devastated she had been and went on to denigrate her mother, her boyfriend and everyone else she was in close contact with stating that she had to keep a 'brave face'. I put it to Ms A that she may feel also that she had to put on a 'brave face' for me which was why she had failed to keep her appointment. Ms A instantly denied this but suddenly started to cry. This was the first time she had allowed herself to cry during a session. It was evident that she found this extremely difficult and appeared to fight back her tears in an attempt to gain some control.

It was on occasions such as these that I felt I was in touch with Ms A's 'true self' and it was also on such occasions that Ms A would abruptly withdraw from therapy and attend intermittently. She has so far been unable and is not yet ready to hand over this role of 'caretaker' to this psychotherapist (Guntripp 1968).

CONCLUSION

Ms A has gained significant insight into the cycle and nature of her offending behaviour, thereby reducing the risk of re-offending which was the initial goal of her treatment plan. However, 'the false self' prevails and continues to cause chaos and confusion within her living relationships. It is possible that should she be any more in touch with 'the true self' she would find this too destructive, leaving suicide as her only option.

Psychotherapy attempts to meet the needs of the patient regardless of the therapist's own insights and beliefs and in Ms A's case her needs were to gain an understanding whilst also respecting her need to maintain 'the false self' in order to exist.

29

Money for Nothing

A Case of 'White Collar' Crime

Gwen Adshead

Clinical vignette

You are asked by defence solicitors to assess a 35-year-old male clerk, who has pleaded guilty to three charges of theft and fraud. When he comes to your office, he is a pleasantly spoken young man, with no prior criminal convictions. He seems calm, and to some extent, unconcerned about the present charges. However, as he gives his history, it is clear that the scale of his offending behaviour is not represented by the charges of which he is convicted. He gives a history of stealing from his parents and siblings since early childhood. As a schoolboy, when employed, he would steal small amounts from his employers but was never detected. While in the army, he stole equipment, which he would sell to local civilians; on one occasion, he was caught and this led to his dismissal from the army.

This current set of charges relates to several years of chequebook fraud, of which only a few offences have come to light. As he speaks of the fraud, he becomes quite animated. Smiling broadly, he tells you that he found cheque-book fraud 'exciting'. What he chiefly enjoyed was the experience of being 'someone else'; of guessing at the character and lifestyle of the name on the chequebook. With the stolen chequebook, he would buy a set of clothes appropriate to the character, then go out for an expensive meal, and then to a club. Sometimes, he would pick up prostitutes, and give them his assumed name. However, he did not obtain or keep any cash, and he always threw the clothes away. When the police arrested him, he was almost penniless and homeless.

ASSESSMENT AND FORMULATION

Stealing is a communication about deprivation and anger. It is also a commentary on an offender's sense of self-worth. This very sad case illustrates many features common to offenders who express their psychological needs by theft.

First, the presentation is a reminder that the offence(s) with which a patient is charged at court often bear little relationship to the extent of the psychopathology. If the assessing therapist had only considered the current charges, then vital information would have been overlooked. In this case, the patient is likely to have provided the missing history, but some offenders are not so forthcoming, especially if they have not entered a plea, and the outcome of the trial is unknown. A comparison of evidence in the statements, and the offender's own evidence may say something about how the offender is thinking about his offences, relating to how much he can bear to think at all. It is therefore essential to get all relevant legal paperwork, especially previous convictions, and victim statements.

Next, the patient seems calm and unconcerned. This conscious exterior, combined with such an extensive history of offending, tells the assessor something about the level of denial and repression of emotion that this man has to impose upon himself. Many offending behaviours have neurotic distress and anxiety as their root, which is never consciously expressed, but is carefully controlled. The control is also manifested in the way in which many of the actual offences are carried out. This man's offender self, which needs so much sustenance which can only be obtained illicitly, is carefully hidden; not only from others, but to some extent from himself.

It is not too much of a generalization to say that deprivation is a common theme in the childhoods of recidivist thieves. Sometimes the deprivation is concrete, in terms of actual abuse, neglect or failure to nurture; sometimes the deprivation is experienced when primary carers fail to 'give' emotionally. In particular, the child is deprived of positive introjects of himself, which he can take into his developing mind. This aspect of insecure attachment results in a gnawing internal anxiety, which needs sustenance. A physical solution may be found in stealing; sometimes food, but usually money, or other items belonging to the parents. The child obtains some sense of satisfaction of his needs, but only by illegal means; he is not really 'allowed' to have anything nurturing, as it were, by right. This reinforces the internal sense that he is unloveable, and that his needs will never be met, with accompanying affects of grief, anxiety, rage and guilt.

Such deprivation, and consequent feelings, contribute to an insecure state of mind with regard to attachment. Furthermore, this state of 'mind' is a false one, insofar as neediness, and awareness of need, is concerned. The notion of anxious and deprived children forming a false self has been described by Winnicott (1984, p.111), with particular relevance to criminal behaviour; in this case, we see a person who is literally constructing 'another self', every time he offends. In the role of the imagined self, he is well fed and clothed, and even loved. But, unconsciously, he knows that the conscious game must end. The clothes are given away, and the cards destroyed. He is so unworthy that he is now not even able to benefit from his offences.

As suggested above, the calmness such patients show is a defence against the storms of unconscious and terrifying feelings. An additional defence, which interacts with denial, is a grandiose one. One aspect of the 'false self' constructed by the deprived child is a grandiose identity in which the child triumphs over others, by virtue of his cleverness and abilities. 'Who needs these hopeless people?' is the internal message. This grandiosity is expressed in the offences; often as a form of respite for the victim, and law enforcement agencies. Such an unconscious defence may become a conscious reality, as the offending behaviour becomes the only area of success. Another aspect of the grandiosity is the conscious experience of 'conning' others, so that only the offender has the true picture, the real knowledge. By this means, he retains an experience of being in control, and also being superior to others.

TREATMENT

The stealing, the success, the evasion of detection and the denial are all defences against rage and grief. Like other perverse solutions, repeated theft and fraud give some relief from internal distress, which is only short-lived. This leads to a pattern of offending which is both compulsive and repetitive. Frequently the behaviour begins to fail as an affect-reliever, and then the offender may experience both sadness and guilt. This may lead to the offender being caught for the first time, as he seeks a concrete attribution of himself as 'guilty'. Insofar as this is the case, then the treatment implications are good, because the patient may be able to tolerate thinking about and experiencing painful feelings.

If the patient is not at this stage, then treatment becomes more difficult. This is partly because the denial will cause the patient to be incurious about himself, which in turn is a measure of the anxiety that he feels about his internal world. It is true that one of earliest effects of successful therapy will be to put such patients in touch with long-suppressed feelings. Thus it is common for such patients to become depressed during therapy, and the risks of suicide need to be considered. Ideally, therefore, treatment should take place with psychiatric input and supervision, to allow for short-term prescriptions of medication or inpatient treatment if necessary. Sadly, it is rare for such patients to be offered treatment, even as a condition of a probation order, because the seriousness of their condition is not recognized, or is minimized by others in the criminal justice system, including defence lawyers and psychiatrists. I shall return to this below.

Sometimes such repetitive theft may be triggered by stressful events in the external world, which act as unconscious reminders of past deprivation, which has otherwise been successfully managed. For example, such offending may begin around the time of the birth of children, when new parents are consciously and unconsciously reminded of the neediness of children. In such circumstances, it may helpful to consider joint work with the partner. It may also be possible to involve other family members in family therapy.

As is common in the psychotherapy of the forensic patient, the therapist can expect to see reenactments of the offences within the sessions. Deprived patients like this may experience any loss of session time as a terrifying deprivation. They may frequently question why the therapist is bothering with them, and portray themselves as unworthy. Less consciously, some patients may maintain their false self for a long time in therapy; or they may attack the therapeutic process by 'conning' the therapist, by being untruthful, or by otherwise acting dishonestly. When this comes to light, it is important to interpret the patient's fear that he is not entitled to an honest benefit, and also the patient's need to triumph over the therapist, who appears to hold all the goodness he needs.

CONCLUSION

The psychopathology of such patients is often well hidden, especially when they come from middle-class backgrounds and may be in good professions, or high-ranking positions. In such circumstances, various aspects of the criminal justice system may collude unconsciously with the patient, to deny both his past traumatic experiences, and his internal distress. Such denial allows both the patient and the court unconsciously to protect his parents (what Fairbairn (1952) called the 'moral' defence). Thus it is not uncommon for quite markedly repetitive offending, which would be taken seriously by the court in other circumstances, to be put down to 'work-stress', or substance abuse. Psychological treatment options are often not sought, even where psychiatric opinions have been obtained.

Another aspect of the courts colluding with offender denial relates to the past experiences of many of the middle-class professionals in the court-room, who may have had similar experience of childhood deprivation. Unlike poorer families, middle-class and moneyed families have the option of dealing with internal distress by acting out, as it were, materially; by the use of material gifts to solve family stress and distress. To any accusations of deprivation, it is possible to say 'My child wanted for nothing'. The tragedy is that this is replayed in latter generations, often with a conscious sense of pride; 'I want him to have what I had' (c.f. Miller 1983).

The best example of this is the English boarding school system; a very expensive part of middle-class and professional identity. The material advantages of such schools are great, and children are expected to be grateful to their parents for sending them away. This not only negates the child's distress; it is also a concrete expression of the view that money is a wholly satisfactory and reasonable alternative to love.

30

Women Who Shoplift

Jane Knowles

In an attempt to delineate between professional 'career' shoplifters and others Dobmeyer (1971) described a second 'non-professional' group of (mostly) women who shoplift unsystematically for goods for personal use.

However, in their study Kolman and Wasserman (1991) found that only a third of their sample of 138 wanted the item they had stolen but could not afford to pay for it. This group represented the younger, less educated women on lower incomes or benefits who had shoplifted since mid-adolescence occasionally.

The remaining two thirds did not want the item(s) stolen and could have afforded to pay for them. This group of women shoplifters have been described as lonely isolated individuals who have no capacity to seek appropriate help for their problems. Although they experience shame and humiliation when arrested, many want none-the-less to be caught, as if the shoplifting is a form of 'cry for help'. Thus the criminal nature of their behaviour is often out of character with the woman's past and overall lifestyle (Brenton 1985; Taylor 1982).

Interestingly, this group also fail to see shoplifting as serious or criminal, a denial presumably based in their confused internal motivation. They cannot equate their own actions with stealing, for instance, because of their lack of interest in the items stolen. Kolman and Wasserman (1991) describe a group treatment programme in which the educational aspects are about shoplifting as a crime and the legal consequences of that crime. In their psychological groups the women talked of anger and frustration as prime motivations for their behaviour. They also talked of feeling sorry for themselves, wanting revenge, needing to be caught and humiliated and of seeking excitement.

I have treated about twenty women shoplifters in NHS psychodynamic psychotherapy individually and in groups over the last fifteen years. Some seek treatment after being arrested for shoplifting and approach therapy as a search for an explanation for behaviour they experience as alien to themselves. Three have admitted to shoplifting during the course of therapy as an apparent response to family crisis but also, I think, as a response to the struggles of therapy. Individual therapy with these women has given me the opportunity of working psychodynamically at the 'trigger' moment immediately prior to the shoplifting behaviour.

Many of these women had an external placidity that was almost saint-like. They sought perfection in their roles of wives and mothers. Orbach and Eisenbaum (1981) have described the social façade that little girls knowingly adopt aged four to five in order to appeal to others. This façade is about being sweet natured, kind, quiet, considerate and nurturing to others. With women shoplifters this façade seems taken to an extreme and adopted unknowingly, unconsciously. Whilst most women knowingly adopt and play these roles, suffering guilt about their hypocrisy in doing so but being trapped by social expectation to continue, women shoplifters seem unconscious that their roles are merely a false sociological self.

Indeed, during the early part of therapy there is often a desperate struggle to recreate the facade of nurturing perfection and deny any discrepancy between that and their shoplifting behaviour. In one psychodynamic psycho-therapy group the two women who had shoplifted were fiercely competitive with the other women members and the woman group leader about nurturing skills. They used the subject of the importance of buying fresh food for their family's nutritional benefit as the vehicle for this competition. One of the women (Esther) started to bring bags of fresh fish, meat and vegetables that she had purchased en route to the group to demonstrate how much better she fed her family than any of the other women in the group.

There was a desperate quality to Esther's behaviour that made it hard to challenge her and interpretations were brushed aside as demonstrations that the woman group leader clearly knew nothing about housekeeping! The need to re-establish the façade of perfection was clear. It was also clear that this reconstruction was not only about finding self-esteem for herself but also about denigrating other women. As one of the male patients commented, it was easy to see why this woman was socially isolated. The women experienced her as hostile and destructive whilst the men thought her 'beyond understanding'.

The group leaders felt that their attempts to contain the hostility and to nurture any expressions of emotion by Esther were attacked and devalued much as is seen in therapy with borderline-type patients. However, Esther did not exhibit other borderline symptoms. In fact if anything the structured order, correctness and total lack of acting out of any form (except shoplifting) in her life were the opposite of the usual borderline chaos. But there was a strong dislike in the group leaders' counter-transference which was described in supervision as a desire brutally to expose Esther as a hypocrite. The leaders could see how much that would mimic the exposure she had experienced when caught 'red-handed'.

Whilst consciously struggling to erect and maintain the façade, the unconscious need to break free of the severe limitations the façade imposed were projected out into others who then experienced the need to attack that façade. Therapeutic breakthrough became possible when Esther had a dream in which the women therapist appeared as half woman and half dragon and breathed fire over the patient's house. Watching the house ablaze filled her with relief, much like the relief she had experienced when arrested. During questioning after her arrest Esther had told the police that her house was full of items she had stolen. She confessed to the group that this was a lie but she had hoped that the police 'would pull the house apart brick by brick to find these goods'.

The extent of her hostility towards her own domesticity then became apparent. The house was experienced as part of her psychological façade and as a hateful trap in which she was the victim. She had hoped that by being caught shoplifting the whole edifice of her life would tumble without her necessarily being seen as responsible for this. She was puzzled that both police and her family had treated her as 'beyond understanding' in exactly the way the men in the group described. She experienced her husband treating her as if frail and ill and related how this felt discrepant with her inner experience of hostility and destructiveness.

Anne, the other woman who had shoplifted in this group, responded to Esther's story by identifying with her descriptions of rage and destructiveness, but she talked of these emotions without affect. She had demonstrated much more emotional energy when discussing shopping and feeding her family. Shopping, for Anne, was an experience of 'coming alive' which she enjoyed more than sexual contact. Indeed during intercourse she would start to write shopping lists because this excited her. However on the day Anne shoplifted she described a feeling of great disappointment and then rage at the shop. She described a sudden 'insight' that shops took all your money but then failed to give you what you had hoped for.

Anne was the first of four children born within five years to a women who had lost her own mother in childhood. Anne's father was frequently absent due to work and his hobby of fishing. Whenever Anne talked of childhood the descriptions had a hollow vacuous ring to them. By the age of five she had become 'a little mother' to the whole family. Anne sustained herself throughout this childhood with hopes and fantasies about the exciting and opulent adult life she would lead. Shop windows had always had a fascination for her as an embodiment of all her hopes.

Interestingly, the three other women in the group who had never shoplifted said that they too had a fascination with shopping with much the same invested hopes of gaining something they had never had. They talked of 'bargain hunting' as an emotional quest to fill whatever was missing in their emotional worlds.

Shopping and nurturing seemed entwined in their inner worlds. Shopping represented the way they expressed caring for others but also the arena in which they hoped to find maternal care for themselves. The shops, full of good and desirable objects, seem to represent their mothers' bodies. Thus when invested with hope of needs being filled the shops were objects of libidinal attention. But when the primary experience had been of disappointment, rage, or envious attack then there was a danger that shopping could trigger a primitive desire to steal from mother. In some women this was transformed into bargain hunting but in Anne the sudden realization that shops took from you as much as they gave back was a 'keyhole' experience that unlocked her early rage at and envy of mother. Her description of her one attempt at shoplifting in which she had managed to drop and break three out of the four bottles of olive oil stolen sounded much more like an envious attack on her mother's breast than a larceny.

The other 'trigger' moment for women who shoplift seems to come from a sudden bringing to consciousness of their fury at the sociologically and self-imposed role perfection. This may be triggered by a family crisis, often in the form of a husband or child being ungrateful for the nurturing that the woman has provided. The woman experiences this as an overwhelming assault on her meaning in life and almost as if in a fugue state precipitated by an overwhelming wave of rage shoplifts.

Mary had a history of shoplifting at moments of family crisis but had not disclosed this either to her GP or myself during her referral and assessment for psychotherapy. She sought help for her intermittent depression which had lasted since the birth of her first child twelve years previously.

In the early stages of therapy her hostility to any expression of empathy was demonstrated and she would dismiss my attempts with a cold sneer. I felt like an inadequate therapist to her and could see that this paralleled Mary's experience of a mother she perceived as inadequate. Mary made several attempts to have me join in with her denigration of this mother even though her mothering sounded ordinary and good enough. When I was non-committal and instead focused on Mary's need to perceive her mother's inadequacies the session became frozen by Mary's mute rage.

The next session was also suffused in cold hostility for twenty minutes until Mary gave a beatific smile and said, with obvious pleasure, that she had been caught shoplifting. I am sure that I felt the same sense of shock that her family had experienced at this news. She related that her husband had told her that he felt physically 'hit' by her arrest, and I had a similar physiological sense of attack. Mary maintained a smiling indifference to these reactions which was completely at odds with the devoted mother and wife she had always portrayed.

The work of the following six months of therapy was to understand the act of shoplifting and to place it in the context of her family life and her therapy. At one point, in an expression of anger and frustration with me, she said of her shoplifting 'I wanted you to know that you had failed completely with me'. When I restated this as my having failed her, Mary came close to tears. Mary had generalized her envy of and contempt for her mother into all relationships with women and all aspects of potential nurturing from her husband or children. Thus the care she yearned for was denigrated and therefore distanced or destroyed.

In the same week that I had commented on the intensity of Mary's need to denigrate mother (and all mothering) her husband had suggested that she return to part-time work and be less involved with the housework and working to relieve her depression. Mary experienced both of these events as an attack on her basic assumptions about being the omnipotently capable mother in the face of everyone else's failed capacity to mother.

She had entered her local supermarket conscious that she was very angry although not certain at whom that rage was directed. She stood under a security camera and proceeded to place items in her bag rather than the trolley in what she later described as a form of 'triumphant revenge for the failures of the whole world'. She expressed surprise that she had been caught, arrested and charged. She had believed that the security men observing her 'would understand' the heroic nature of her actions.

What is evident in all psychological work with women who shoplift is the desperateness that arises from the inherent instability of the massive discrepancy between their inner world experiences and their external world façade. Such a discrepancy is bound to leave the woman vulnerable to disappointment in self and others and subsequent exposure and disappointment of others with self. This is acted out in therapy and can become rapidly anti-therapeutic if not understood and confronted. As the psychological façade is so in line with social expectations it is reinforced and encouraged in all arenas of the women's life. Unlike women who know that their own external image is as much a façade as the advertising of expectations that mirror it back to them, women who shoplift seem unaware of their inner hostility and destructiveness, and their denial of it is often strong enough to survive arrest, exposure and humiliation. Important others will join in that denial because the women's nurturing facade is useful to the family and society more generally.

The extent of the underlying psychopathology becomes clear in the therapeutic alliance, an alliance that is difficult to achieve in the face of the woman's hostility to and contemptuous envy of nurture and empathy. Yet the need these women have for that nurture and empathy is the time-bomb that ticks away, awaiting a trigger moment of massive disappointment or rage at confrontation of basic assumptions. Of course shops know that they play to their customers' hopes and fantasies for fulfilment, and advertising is rooted in that concept. People who had never shoplifted in the mixed outpatient group shared many of the emotions about shopping, its libidinal fascination and the potential for both disappointment and provoking a need to steal (expressed more healthily between clients and shops by 'bargains' and 'sales').

The shoplifters were isolated and lonely because of their need to denigrate any form of help, support or love. Their façades of omnipotent perfect mother and wife were constructions based in the denigration of all others rather than a strong esteem for self. This makes them vulnerable façades to hide the desperate emptiness within. In at least two of the cases discussed there were moments when I feared that suicide was an active thought, although this was always denied. There must be a possibility of the false self turning and discovering that there is no true self to protect with such women. I think this is why it is so important to work through the anti-therapeutic phase of therapy as soon as possible and establish some form of alliance if allowed. Even experienced therapists may need supervision to contend with the powerful counter-transference issues involved in this work.

31

A Delinquent
in the Therapeutic Community
Actions Speak Louder than Words

Gill McGauley

INTRODUCTION

Clinical vignette

Mr A has endured a childhood and adolescence characterized by neglect and deprivation. The legacy of his inadequate parenting and prolonged institutionalism, during his several foster home placements, is that he is distrustful and suspicious of anyone he perceives to be in a position of authority. This view of others means that he finds it extremely difficult to accept and benefit from help as evidenced by the long string of failed therapeutic interventions.

In my examination of Mr A, I could find no evidence of formal psychiatric illness. His antisocial and delinquent behaviour, the roots of which can be traced back to early adolescence, are symptoms of a severe personality disorder of both an anti-social and borderline type, using DSM-IV criteria.

The absence of formal psychiatric illness does not mean that this young man is not in need of help. Unfortunately, up to now he has not responded to treatment. Indeed, therapeutic interventions can be linked chronologically to subsequent escalations in his offending behaviour.

In the light of his previously failed probation orders, some of which have included conditions of treatment, it is unlikely that he would adhere to a new order; however, this remains an option open to the court. Sadly, I have no recommendations to assist the court in sentencing this man.

The above fictitious court report opinion and recommendations is one that is only too familiar to professionals involved in the care of young men whose disordered personalities lead them to offend and to their subsequent involvement with the criminal justice system. Repeated treatment failures can quickly lead to therapeutic despair in the minds of their carers. However, such failures are not altogether unpredictable when the background and style of relating of these patients is considered. Often such patients unconsciously provoke individuals and systems to behave towards them in a punitive, authoritarian way. This style of interaction frequently becomes fixed in a frustrating and repetitive cycle of sado-masochistic relating.

TREATMENT IN A THERAPEUTIC COMMUNITY

The above recommendation does not consider how Mr A might respond in a therapeutic community. In the following case study this treatment option has been provided for Mr A, his progress is charted through a particular therapeutic community, Henderson Hospital, which specializes in treating young adults with personality disorder. Henderson operates as a democratic-analytic therapeutic community, using both group analytic psychotherapy and socio-therapy as the backbone of its treatment (Norton 1992).

Readers are referred to the following references for a full account of the historical development of therapeutic communities in Britain (Kennard 1983 and 1988; McGauley 1996). Although individual therapeutic communities vary in their entry criteria, treatment programmes, community structure and rules, democratic-analytic style communities are united in sharing the following common principles.

(1) They aim to help the individual take responsibility for his or her difficulties, their role in maintaining or perpetuating these and their effect on the patient's relationships. These aims are fostered by patients becoming involved in understanding the meaning of their symptoms and in helping one another 'as a community'. Within such communities, professionals are less hierarchical and patients are often referred to as 'residents' to denote their active involvement in the running of the community.

(2) They aim to achieve a 'culture of enquiry' (Main 1983) where the *meaning* of an individual's feelings, actions and relationships with others (residents and staff) is examined.

Entry and Early Months in the Community – Challenging Times

There was scant information in Andy's (Mr A) referral letter. His mother died when he was eleven and he blamed the medical profession for not diagnosing and treating her cancer more effectively. He endured his step-father's drunken physical attacks on him for two years before he ran away to live on the streets. He spent the rest of his adolescence in and out of child care institutions. His forensic history began when he was aged thirteen and by the time he was referred he had collected a long string of offences relating to stealing, shoplifting, damaging property and, latterly, breaking and entering. He was referred to psychiatric services because of his increasing alcohol and drug misuse and a previous overdose. He had no contact with his family; the only relationship he sustained was with a probation officer.

Potential residents are chosen on the basis of a group selection interview where residents outnumber staff so that they have the major say in who is admitted, an example of 'democratization' (Rapoport 1960). One of the medical staff in the group knew Andy from a previous psychiatric assessment, during which the doctor remembered feeling ridiculed and humiliated as he could not answer the questions Andy provocatively threw at him. He recalled writing a terse letter discharging him back to his referrer. On the occasion of the selection group it was noted that:

> Andy was a thin, pale young man who came wearing a t-shirt and jeans, although it was winter. He shivered and stared at the floor, hiding behind his lank hair for the first part of the group. The doctor was surprised that he did not 'rubbish' the community or shout and swear but struggled to respond to the residents' questions. Andy was accepted and moved in right away. The doctor that had previously met him wondered if Andy had felt less compelled to re-enact his adversarial style of relating to authority figures in a group where residents outnumbered staff.

The community quickly saw evidence of Andy's poor impulse control and low frustration tolerance. These were most visible when his unrealistic expectations were not met and he was overwhelmed with feelings of rage, which he then vented on the fabric of the community. The following episode was frequently re-enacted, in various guises.

> Residents and staff had explained to Andy that his social benefit would take at least three weeks to arrive. He would then receive all the back pay owed to him but, in the meantime, he could arrange for a loan from community funds.
> On his second day, when his benefit cheque had not arrived, Andy stormed out of the community meeting and hurled a large plant pot through

a glass window. By damaging property he had broken one of the main rules of the community and had automatically discharged himself, but could ask the community for reinstatement.

One of the most difficult tasks in treating severely personality disordered 'delinquent' individuals is engaging them in treatment and then maintaining the fragile treatment alliance, which is repeatedly tested by destructive, acting-out behaviour.

Norton and Dolan (Norton and Dolan 1995) emphasized that the type of response 'chosen' by an institution to such an incident is crucial as to whether the treatment alliance is repaired or irreversibly damaged. More traditional psychiatric institutions often aim to contain such behaviour by the use of drugs, close observation, seclusion or moving the patient to another institution. At Henderson, staff and residents struggle to try and understand and explore the less conscious motives underpinning such behaviour. The response to Andy's violence was the convening, by the three senior residents, of an emergency meeting, attended by all staff and residents. Andy was expected to give an account of his actions; their antecedents and consequences were discussed and the community voted him back in.

Middle Months – Therapeutic Impasse

As a resident settles in, there is an expectation that they will participate fully in community life, engaging in the wide range of groups offered and taking on household tasks, such as cooking and cleaning, essential for the running of the community. Furthermore, if an established resident breaks the rules, the community listens for evidence that he has learnt from his experience and is committed to future change. His account of his actions should contain an increasing awareness of his emotional state of mind and realization of the effect of his behaviour on others.

These were markedly absent in Andy's accounts. Although he sat hunched in the corner of meetings and said nothing, everyone was acutely aware of his presence and expected an explosive outburst. He would restlessly fidget, tying and untying his shoelaces. When the community talked to him about his feelings or behaviour, he would clasp his hands over his ears and shout that they were giving him a headache or drown any discussion by swearing and storming out.

He would not participate in any community tasks and the only contributions Andy made to community life were ones that he accomplished alone. His only tenuous niche seemed to be in the 'gardening and maintenance' work group, where he would labour away from the rest of the group, furiously digging a piece of ground in a haphazard way.

There was increasing discussion about Andy in staff supervision groups. The therapists in his three times a week psychotherapy group described that being in a small room with him felt like sitting near an unexploded bomb. When the female therapist pressed Andy to participate in the group, he leapt up and loomed over her. She felt frightened that he was about to punch her in the face.

Intellectually, staff knew that Andy's internal world was a harsh and cruel place which he often externalized so that staff and. residents became the persecutors responsible for his headaches and other problems. These projections, if unthinkingly responded to, would result in the community relating to him in a punitive, sadistic way. Andy's unconscious request for a relationship with the community, founded on a sado-masochistic dynamic, would be fulfilled. His style of relating to the community was at risk of becoming fixed in a cycle where he and the community oscillated between the positions of victim and perpetrator.

Staff also thought that these unconscious defensive strategies protected him from profound feelings of unworthiness. He also projected these into the community, which then became useless and 'rubbish', freeing him to take an aloof, contemptuous position in relation to the rest of the community, further invoking their anger.

This understanding resided mainly in the minds of the staff, and did not seem to help them modify their intense emotional response to Andy, which varied from wishing to eject him sadistically from the community to contemptuously ignoring him.

The therapeutic challenge was how to open a dialogue with Andy, based on empathic understanding as opposed to identifying with his projections and acting on the reactive counter-transference feelings they produced.

Closing Months – Actions Speak Louder than Words

Most of the resident group opted for a quiet life in their dealings with Andy so that he became more and more marginalized. The gardening and maintenance group seemed the only place where his membership was valued and Andy felt he belonged. Staff noticed that he often volunteered for the unsavoury tasks such as repairing the drains or clearing the garden of rubbish. He had also formed a tentative friendship with Pauline, an older female resident in the group.

One afternoon, Andy was clearing away the rubbish which had piled up because of a refuse collection strike and was beginning to smell. Pauline went to help and passed him a bag which, unbeknowns to her, had burst. The rotting, liquid contents spilt over Andy's jeans. Andy exploded at her, saying it was her fault, within earshot of a group of senior residents, who agreed that his demeanour was aggressive and threatening. An emergency meeting followed, at which the community expressed their increasing intolerance of his behaviour. Andy was put on a 'treatability vote' which meant he must attend and participate in all his groups for the next three days while everyone considered whether he was able to benefit from being a community member. The next morning, Andy was absent from the community meeting. People called for his vote to be held early as he was obviously not interested in staying. Pauline protested, saying that was altering the rules and that Andy should be given a chance to explain his absence. She volunteered to see if he would come down.

Five minutes later, a sullen looking Andy appeared and staff and residents could not resist interupting the agenda of the meeting to ask him to explain his lateness. Their enquiries were met with silence. Pauline broke the impasse, saying that she felt partly responsible for the situation and, if Andy would not speak, she would. She said she had found him in tears. Andy took over and hesitantly explained that he had washed his jeans the previous night, leaving them to dry in the laundry room, but this morning they were missing. He had only one pair of trousers, no pyjamas and no dressing gown. He felt too ashamed to come to the meeting. He went on to ask if he could use a jumper that had lain unclaimed for weeks in the laundry room as he had no warm clothes to face the winter. The community agreed, no more was said and the meeting continued in a subdued atmosphere.

The next day was Andy's birthday. At the morning meeting the residents gave him a birthday card and a pair of jeans, an expensive present for people living on a few pounds a week. One resident said that he wished Andy could have had them two days previously when he most needed them. Andy smiled and said that he had only ever received one birthday card which was from his mother before she died.

The residents had been able to tolerate Andy's delinquent behaviour and had emotionally understood something of his projected feelings of unworthiness and abandonment which fuelled his rage. They had responded by an empathic action at a level of attunement that he could accept.

Residents can stay up to a year in the community. Andy remained for eight months, an average length stay. Although in the above interaction he was able to accept help, he more often provoked a punitive response from the community.

He left hurriedly after the community persisted in their attempts to help him face and take responsibility for his actions and style of relating. During Andy's stay, Henderson did not have a follow-up system so the community heard informally that he had found a hostel placement. In general, people felt that his precipitous departure did not bode well in spite of the sporadic progress he had made.

CONCLUSION

A therapeutic community placement can be overlooked as a treatment option for people like Andy, who are sometimes labelled as 'delinquent'.

Violent, disturbed behaviour can often be contained by the community's culture and its 'choice' of response to such incidents. De-emphasizing staff hierarchy in favour of a deliberately structured resident hierarchy helps to engage residents who are distrustful of traditional authority. Their defensive style of lashing out at an authoritarian system is challenged when they find themselves hitting out at fellow residents, who occupy the senior positions. A healthy culture, where both residents and staff examine the meaning of an individual's actions and feelings, reduces the likelihood of a sado-masochistic style of relating establishing itself.

Like Andy, many residents have difficulty in thinking about and verbalizing their feelings, so they find traditional psychotherapy groups difficult. The structure of the programme, where work groups and creative therapy groups lie side by side with more formal psychotherapy groups affords a range of therapeutic arenas where, through their actions, residents express some aspects of their internal world. In Andy's case the community provided an opportunity for him to take the first tentative steps in developing and testing out a different style of relating.

32

Working on the Borderline
Can We Continue to Turn a Blind Eye?

Felicity de Zulueta

In the struggle to help a group of five individuals (in a therapeutic group) described as suffering from a 'borderline personality disorder', I discover how hard such a task is. What these three women and two men share is a history of violent abuse, be it physical, sexual or emotional. Their recent past lives testify to the pain they endured as children. Lydia, Anne and Rita spent their early adulthood being battered by the men they lived with, reliving and repeating what they had lived through in childhood. As for Peter, he was to rediscover the unbearable pain of not 'being' when his wife died. Patrick sought refuge from rejection and sexual abuse in total anonymity.

These five patients and two others who dropped out early in treatment were on our waiting list until such time as a suitably skilled therapist could be found to treat them, or a bed became available in the local therapeutic community. As both options became less and less likely, we decided to offer these men and women a therapeutic programme which would involve both weekly individual psychoanalytic psychotherapy and group therapy for a minimum period of three years. Funding had to be obtained to pay for the different individual therapists, the group therapist and the co-ordinator of the team who would supervise the therapists and liaise with the patients' psychiatric teams. The local health authority agreed to pay for the three year treatment programme which has now been running for over a year.

I shall focus here on the structure which has gradually been set up in order to protect the children of these individuals. It is known that, during therapy, patients who have suffered childhood traumas can recall, feel, relive and, at times, re-enact the violence of their past (Zulueta 1993). Four of these patients have small children to look after. Peter is a single father looking after a four-year-old daughter. Anne is also a single parent with a young daughter; her three older children ended up in care because they were seen to be at risk of violence at the time when Anne lived with her partner. Lydia is married with two young boys to bring up. Rita is also married with a nine-year-old son.

Some people may wonder why we worry about these children who are not directly our patients. Why do we fear for them when we are providing their parents with the possibility of being able to overcome their past and live less destructive lives?

The simple answer is that our patients suffer from the long-term effects of psychological trauma endured in childhood. Lindemann (1944) defines these as a 'sudden, uncontrollable disruption of the affiliative bonds' with all that this implies in terms of disrupted attachments and violent feelings (Zulueta 1993, p.294). We now know that children do suffer from psychological trauma, much as adults do, with the additional complication that it happens during emotional, intellectual and physical development. Like adults who have been traumatized, children tend to relive their past or try to to cut themselves off from these terrifying memories through denial, dissociation, projective identi-fication or by attempting to 'medicate' their pain through addictive patterns of behaviour including self damage, drugs, alcohol and perhaps most important here, through the re-enactment of their abusive experience but, this time, in identification with their abuser. It is this last defensive and often perverse manoeuvre which can cause us the most concern, not only for our patients but also for their children.

As co-ordinator of the project, I feel I have to bear these children in mind whilst I attempt to offer their parents the opportunity to change and, one hopes, end their cycle of abuse. Such a venture is ambitious and does not work overnight. In the attempt to come to grips with with what has been done to them, Rita, Anne, Lydia and Peter can be so aroused by what they feel that the likelihood of their recreating what they went through at home cannot be ignored.

With these concerns in mind, I aimed to set up a web of mental health workers to attend to these families when in need. All the patients have been allocated a psychiatrist from whom they can obtain medication or support when their therapists are on leave or unavailable. Only Anne and Lydia use this facility.

When Anne joined us she already had mental health workers involved with her to help with her daughter. This was essential for Anne who had already lost the care of her three older children because of the violence she and her husband exposed them to. Anne subsequently decided to leave him and mother her little one alone with the help of the psychiatric services. Whilst she was herself subjected to severe deprivation and horrendous physical abuse as well as sexual abuse as a child, Anne believes she can avoid doing what her mother

did to her by giving her daughter all she needs materially and never disciplin-
ing her. However, we know without going into any details that her child often
witnessed the effects of her mother's violent past. She began to behave
aggressively at school and this led to both her and her mother being provided
with professional help outside the confines of our therapeutic programme.

As for Lydia and her three children, two sons and a daughter, we were less
concerned because she has a caring husband who supports her. However, this
fragile set up nearly collapsed when he was threatened with imprisonment for
an offence which did not involve his family. Lydia sought help from us which
we gave in the form of a report for the Court outlining the needs of the family
and the dangers the children would face if left with a distraught and potentially
violent or rejecting mother. Her husband was finally not convicted, and Lydia
had to face the pain of realizing just how much she needed us all, a realization
she tried very hard to avoid by putting herself in danger and almost enjoying
the excitement it gave her. For Lydia to admit to her needs meant facing the
terror of being abandoned and abused yet again, an outcome which seemed
quite likely when, faced with the loss of her partner, she began to court the
idea of meeting with her violent ex-partner.

Peter began to cause us some alarm when he spoke to his therapist of how,
at times, he could not respond to his two-year-old daughter, forgetting to feed
her and going to his bed for days at a time, in the grip of disturbing psychotic
experiences. He was given the opportunity to meet the project co-ordinator to
discuss whether he wanted assistance in the form of medication and help with
his daughter who was perhaps being exposed to the same absent parent as he
had. He could acknowledge that our fears were valid but refused professional
help saying that he preferred to make greater use of a person he knew who is
willing to take his daughter on for days at a time if necessary when he feels
unable to parent. We continue to feel concerned about this arrangement but as
he is beginning to voice his own worries about his daughter in therapy, we,
rightly or wrongly, hold onto our anxieties.

Rita is quite open about her fears of hurting her children and often shares
her worries and educational concerns in the group, where she is either given
support or, at times, criticized. She recently informed us that the school staff
are concerned about her son getting into trouble at school because he was
isolating himself and seeing the nurse for physical complaints which appeared
to have no cause. We heard that a medical visit has been arranged. All the
therapists felt concerned about what might be going on in this family but, in
view of the fact that other professionals have been alerted and that our patient
was sharing this with us, we decided not to intervene for the time being. The
need for some form of intervention may arise in the future but we would have
to begin by consulting with Rita.

Clearly, such a set up is far from ideal. When we began this project, we only had our five patients in mind. It is only as we learnt more about them and their families that we could no longer blind ourselves to the reverberations that their pain and violence could be having on their children. The latter are totally dependent on their parents and we now know through recent research in attachment just how much psychological damage traumatized parents can inflict on their children (Main and Hesse 1992). However, short of admitting these families during treatment, which can still be done in the Cassel Hospital with very severely damaged families, what can therapists like ourselves do when working with traumatized individuals? What I have attempted to describe is how we have tried to create a therapeutic system which has some holding function for both our patients, their families and, perhaps equally important, for the therapists in the programme.

CONCLUSION

Perhaps by attempting to respond concretely to our anxieties about our patients' children, I am still dodging the issue that I feel needs to be addressed in the treatment of patients with early experiences of severe trauma who present with the symptoms of a borderline personality disorder. The therapists in this programme have nearly all been psychoanalytically trained and have worked mainly in private settings. A comforting aspect of the psychoanalytic approach is the tendency to believe that the patient's psychopathology is located within the individual. By focusing on his or her patient's internal world the psycho-analytic psychotherapist can usually feel that she is fulfilling her obligation. However, with this particular group of patients few therapists feel satisfied with what they are doing. Such feelings are almost the *sine qua non* of the task. Indeed, there is little doubt that the psychoanalytic treatment of this particular group of patients is particularly difficult. Endless papers have been written on the destructive potential of 'borderline patients' which is often attributed to the manifestation of some innate aggressive drive. The trouble with such an approach is two-fold. On the one hand, it confirms these individuals' most deeply held belief in their own badness, a belief which in Fairbairn's (1952) view is a defence against the terrible realization that those who rejected and abused them were usually the very people on whom they totally depended and yet whose love was unavailable to them. And, furthermore, recent evidence also highlights how, in feeling to blame for their abuse, these survivors are also voicing what their abusers made them believe. Kernberg's (1984) apt descrip-tion of the borderline patient's 'sadistic attacker' could be understood as the manifestation of this internalized abuser, an internalization which is bolstered by the defensive need to preserve the hope of a better world. In a nutshell, to collude with these patients' belief in their inherent badness could be seen as reinforcing both their moral defence, as Fairbairn called it, and their identification with their abuser, and thereby prolonging their treatment.

In my experience, when working with those who have a past history of abuse or severe early loss, it is increasingly difficult to justify an old fashioned psychoanalytic approach in the face of new findings in the field of attachment and psychological trauma. Again and again, individuals with a history of such trauma describe to me how certain experiences keep on plunging them back into states of terror and destructive rage over which they have little or no control. This often happens without their realizing at the time that it is taking place. It comes as no surprise to discover that these states can be triggered off both out of therapy and within therapy, either through memories or through interactive experiences with the therapist or other group members. The group analyst in our therapeutic programme has learnt to modify his approach in order to limit and contain such flashbacks or attempts at victimization or abuse. Some of the individual therapists are beginning to see the need for similar modifications in their treatment. An understanding of how past memories involving smells, sounds, behaviours and feelings can act as triggers to past unresolved experiences of trauma and abuse can be helpful for both patients and therapists in making sense of what happens in and between sessions. It is through this understanding that we have come to realize how similar processes can take place in the patient's home, particularly when the individual is in a state of high arousal as a result of therapy. Linking past with present and undoing defences used to protect the survivor in the here and now can make the therapeutic task a very frightening one for patients both within and outside the therapeutic structure of the group. To deprive ourselves and our patients of some understanding of what they may be struggling with in terms of the past traumatic experiences and its physiological and cognitive effects can leave us all groping in the dark. Trying to make sense of the horrifying manifestations of our patients' violence, we can cling, as they do, to the prevailing view that what we are witnessing are the manifestations of their intrinsically evil nature and not, as I see it, the psychobiological manifestations of our patients' wounded attachment system.

PART III

Society, Law and Psychiatry

33

The Court, the Lawyer, the Psychiatrist and the Legal System

Debbie Taylor

INTRODUCTION

It is common knowledge among criminal lawyers that most defendants would, if they could, prefer to be represented by Horace Rumpole. Not only because the tense court room drama (including of course a show of healthy contempt for the trial judge) is followed by the assured acquittal, but because (usually) *en route* Rumpole dismembers, limb by limb, the testimony of the pompous expert witness. His ability to expose the professional fraud to public humiliation is unsurpassed. Whilst criminal lawyers may not go so far as to admit to wanting to be Rumpole, most would confess to wanting his legendary forensic skill.

A psychiatrist giving evidence in court proceedings will usually do so as an expert witness. An expert witness has the right to give opinion evidence about matters within the area of expertise, as well as evidence of facts. The right to give opinion evidence distinguishes the expert witness from any other witness called, who may only give evidence about facts. By virtue of the clientele, the psychiatrist may appear before any level of court from Magistrate's Court to Court of Appeal, as well as before tribunals, panels and committees of enquiry.

With the exception of when appearing before a Magistrate's Court comprised entirely of a lay bench (i.e. no legal member), the psychiatrist called to give oral evidence will inevitably be questioned by a lawyer, probably more than one and including the judge. In our jurisdiction the legal professional is divided into two branches: barristers and solicitors, with 'lawyer' being the generic term for both. Students spend a minimum of four years studying law before taking either the 'solicitor's finals' or the 'bar exams', depending upon the branch of the profession in which they want to practice. A further period of practical apprenticeship with experienced practitioners, called 'articles' for solicitors and 'pupillage' for barristers, must be spent by both before either the newly qualified solicitor or barrister is considered ready to be unleashed on an unsuspecting public.

Each branch of the profession has a different job to do. The solicitor sees the client and any witnesses from whom statements need to be taken and bears the responsibility of ensuring that all the material relevant to the proper representation of the client has been gathered. The barrister will analyze the material the solicitor sends him ('the brief') and present the client's case to the court. A good barrister is a persuasive advocate with a sound knowledge of the relevant facts and law in the particular case. With increasing frequency he will specialize in a particular area of law and not pretend to know anything outside it. He may be instructed because of his expertise or reputation or both. The tasks of the solicitor and barrister are complementary, a comparison frequently being drawn between the roles of general practitioner and specialist. The division of labour between the two branches of the legal profession as described above applies in general terms; however, there is some overlap between the two as some solicitors also act as advocates, particularly in the Magistrate's Courts and in cases concerning children, and some barristers spend most of their time doing written work and rarely appear in court.

In general, solicitors practice in firms and may be in partnership with other solicitors or employees of the firm. They may be employed in the legal department of a company or branch of government. A firm of solicitors is directly accessible to the public.

In contrast, barristers are all self-employed and, with the exception of rules permitting direct access by other professions such as accountants and architects, may only be consulted directly by the lay client when accompanied by the professional client, the solicitor. Barristers practice in groups called sets of chambers, known by their street address ('3 Equity Court') or the name of the incumbent head of chambers ('the Chambers of Guthrie Featherstone QC'). Most barristers in England and Wales practice in sets of chambers located in and around the four Inns of Court near the Royal Courts of Justice in London, with smaller groups practising in many of the larger cities throughout the country. The most able and experienced members of the Bar become Queen's Counsel, and are recognized by the initials 'QC' after their name. The terms 'leader', 'silk' and 'QC' are all used to describe Queen's Counsel.

Neither branch of the profession likes to be mistaken for the other. At a very basic level the difference may seem to be simply the mode of dress; for example, wigs and gowns are the prerogative of the Bar.

The psychiatrist as expert witness in court will be wise to remember his audience. The judge was once a practising lawyer whose ability and integrity have seen him rewarded with judicial office. An appointment may be a blessing and a burden: the honour, responsibility and challenge afforded any judge must often be weighed against the substantial loss in income a successful practitioner will incur on accepting an 'appointment to the Bench'. His relationship with his former colleagues will also change, judges being known to mourn the loss of their former life as elevation demands a distance be maintained between Bench and the legal profession. The judge will of necessity form an impression of the expert's character and personality, as well as his professed expertise. A psychiatrist should be aware that his appearance and demeanour in court may have a direct bearing upon the effectiveness of his evidence.

The legal profession is inherently conservative. Most judges were practising barristers before their appointments. Less often they were solicitors in private practice or women. Many are products of Oxbridge, and the major public schools before that. A judge's seniority may be gleaned from his attire (a Circuit Judge wears purple, a High Court Judge wears red; the more ermine and gold the more senior the judge) and the mode by which he is addressed. Magistrates, whether legally qualified (stipendiary) or not (lay), and District Judges should be addressed as 'Sir', 'Ma'am' or 'Madam' ('Your Worship' is a term favoured by television producers and police officers, but not by lawyers.) Circuit judges and recorders (part-time appointments of practising lawyers) sitting in the County Courts hearing civil cases should be addressed as 'Your Honour'. Crown Court judges should be addressed as 'Your Honour' unless sitting at the Central Criminal Court (Old Bailey) in London when, by tradition, they are addressed as 'My Lord/Lady'. A High Court judge is always addressed as 'My Lord/Lady' or 'Your Lordship/Ladyship', even when sitting in the Crown Court in cases of major importance.

The vital role of psychiatric evidence in court proceedings has long been recognized by the legal profession and the judiciary. In recent years demands by the legal profession upon the time and skill of what in reality is a small pool of expertise has placed considerable pressure upon the medical profession. Judges regard experts as essential resources too invaluable to be the subject of profligate use. Lawyers tend to be less restrained. In a series of reported cases, judges have endeavoured to provide the legal profession with clear guidance on the preparation of reports and the giving of evidence by expert witnesses in cases concerning the welfare of children. Wall J has emphasized the non-adversarial nature of children's proceedings and stressed the vital importance of expert evidence in assisting judges to reach the right solutions.[1]

Best practice now dictates that lawyers apply their minds at an early stage of the proceedings to the issues in the cases to which medical evidence will be

---

1   Re M (Minors) (Care Proceedings) (Child's Wishes) [1994] 1 FLR 749.

relevant. Lawyers are encouraged to make applications for leave to instruct an expert or experts at as early a stage as is possible.

In Re R (A Minor) (Experts' Evidence) [1991] 1 FLR 291 Cazalet J refers to the need for the expert, once instructed, to express only opinions which they genuinely hold and which are not biased in favour of one particular party. The expert should not mislead by omissions. He should consider all the material facts in reaching his conclusions, and must not omit to consider the material facts which could detract from his concluded opinion. The expert's report should (1) provide a straightforward and not misleading opinion; (2) be objective and not omit factors which do not support their opinion; and (3) be properly researched. If an opinion is based upon insufficient data because that data is unavailable, the expert should say so and indicate that his opinion is only provisional for this reason.

CIVIL LAW

In England and Wales the civil jurisdiction is exercised mainly by the High Court and the County Court. There are about 270 County Courts serving surrounding districts whilst the High Court sits at the Royal Courts of Justice in London or at one of the 133 district registries across the country. The vast majority of civil cases requiring evidence from those working in the field of forensic psychiatry concern either personal injury claims or children.

Personal injury claims are brought with the aim of receiving damages (money) to compensate for injury and/or loss caused by negligence. The plaintiff brings the case against the defendant(s) and commences proceedings in either the Queen's Bench Division of the High Court or the County Court depending on the nature and gravity of the claim and the sum he expects to receive. The claim must be commenced in the County Court where the plaintiff does not expect to recover more than £50,000.

In order to succeed a plaintiff must prove his case on a balance of probabilities. This is in contrast to the higher standard of proof required in criminal cases – proof beyond reasonable doubt. The plaintiff bears the burden of proving the case to the standard applied in all civil cases. Should he fail to persuade the court to the necessary standard, he will have failed to discharge the burden placed upon him and face the likelihood of paying the defendant's costs as well as his own. In civil cases, costs generally 'follow the event', which means that whoever loses pays the costs of the other party.

Proceedings in the civil courts not concerned with children are adversarial. Routine preparation of a personal injury case by any party, whether plaintiff or defendant, will involve the gathering of medical evidence essential for the desired outcome, if available. When an expert is first instructed he is usually asked to produce a written opinion in the form of a report. Any report made for the purposes of pending or contemplated litigation is privileged and does not have to be disclosed to the other side unless it is going to be adduced at trial. Either side is able to seek the most favourable opinion without disclosing damaging reports to the other side. It is not a procedure designed to establish the truth. Generally expert evidence is only admissible at trial where the court has given permission for it to be filed. The court will usually direct that the substance of the expert reports be mutually disclosed in a written report. A direction is often given for the exchange of lists of any published or unpublished material likely to be relied upon in reaching an opinion. This material may be produced during the course of the expert witness's testimony.

If the case cannot be resolved without a contested hearing the expert will be called to give oral evidence at the trial unless the substance of his written report is accepted unreservedly. He may be asked to listen to the testimony of other witnesses, both before and after giving evidence himself.

If called to give oral evidence the expert will go into the witness box and take the oath or affirmation. He will be called by counsel (the barrister) for the party instructing him, who may ask him non-leading questions in examination-in-chief. He will be asked questions about his qualifications and experience. His report, which the judge will have read, is almost always put in evidence at the beginning of examination-in-chief. The expert may be asked to explain, comment upon or up-date the report. The rest of examination-in-chief will generally be spent dealing with the other expert's report, focusing on matters of dispute, and providing an opportunity to clarify and expand on the report. The expert will then be tendered for cross-examination by counsel for the other party.

The purpose of cross-examination is to cast doubt on an expert's opinion. The manner in which this is done if at all will depend on the skill of the advocate. The approach may be by way of a wolf in sheep's clothing that elicits extra, useful facts that put in question the factual material upon which the opinion is based. This is often followed by questions designed to maximize the expert's discomfort before a lifeline is thrown in the form of a question such as 'of course, doctor, had you known about the patient's drug abuse, would you have come to the same conclusion?' – that enables the expert to retract his opinion and save face. Or, the approach may resemble the slash and burn method of farming in the course of which sight is lost of the fact that it is the evidence, and not the witness personally, that needs to be discredited.

If the facts in the case are not in issue, counsel will try to place a different interpretation upon them by challenging the expert's reasoning, methods and experience. Questions put to an expert will tend to be 'closed' questions requiring specific answers which enable counsel to control the direction of cross-examination. Leading questions (that suggest the answer) may be asked and counsel will generally take the opportunity to re-state his own expert's opinion. Counsel will attempt to undermine an opinion by establishing that a particular field of expertise cannot provide a definitive answer. Hypothetical facts will often be put to an expert to test an opinion.

An expert is not an advocate and his opinion on matters within his expertise should be independent and unbiased. However, courts are more than familiar with degrees of objectivity and expert witnesses who are not always as unbiased as their role would suggest.

FAMILY LAW

Where the court is concerned with the interests of children and family law an inquisitorial approach is taken by the judge, whose duty requires him to consider all matters relevant to the decision he has to make. In most cases concerning children the welfare of the child is paramount and all information relevant to the issues to be determined must be disclosed by the parties to the proceedings. An adverse medical report about the mental health of a parent, for example, must be disclosed.

There are three levels of court where a family law case may be heard:

(1)   the High Court

(2)   the County Court

(3)   the Magistrate's Court and the Family Proceedings Court.

The tribunal before whom the case is heard is determined by the nature and gravity of the case, the complexity of the issues and the likely length of hearing. Most cases in which expert evidence about a party's mental health is called will be heard by a High Court Judge of the Family Division, or a Circuit Judge in the County Court, or a District Judge at the Principal Registry of the Family Division at Somerset House in London.

Family law proceedings are divided into two types:

(1)   Public law

(2)   Private law

Public law proceedings are usually brought by a public body such as a local authority about matters of general public interest or concern. Private law proceedings are brought by individuals, usually against other members of the family, often as a result of the breakdown of relationships within the family, and may result in divorce. The proceedings are not mutually exclusive and in complex cases, often involving child protection issues, there is an overlap between the two, with public and private law proceedings being heard together. In both sets of proceedings parties apply to the court for an order to be made. The court considers the written and oral evidence and submissions made by counsel about the facts and law before deciding whether to make an order at all, and if so which order is best to make in the circumstances.

Before 1989 family law was found in a number of different and disjunctive pieces of legislation. Even the initiated found it disjointed and lacking in uniformity and consistency. The Children Act 1989 was described in the House of Commons during the debate prior to its enactment as 'the most comprehensive and far-reaching reform of this branch of the law ever introduced'. The Children Act 1989 went some way towards creating a 'family court' amongst the three levels of court. It abolished orders for 'custody' and 'access'. 'Residence' and 'contact' were the new terms. Under the Children Act the court must apply the same criteria in deciding what, if any, order to make.

In most proceedings relating to children, the child's welfare must be the paramount consideration. The court does take other factors into consideration but the final question is 'what is in the best interests of the child'. When deciding this question the court must apply what is commonly known as the 'welfare checklist'. It must have regard to the following,

- the wishes and feelings of the child, depending on how old they are and how much they understand
- the child's physical, emotional and educational needs
- the likely effect on the child of any change in circumstances
- the child's age, sex, background and other relevant circumstances
- any harm the child has suffered or is at risk of suffering
- how capable the parents or anyone else are of meeting the child's needs
- the powers available to the court.

The most common orders made under the Children Act in public law proceedings are orders placing a child in the care or under the supervision of the local authority. A court may only make a care order or supervision order if it is satisfied that the child concerned is suffering or is likely to suffer significant harm. The harm can be physical or emotional and must be attributable to the care given to the child by the parent(s) not being what it should be.

In private law proceedings commenced to resolve disputes between members of the same family the main orders are as follows:

(1) Residence order; this determines where the child lives

(2) Contact order; this requires the person with whom the child lives to allow the child to visit or stay with the person named in the order – usually the other parent or a grandparent, or a sibling

(3) Prohibits Steps order; this prevents someone doing something without the court's consent

(4)   Specific Issue order; the court determines a specific question that
      may have arisen, perhaps to do with medical treatment or religion.

CONCLUSION

It is not surprising that the doctor and lawyer may gaze at each other from
their respective corners of the court room with several degrees of suspicion.
Much may be born of ignorance of the other's discipline and training. More
may derive from fundamentally different approaches to the same problem. The
only common ground may be the patient, for whom each wants something
different.

34

The Adversarial Process
Trial by Ordeal?

Penelope Barrett

It may be that the functions of forensic psychotherapy are irrevocably at odds with a trial process based on confrontation and conflict. If the aims of forensic psychotherapy are to understand and treat, the aims of the prosecution and trial processes are clearly not the same. Even if they purported to fulfil such aims in part, in spite of carefully drafted guidelines and rules, they fail. The *Code For Crown Prosecutors*[1] emphasizes that Crown Prosecutors must be 'fair, independent and objective... They must not be affected by improper or undue pressure from any source'. These may be admirable sentiments, but I suggest that they are meaningless in view of the political considerations and media attention which underpin the appearance of the mentally disordered offender before the courts. In my view it is nonsensical to suggest that the political profile and importance of the policy of Care In the Community or the baying of the press when a mentally disordered offender (MDO) commits a serious offence, have no repercussions for the prosecution and the sentencing of *all* mentally disordered offenders.

No social worker wants to be the person who recommends discharge of a patient to a Mental Health Review Tribunal if the patient immediately upon release commits a serious violent offence. No Prosecutor wants to drop the minor assault case against the mentally disordered man or woman who, perhaps unpredictably, then goes out and kills. No Judge wants to entrust the decision about when a violent mentally disordered offender is released from hospital to

---

1 Available from the Crown Prosecution Service Information Branch, 50 Ludgate Hill, London EC4M 7EX.

doctors, whose primary concern is seen as the welfare of the patient, when it is the Judge who takes the brunt of media attention if things go wrong. It is 'safer' to opt for a s.47 Restriction Order and leave the decision to the Home Secretary.

THE DECISION TO PROSECUTE

There are two stages to the decision to prosecute. The first stage is the *evidential test*. If the case does not pass this it must not go ahead, no matter how serious or important it may be. If a case does pass this test, Crown Prosecutors must decide if a prosecution is needed in the public interest. This second stage is the *public interest test*.

The Evidential Test

The evidential test requires the Crown Prosecutor to decide if there is enough evidence to provide a 'realistic prospect of conviction' against a defendant on each charge; that is, that the tribunal of fact (magistrates or jury) is more likely than not to convict. They must consider whether the evidence available is admissible and whether it is reliable. They will on the latter issue specifically consider whether it is likely that a confession is unreliable, 'for example because of the defendant's age, intelligence or lack of understanding'. There is in the passage quoted no specific reference to the MDO. Equally, s. 77 of the Police and Criminal Evidence Act 1984, which requires a Judge to give a warning to the jury of the special need for caution before convicting a mentally handicapped defendant by relying on his/her own confession to the crime of which he/she is accused, does not specifically include an accused who is mentally disordered. Rather it defines 'mentally handicapped' in sub-section 3 as being 'in a state of arrested or incomplete development of mind which includes significant impairment of intelligence and social functioning'.

The Public Interest Test

In the public interest test we might expect to find more protections for the MDO. Instead we are disappointed. It is stated that 'In cases of any seriousness a prosecution will usually take place unless there are public interest factors tending against a prosecution which clearly outweigh those tending in favour. Although there may be public interest factors against prosecution in a particular case, often the prosecution should go ahead and those factors should be put to the court for consideration when sentence is being passed.'

Common public interest factors in favour of prosecution include that a conviction is likely to result in a significant sentence, a weapon was used or violence was *threatened* (my emphasis) during the commission of the offence, the offence was committed against a person serving the public (for example a police or prison officer, or a nurse – psychiatrists and/or psychotherapists are not specified!), and that there are grounds for believing that the offence is likely to be continued or repeated, for example by a history of recurring conduct. I venture to suggest that many of these factors are heavily weighted against MDOs, or at least give those who make the decision to prosecute scope for operating under commonly held prejudices and ignorance about this group of offenders.

What then are the public interest factors against prosecution? They include that the court is likely to impose a small or nominal penalty, that the offence was committed as a result of a genuine mistake or misunderstanding, that the loss or harm can be described as minor, that the defendant is elderly or is, or was suffering from significant mental or physical ill health, unless the offence is so serious or there is a real possibility that it may be repeated.

How do these principles work in practice? As recently as April of 1996 an MDO who was of previous good character was prosecuted for 'theft by finding' of a stolen driving licence and birth certificate. Last year an 86-year-old man who was plainly suffering from dementia (evidence clearly supported by both prosecution and defence experts) was prosecuted for the most minor of indecent acts against a young relative. The evidence was that the child had recovered, was still devoted to the old man, and in any event the family had taken steps to avoid the man being alone in the company of the child. The old man did not make it to his trial. While awaiting a hearing on whether he was fit to plead he went missing and was found dead alone in his flat some days later. If such cases reflect the way in which the code is applied it seems to me that the code has failed.

THE TRIAL ITSELF

The adversarial system is not about the search for truth. Nor is it about the unfettered disclosure to the jury of information in order to assist them in reaching a proper decision. It is about contest. It mostly involves confrontation. A trial is not designed to understand the offender or the offence, only to see whether, within the framework of the burden of proof, blame can be placed and responsibility apportioned. Over the years convoluted principles of law and evidence evolved within the common law have been supplemented, amended or completely reframed by statute. Lawyers have tried to define and particularize concepts of knowledge, intention, recklessness and responsibility, in a way which allows them to determine whether a person should be found guilty for a criminal act or not. To psychotherapists the efforts of lawyers to answer the question of whether a defendant was responsible for his/her actions or not must seem at best pedestrian and at worst ludicrous. They are founded on our need to punish others and absolve ourselves of guilt – guilt for allowing inequality, discrimination, poverty and greed to subsist unchecked; guilt for society's inhumanity to its weaker members. If we condemn the criminals, we are not like them. Notions of intention and responsibility, self-defence and provocation as currently defined by the law are almost meaningless when dealing with the mentally disordered.

The primary tool utilized within the adversarial process is that of cross-examination. It is said that cross-examination is the crucible within which we pound out the truth. A notion exists and is nurtured that if we question someone sufficiently closely about his/her account of events the truth will emerge. But what truth? And will getting at the truth always bring justice? I think of an ex-client of mine who was tried on an assault case. It was alleged that she had bitten a police officer's nose. She claimed that she had acted to defend herself against excess force used in an unlawful arrest. The police evidence was in tatters at the end of the prosecution case and she would almost certainly have been acquitted if matters had been left there. But she insisted on giving evidence. Before she stepped into the witness box the jury were plainly on her side. Until she started sharing with them the real reason for the police assaulting her: which was that they were in league with the local authority and her neighbours in sending telepathic messages to drive her out of her home, and when this tactic failed they decided to use force. She was convicted. But it was her truth. And the evidence called for the prosecution had been highly unsatisfactory.

This case illustrates what in my view are important ways in which the MDO is ill-served by the trial process.

(1) Prejudice and Ignorance

A trial does not exist in a vacuum and cannot therefore protect a mentally disordered defendant against the manifest prejudice and ignorance allowed and in some quarters encouraged to flourish in society. Sadly, it seems to me that precious little effort is made within the confines of the adversarial process to dispel such prejudice and ignorance. Indeed, the lack of consideration often shown to MDOs at court helps to fuel such attitudes.

(2) Amelioration of Stress

If a mentally disordered offender wishes to give evidence there are no provisions to ameliorate the stresses of appearing in the witness box unless s/he can be brought within other provisions (the only statutory example I can find is if s/he is under 17 and giving evidence about certain offences of a violent or sexual nature, when s/he might be able to give evidence via video-link).

(3) Right to Silence

Most important, there is built into the Criminal Justice and Public Order Act 1994 an expectation that an offender will give replies when interviewed by the police and give evidence at trial. No longer is a defendant, even if mentally disordered, *entitled* to sit back and say nothing but have the jury told that they must not infer anything adverse from his/her silence. By sections 34–37 inclusive of that Act the jury is allowed to draw 'proper inferences' from the fact that a defendant does not disclose in police interview matters upon which s/he relies in her/his defence at trial, from failure or refusal to account for objects, substances or marks (and for presence at a particular place) and from a defendant's silence at trial. The MDO is in theory protected at least in the case of silence at trial in that the inference does not arise if 'it appears to the court that the physical or mental condition of the accused makes it undesirable for him to give evidence' (see section 35(1)(b)). In my view the subjectivity of this test leaves too much to chance. I am aware of one case where in spite of psychiatric evidence that the defendant suffered from a depressive illness, had attempted suicide and remained a suicide risk as a result of the pressure of the proceedings the Judge ruled that the defendant was fit to give evidence provided that he was given sufficient breaks and supplied with suitable medication.

In addition, no specific provision is made in respect of the other inferences, just a general discretion, as in section 35, that the court *may* (and by implication therefore may not) draw such inferences.

As there has been so much publicity surrounding these provisions few jurors are unaware that the unqualified 'right to silence' has now gone. The advocate may therefore feel forced into calling evidence of her/his client's mental disorder, which will both stigmatize the defendant and almost certainly affect the jury's approach to the evidence, as a way of 'rebutting' the inference. I will go on record now and say that I and many others who work in the Criminal Justice System (including some Judges and some of those who mostly prosecute) are ashamed that such provisions have become part of our law.

(4) Respect for Authority

There is another way in which fundamentally the adversarial process does not take account of the needs of the MDO, and that is in its obsession with order and respect for authority. Judges do not take kindly to those who flout their authority or appear to be trying to manipulate the process of the court. In my experience even some senior and supposedly specially trained Judges cannot understand or accept that sometimes manipulative behaviour is a symptom of the defendant's illness. In one recent case a defendant's bail was withdrawn during trial although he was an in-patient at a hospital (he had voluntarily admitted himself on the day before the trial started) and attended court with a nurse who was intending to escort him back to the bed which had been kept for him. She left court without the defendant. Plainly the Judge had formed the view that the defendant had tried to avoid trial by self-admitting, but whether that was or was not the case there appeared to be no ground for believing (since he had attended on that occasion) that he would not attend court again. The effect of a remand in custody on the defendant, however, was to heighten his anxiety and increase the manifestations of his personality disorder. This in turn had an inevitable and adverse effect on his trial.

(5) Ethical Questions

There are also a number of important ethical problems surrounding the appearance of a mentally disordered offender before the courts. To whom does an expert instructed by either side owe a duty? How far do the boundaries of confidentiality between patient and 'doctor' go? This question is by no means academic. According to case law [R v McDonald [1991] CLR 122 and R v Gayle [1994] CLR 679] there is no absolute prohibition on the prosecution relying on a confession given to a psychiatrist who examines a defendant for the purpose of determining whether he is fit to plead. The court in those cases did however express the view that it would be *rare* to seek to adduce evidence of what a defendant said to a doctor on a non-medical issue.

So, too, the ethical questions for an advocate are of nightmarish proportions, and are affected by the attitude which s/he brings to the representation of the MDO. Does the advocate act as though the MDO is not able to make informed decisions and therefore 'take charge'? Again my experience is that many Judges expect advocates to act as though they are *in loco parentis* to the MDO client. I and others take a different view. As far as I am concerned once a defendant is said to be fit to plead and give instructions, then as far as possible I will accord her/him no less right to participate in the decisions affecting the conduct of her/his case than I would accord to any other client. After all, just because a client is 'not too bright' one does not say s/he forfeits a right to give informed consent to the conduct of her/his case. Yet label a client mentally disordered and some advocates think it not just their right but their duty to 'play God' and take all the important decisions either without consulting the client or in direct conflict with their client's expressed wishes. If the defendant complains the lawyer concerned can be fairly confident that the client's mental disorder will count against her/him when the decision is made as to whether the lawyer acted properly. I clearly remember being harangued in a robing room by just such a lawyer, who thought it outrageous that I had mitigated towards a suspended sentence for a client (who had no previous convictions and on all of the facts was unlikely to offend again) when there was the option of probation available. It mattered not to him that my client was a highly intelligent, articulate lawyer, who had specifically instructed me to do so. The problem for him was that she was mentally disordered, and therefore according to him 'was incapable of knowing what was best for her'. She was fit to plead but suffered from delusions. One of her delusions was that the probation service were in conspiracy with the police and local council against her. Probation requires not just the consent but the co-operation of the defendant. I still believe that I did the right thing. She did not reoffend.

I cannot begin to address the lawyer's duty where a client on the evidence is unfit to plead and give instructions. There are those who would say that it is obvious that the lawyer must then take charge. However, I sometimes represent clients who have no mental disorder yet whose instructions are at least as far-fetched as those emanating from an 'unfit' client. Since I am supposed if such 'normal' clients insist to put their instructions into effect, there are many who would argue that the client who is 'unfit' has no less *right* to get their case *wrong*!

CONCLUSION

This chapter is too short to address in any detail what reforms of the adversarial process might be made to protect the MDO. In any event I fear that such reforms are not high on the legislature's list of priorities. My perception of the criminal justice system is that it reflects society's attitudes to those who are mentally disordered: it views them with suspicion, fear and something little short of contempt. Alternatively it patronizes them. While the political parties are competing for the 'moral high ground' as to who is 'toughest on crime', and the current government is seriously considering a 'three strikes and you're out' sentencing policy, while insufficient beds are available to accommodate mentally disordered patients, and while prison hospital wings are so overcrowded that mentally ill prisoners are sometimes kept on ordinary wings, the future does not look good for better treatment of the MDO.

But then perhaps neither the public nor the courts really want to grapple with the problems which MDOs present. It involves after all wrestling with what can go wrong with the human mind – and therefore with what can go wrong with all of us.

35

Forensic Psychotherapy Assessments and the Legal System

Carine Minne

In order to avoid misunderstandings, forensic psychotherapists should acquaint themselves with the law and learn to translate their psychodynamic formulations into a language that is comprehensible by lawyers. Law is the body of rules formally sanctioned by Parliament and the Courts, involving two kinds of legal procedure, criminal and civil. The civil law is concerned with private rights and involves one 'individual' against another. Criminal law involves the State against the individual and is concerned primarily with the question of whether criminals are to be punished or treated. Where Parliament and/or the Courts have defined an activity as a crime, the state has the right to initiate proceedings on behalf of society. The police are charged with enforcing the criminal law in respect of the major crimes against the person, property and public order, and in respect of driving offences and miscellaneous minor offences. Prosecution may also be instituted by the Director of Public Prosecutions, particularly in the more difficult or serious cases. Psychiatrists and other mental health professionals can be involved in both civil or criminal legal matters in relation to assessing people for a wide range of reasons.

For the legal system to benefit from forensic psychotherapists, it may be necessary for lawyers to acquaint themselves with some basic psychodynamic principles or at least be open to these. These issues were addressed at conferences for psychodynamic practitioners and both the criminal and the family justice systems (Windsor 1994; Dartington 1995). More such conferences are required. The International Association for Forensic Psychotherapy is another medium through which the forensic psychotherapy and interested legal bodies can further their understanding and educate each other.

It may be helpful to demonstrate the application of psychodynamic assessments to the legal system by offering two examples.

Clinical vignette

A 42-year-old professional woman was charged with reckless driving and assault. A psychiatric assessment prepared for court made the diagnosis of borderline personality disorder (as defined in the American Diagnostic and Statistical Manual of Mental Disorders, third edition revised) and recommended psychotherapy as the most appropriate treatment should the court consider a non-custodial sentence. The woman was placed on a probation order with a condition of treatment and a psychotherapist was then sought to provide this treatment.

There are two main problems in this example. First, if psychoanalytic psychotherapy is thought to be appropriate by the assessing mental health professional (for example a forensic psychiatrist) then a psychotherapy assessment should be undertaken prior to recommending such treatment in a report, in order to confirm suitability for treatment. Second, if such treatment is recommended, it should generally not be a condition of the probation order as this could interfere with the therapeutic alliance by rendering the patient's motivation questionable and raising major confidentiality issues. Indeed, this proved to be the case with this particular patient who dropped out of treatment after eight months and was subsequently in breach of her Probation Order. An alternative would have been to have psychiatric treatment as the condition, with voluntary attendance for psychotherapy should the patient show any motivation.

The issue of conditions of treatment proved to be a complicated matter in the above case. Ideally, a patient should be seen for psychotherapeutic treatment on a voluntary basis when the motivation to receive help with their offending behaviour is clearly internally driven. If a patient is obliged under a Court Order to attend, not only is their motivation questionable but their relationship with 'authority' figures can be re-enacted in a pathological way without the possibility of being addressed. If offending behaviour occurs as a solution to mental conflict then it is not surprising if the offender reverts to similar solutions when faced with further conflict within the legal framework, particularly if the therapist is seen as part of this. Confidentiality can also become a major stumbling block when the patient is, understandably, anxious that the therapist might repeat what is said in a session to the probation officer and cannot accept reassurances that only a general report on attendance is supplied. This can develop into the main form of resistance by the patient. In addition, if a patient fails to attend treatment, they can be reported as being in breach of their Order. The therapist may become in the transference an 'authority' figure who is telling them what to do. The therapist, like other authorities in the patient's life, may be dealt with by defiance. Alternatively, some patients actually request to be placed on a condition of treatment which they believe will provide extra containment for them. Obviously a balance must be reached between confidentiality and containment – one of the main features of forensic psychotherapy.

From the criminal justice perspective, it may not be acceptable to accept a treatment recommendation which appears as a 'soft option' and too risky in terms of re-offending possibilities. If a patient attends voluntarily for treatment without an Order having been imposed, there is a risk that the therapist will be left to 'carry' all the anxiety about any re-offending. If an Order is in place, a network of other professionals is available to offer support to the therapist as well as to the patient. It is helpful to consider the allocation of a manager who can relate to the psychiatrist, psychotherapist, probation officer and other professionals involved in a case. This can protect the therapist from undermining the patient's confidence by contacting other professionals and can also prevent *splitting*, a common feature in teams attempting to work with disturbed patients.

Clinical vignette

A 21-year-old man made a number of hoax calls to people whose names he plucked at random from a telephone directory and he was charged with making threats to kill. He explained that previously he had made hoax 999 calls but he had started to make threatening phone calls to strangers after having been turned down for another job. He was remanded in custody which he described as offering him time to 'cool down'. However, his behaviour was, at times, disturbed and he smashed up his cell on a couple of occasions and complained that no-one would speak to him. A nursing prison officer described him as being strange, distant looking, very lonely and wanting to attract attention. In view of his behaviour, a psychiatric report was requested and provided by a general psychiatrist. This psychiatrist was of the opinion that a psychotherapy assessment would be beneficial in this case and requested that one be provided in time for his trial. An assessment was carried out in the prison over a period of three sessions, as there was sufficient time before the court case. The patient was considered to suffer from a personality disorder with prominent schizoid traits and he was thought to be possibly susceptible to psychotherapy treatment which was recommended in the report, emphasizing that this should be voluntary and not part of a condition. The patient was placed on a two-year probation order with a condition of treatment that he should attend his psychiatrist on a regular basis. The patient was also encouraged in court to attend psychotherapy treatment, but this was not specified as a condition of the Probation Order. This patient completed his Probation Order without complications and attended weekly individual psychodynamic psychotherapy throughout the order where he was able to start making a link between his offences and his own state of mind. He continued to attend psychotherapy sessions long after the end of his Probation Order. He made further progress in therapy where earlier childhood traumas eventually emerged and he was able to see connections between these and his sense of helplessness then and that which he made his victims feel in order to regain power and control. He had changed his status from victim to victimizer.

Both these cases illustrate a number of the difficulties that one has to be aware of in preparing such assessments. In the first case, psychotherapeutic treatment came to a premature ending as the condition of treatment interfered too much with the therapeutic alliance. In the second case, the patient successfully completed his two-year probation order and is still in weekly individual psychotherapy treatment.

These cases also illustrate the need for forensic psychotherapy reports to present individually tailored recommendations which take into consideration treatment needs and availability, and patient suitability for such treatment. Furthermore, they should include consideration of security and containment needs that a Court would request given its requirement to apply justice and protect the public on society's behalf. By focusing on the individual, it is possible to achieve a balance between addressing both the needs of that individual and those of society in offering a psychodynamic perspective of an offender to the legal system. A psychodynamic assessment in the legal system can, it is hoped, offer space for all involved to think rather than react.

GUIDELINES ON PREPARING REPORTS FOR COURT

Preliminary Matters

(1)   Who can refer?

- o Probation officers

- o Defence solicitors

- o Crown Prosecution Service

- o Other mental health professionals

- o Social services (in cases involving a risk assessment of parents, best to request that the referral come from the solicitor representing the Guardian ad Litem to the child rather than either parents' solicitor, as this is in the best interests of the child).

(2)   Ensure that the instructions are adequate and that the request for such a report is within your remit. Clarify exactly which forum the report will be used in so you can be sure of its final destination. Request all

available documents from the referrer, e.g., previous psychiatric notes, social enquiry reports, depositions and criminal records of offences etc.

(3)   Try to decide approximately how many interviews you are likely to need to see the person and arrange these in advance. For example, you may need 2–3 interviews when assessing an individual to allow the opportunity for the evolution of a rapport as well as to have time to obtain a full history.

(4)   At the beginning of the first interview make sure the person is aware that the purpose of the assessment is to provide a report to the court and that any matters that arise during the assessment may be mentioned in the report. It is always wise to obtain the person's written consent for you to have access to any medical or other relevant files you may wish to request.

Planning the Written Report

(1)   State the name and date of birth of the person assessed.

(2)   Introductory paragraph including who referred, why, and the assessed person's current situation (e.g., in the community on bail or detained under a specific section of the 1983 Mental Health Act in a certain hospital). If the person has been charged, then state what s/he has been charged with and how s/he is pleading. Refer to the dates and places of the interviews held and any documents or informants information made available to you.

(3)   For the sake of clarity, it is sensible to begin the background history with the person's family history, including any psychiatric or forensic history and an impression of the family dynamics if this is possible from the material available. This can be followed by the personal history to include birth and development, schooling, qualifications, employment record, drugs and alcohol history, forensic history, medical history, psychosexual history and psychiatric history under the relevant headings if possible.

(4)   The next section should be an account of the index offence (or problems leading to the referral) and the circumstances surrounding this. It is helpful to give the person's own account and compare this with other information available. Any relevant psychological factors or aspects of the person's mental state at the time should be included.

(5)   The person's current mental state should now be described. Whereas a psychiatric report would tend to present this in a formal manner, in a forensic psychotherapy assessment, it can be helpful to describe not just the presence or absence of any psychiatric symptoms, but also

references to the transference (and counter-transference) as it emerged during the interviews. This should be written in clear terms with minimal use of technical terms. Any technical terms used should be clarified in lay terms within brackets.

(6) The last section of the report should consist of your opinion and recommendations and be headed 'Conclusions'. Give a brief résumé or outline of the background and personal history. Give your opinion on any diagnosis (if this is within your remit) and implications within the 1983 Mental Health Act if this is relevant. Refer to the offence and your opinion on the importance of any psychological factors at that time. Offer a psychodynamic formulation which includes current psychopathology, aetiological factors and maintaining factors. This too should be written clearly and in lay terms as much as possible. The purpose is to offer the court an understanding of the person's internal world and the offence or presenting difficulties. An opinion on suitability for treatment should be given and if treatment is considered, then appropriate recommendations ought to be listed. These recommendations must be within the remit of the court (and this must be checked prior to recommending) and ought to be available. It is sensible to make recommendations respectfully to the court and to mention the concerns you may have if such treatment cannot be provided (e.g., by the person being sent to prison if the court did not accept your recommendations). A comment on prognosis is often appreciated but not always possible.

(7) State your name and qualifications at the end of the report and your current status within your profession. Date the report.

N.B. Do not write anything in your report that you cannot explain or that is irrelevant.

APPEARING IN COURT

(1) **Preparation**

Read your report again to be familiar with its contents. It can be helpful to read any literature which can support your opinion and recommendations. If a long time has lapsed since the preparation of the report, you may need to consider a further interview with the person and provide an addendum to your report prior to the hearing.

(2) It is helpful to make yourself familiar with court procedures as this can help overcome feelings of anxiety induced by what may be perceived as a strange, threatening or even hostile atmosphere. Note which court

you are appearing in, for example, Magistrates Court, Crown Court, High Court or Central Criminal Court.

(3)   It is best to respect dress code and time. Generally, courts are very appreciative of professionals giving their time to assist.

(4)   The following notes apply to all courts:

- Announce your arrival to the clerk.

- Bow to the bench when you enter.

- You will be shown where to sit.

- Be prepared for how you will want to be sworn in, as you will be asked.

- When you say the oath, use this as an opportunity to gauge your voice projection.

- Check how to address the bench; for example, the judge will be addressed as

    'Your Honour' in Crown Court, and 'My Lord' or 'My Lady' in High Court

- In the witness box, bring only your report and any notes you have prepared that you have checked can be disclosed as this may be requested.

- Answer questions succinctly and do not attempt to answer questions beyond your remit especially when you are feeling pressed to do so.

- When asked a question by a barrister or Queen's Counsel, turn towards the bench when replying. S/he is the person you are answering to.

- Remember that you are an impartial witness there to assist the court.

- When you leave the court, remember to bow again.

(5)   It may be helpful to discuss your experience in court with colleagues afterwards, especially if you have had a difficult cross-examination.

36

Medico-Legal Ethics in Forensic Psychotherapy

Julie Stone

INTRODUCTION

Imagine that you are a student counsellor. A student who you have been seeing for some time confesses to you that he intends to harm a woman who has rejected his advances. You try and assess the seriousness of his threat and whether you should breach confidentiality and warn the woman or the police that she might be in danger. You decide to respect your client's confidentiality. Your client carries out his threat and kills the young woman. The woman's family sue your employers. What issues does this raise? With foresight, would you have acted differently? (Tarasoff v. Regents of the University of California (1976 SSI p 2d 223))

The above scenario is based on a real case and highlights just some of the ethical dilemmas which may arise in practice. The inherently value-laden nature of psychotherapy demands that ethical decisions are critically analyzed. This need is intensified in forensic psychotherapy because the patient's wellbeing will not always be the practitioner's sole consideration. Although therapists may have come across certain ethical concepts, such as the principle of respect for autonomy, within their clinical training, the centrality of moral judgments in psychotherapy means that therapists need to develop a specific awareness of the ethical implications of their interactions. Professional ethics is a branch of applied philosophy which provides an opportunity for reflection about the assumptions and values upon which decisions are made. Whilst there are no right or wrong answers, ethical debate can at least help to ensure that decisions are made on the basis of consistent and morally defensible arguments.

For the purposes of this chapter, I shall use the terms 'ethics' to connote obligations of a moral nature which govern the health care practice. Ethics is concerned, in essence, with the rightness or wrongness of behaviour. In terms of ethical analysis, two distinct generalizable types of ethical theory can be identified: deontological theories, which focus on special duties and responsibilities to others born out of certain types of relationship, and consequentialist theories, such as utilitarianism, which judge conduct in the context of consequences or likely consequences attendant upon such action.

NATURE AND EXTENT OF THERAPISTS' DUTY OF CARE

The forensic dimension of the therapeutic relationship may give rise to some acute ethical dilemmas, but the same fundamental ethical principles underpin this relationship as apply in other clinical settings, even though a certain reordering of principles may be required. Thus, therapists must still ask themselves whether their actions are beneficial to patients or harmful, whether they have the requisite skills and resources to achieve the desired goals and whether they are justified in overriding the patient's autonomy for the protection of others.

To whom do forensic psychotherapists owe a duty of care and why? Any therapeutic relationship gives rise to ethical responsibilities. Benefitting the patient is the guiding Hippocratic principle. Whilst all therapists would accept that treating a patient may have consequences for third parties, ordinarily, their duty as therapists lies in helping the individual. In a forensic setting, that position is fundamentally different. The very purpose of forensic psychotherapy is to help offenders understand their actions in the hope that this will prevent them from re-offending. The raison d'etre of forensic psychotherapy envisages broader responsibilities. Forensic psychotherapists also have direct responsibilities to the State as their employers. This ambiguity has profound ethical implications. Who does the forensic psychotherapist serve? The patient? The institution? Society as a whole?

How far do forensic psychotherapists' duties extend towards third parties? If, for example, it transpires that a patient harbours resentment against a specific individual and is seeking to exact revenge, should this knowledge be disclosed to the authorities, or brought to the attention of the Mental Health Review Tribunal? Do therapists have a right, or even a duty to breach confidentiality in such circumstances? Although the Tarasoff case which introduced this chapter supported breaches of confidentiality where threats of harm were made about a specific, named individual, subsequent cases have extended this duty even further.

Forensic psychotherapists may be the only member of the team the patient can actually talk to. Because patients may see their therapist as being more trustworthy and sympathetic than other authority figures, they may be inclined to reveal matters which might subsequently incriminate themselves. Psychotherapists should explain that they may not be able to maintain strict confidentiality to their clients at the outset of the encounter, but should nonetheless attempt to secure the patient's consent before disclosing confidential information to others.

RECONCILING CONFLICTING DUTIES

Can therapists reconcile their conflicting responsibilities? To respect the patient's autonomy in full, including the patient's right to have his or her confidences kept, not to mention the right to liberty, may disrupt the smooth running of the institution and place others at risk. Yet, to place the interests of others before the interests of the patient fails to respect that person as an individual and will damage the sense of trust which is vital to the therapeutic encounter. For this reason, it is essential to be open with patients and explain the constraints within which the therapeutic interchange must operate.

The Need for Consent

The principle of respect for autonomy is manifested by the need to obtain consent. Ordinarily, adult patients of a sound mind have a right to consent to and refuse medical treatment. In order for consent to be valid, the patient must be given adequate information, must have the capacity to comprehend that information and must be able to come to a decision free from coercion (although compulsorily detained patients may be given treatment for mental disorder under the Mental Health Act 1983 without their consent *even if they are competent*). Compulsory treatment clearly overrides a person's autonomy and should be seen as a last resort option. Whilst there are strong reasons for overriding autonomy for the protection of others, it is harder to find ethical justifications for protecting patients from themselves.

Labelling all psychiatric patients as irrational, and thus, non-autonomous is unhelpful. Capacity to consent should be decided according to the patient's functional ability. In seeking the patients' consent, therapists should explain that therapy can be a distressing process and may make the patient feel worse not better. An institutionalized setting may significantly hamper a patient's ability to consent to therapy. The ethics of compulsory treatment take on a particular relevance in a psychodynamic situation which requires the active participation of the client. Is it possible for individual or group psychotherapy to be foisted on unwilling patients? How efficacious will treatment be when it is entered into as part of a court's disposal, rather than a conscious choice?

Respect for Confidentiality in a Forensic Setting

Respect for confidentiality is a vital component of respect for a person's autonomy. However, the duty of confidentiality will be compromised by (i) the need within an institutionalized setting to place safety before individual rights (ii) the multi-disciplinary approach of forensic work, which may require a number of professionals to have access to case notes (including the psychotherapist's supervisor). Despite these constraints, confidentiality must be respected to the extent that the forensic context allows. Respect for the individual's autonomy necessitates the patient being informed that information may be given to third parties. Practitioners need to appraise themselves of an institution's policy on confidentiality, and decide whether they can work within it.

Role of Therapist in Case Conferences and Tribunals

Psychotherapists should facilitate access to Mental Health Review Tribunals as a means of ensuring some independent review of the patient's treatment regimen. Here, however, a balance must be struck between protecting the patient's trust and giving evidence which could result in their continued confinement.

DO NO HARM

The forensic aspect of the relationship means that a wholly therapeutic relationship may not be achievable. If this is the case, therapists must still, even when acting as an agent of the state, adhere to the principle *primum non nocere*, and attempt not to cause harm to the patient. Although what might constitute doing harm is less obvious in a psychotherapeutic context than in other clinical scenarios, all therapeutic interventions are potentially harmful. The justification for treatment is that the benefits outweigh their risks. In other clinical situations, the patient usually makes that assessment on the basis of his or her own values. However, the tendency towards paternalism in dealing with psychiatric patients means that professional opinion will usually determine what treatment is appropriate as being in the patient's best interests. The problem is that psychotherapy is a two-way enterprise which cannot be effective unless the patient is willing to engage.

Psychotherapy carries with it the risk of causing emotional harm. What degree of distress is legitimate? Therapists must be sensitive to the dangers of upsetting already vulnerable patients whose institutional confinement may deny them the emotional support they require, thus increasing dependency on the therapist, and the effect of which could lead to disruptive behaviour which would pose a threat to others. These are issues of clinical judgment, although the professional competence is itself an ethical issue.

In this context, abuse of power is both professionally and ethically unacceptable. Physical, emotional or sexual abuse runs counter to any therapeutic relationship, and would have a particularly damaging effect on the particular client group.

Training

The ability to help patients rather than harm them depends on effective training, and adequate support and supervision. Candidates may well be drawn from other disciplines, bringing the advantages of wider theoretical bases. The demanding nature of the work makes selection criteria very important. As well as being aware of clinical developments, therapists need to appreciate the legal implications of their work and to keep up to date with developments in this field. Training must challenge therapists' personal prejudices and assumptions. Forensic psychotherapists need to be realistic about what they can achieve in this particular environment and appreciate the limitations of adopting a purist ideological approach to their work.

Recognizing Limits of Competence

As with any treatment, psychotherapeutic interventions poses risks as well as benefits. Given the client group, adverse outcomes may have dire consequences. Therapists must be aware of their limitations and lack of experience and be particularly aware of counter-transference. When advising tribunals and the Home Office on the progress of treatment, or indeed on treatability, practitioners should freely admit the shortcomings of their knowledge. The prediction of dangerousness is a particularly contentious area, not least of all, because of its inherent unreliability. Practitioners must be certain to differentiate between fact and opinion.

Effectiveness of Psychotherapy in a Forensic Setting

The moral legitimacy of forensic psychotherapy, rather than that of individual practitioners, depends on whether forensic psychotherapy works. Does a psychodynamic understanding of why people offend assist in preventing them from re-offending? There are immeasurable difficulties in assessing efficacy. What counts as an effective outcome? Does greater insight on the part of the offender constitute therapeutic success, or is the re-offending rate a more appropriate determinant? Therapists cannot benefit their patients unless theoretical justifications for forensic psychotherapy are validated. There should thus be a commitment to research at both an individual and a collective level.

Whilst research into the efficacy of forensic psychotherapy is vital, the combined factors of possible mental disorder and compulsory detention question the ability of an offender patient to consent to participate in research. Given the constraints on autonomy, non-therapeutic research would not be ethically permissible and even therapeutic research is highly problematic. The dangers of coercion within an institutionalized setting are obvious, although there is a somewhat unconvincing counterargument that detained persons should not be deprived of the opportunity to be altruistic by contributing to medical research. Whilst obtaining consent undoubtedly requires far greater vigilance on the part of researchers, such data is necessary if forensic psychotherapy is to continue to establish itself as a valuable tool in dealing with offenders. Where appropriate, research protocols should be approved by a local research ethics committee.

Resources

A further ethical issue is whether therapists can operate in an underfunded system in which they are unable to provide as much therapeutic support as they would wish. These difficulties may be compounded in a prison setting, which may have even less funding to provide psychotherapy services and where the environment is anti-therapeutic, with an emphasis on punishment rather than rehabilitation. The justification for detaining ill people is that they should be treated. If such treatment cannot be funded, the legitimacy to hold people is called into question. Therapists, as part of a broader duty of beneficence, may find themselves acting as advocates for patients, campaigning for resources necessary to provide treatment.

CONCLUSION

Forensic psychotherapy poses a number of ethical dilemmas. Many of these need, ultimately, to be discussed at a collective level, and the development of consistent and ethically defensible guidelines is to be encouraged. Nonetheless, practitioners must be sufficiently aware of the individual ethical issues confronting them and should strive towards securing appropriate treatment for forensic patients and not further undermining such restricted autonomy as they may have.

PART IV

Research and Audit

37

Research

Alice Levinson

INTRODUCTION

A chapter on research would traditionally review the research of the field, but for forensic psychotherapy the situation is different, due to the relative recency of the discipline and the subsequent poverty of such research. In view of this situation, the more appropriate and challenging task is to prepare the ground for future research. Ideas for research should come from essential clinical concerns, the research will then be of help in modifying and shaping the discipline. Forensic psychotherapy has emerged as a new discipline that is distinct in itself, but to do so it needs to be cross-fertilized by its parent disciplines, forensic psychiatry and psychotherapy. In the creation of research in this field we should learn from research in these parent disciplines, as well as from other psychological research. By doing so, we will then be in the advantageous position of being able to avoid repeating some of the shortcomings that are common in psychotherapy research. Psychotherapy research has often been criticized for its poor methodology, including samples that are too small and inadequately defined, the lack of operationalized diagnostic criteria, the use of unstandardized measures, being uncontrolled, retrospective in design and with insufficient follow up.

The aim of this chapter is to provide some concepts for designing different research projects, which independent of whether the results are significant or not, can produce interesting findings. An overview of the different approaches will be given, with the hope of stimulating interest and the development of valuable research in this area.

GOALS

In the broadest sense, the goal of psychotherapy research is to help in the clarification of clinical concepts. It should advance our understanding of psychopathology, so that we are able to create more appropriate hypotheses, in our clinical work and for further research. It therefore assists in shaping the clinical discipline, by providing a sound conceptual framework that structures the clinical field, and which enables clearer and more accurate thinking.

The specific goal of a research project will depend on the questions being asked by it and the type of psychotherapy. For psychodynamic psychotherapy, the final goal is to investigate mechanisms of psychic change, by furthering our understanding of intrapsychic and interpersonal processes. In treatment evaluation studies the aim will be to show that psychotherapy is effective, in comparison with no treatment or a different form of treatment; it should also be possible to examine prognostic factors, in order to provide predictive information to assist in the assessment of individuals for psychotherapy.

METHODS

There is a wide range of research methods. A conceptual dichotomy has been created between qualitative and quantitative research: descriptive versus experimental designs, case studies and small single samples versus large group comparison studies, and process versus outcome studies. This dichotomy has provided some conceptual structure but it is artificial. Process research – such as the examination of the therapist–patient relationship – will also, over time, tell us about outcome; and some information about process can be gained from outcome studies if appropriate measures are conducted temporally. I think one of the interests in outcome studies is their potential to further our understanding of the process of change.

In order to develop as 'whole' an understanding of a subject as possible, a range of different methods needs to be employed and their findings integrated. Each method on its own has limitations. Case studies may provide intricate details about the individual, but these findings cannot be generalized to other subjects. Group comparison studies, on the other hand, provide data that can be generalized to similar populations and compared with other groups, but they do not provide information about the individual subjects. The information they do supply is coarse-grained and cannot reflect the complexity and subtle nature of the mind's subjectivity, which is the field of study. Large statistical studies have been criticized by clinicians for only proving what is already clinically understood. For this reason there is a requirement for a variety of research methods which have different focuses and from which findings can be collated. The overall principle for research is that the methodology is sound so that the results can be respected, and that the study is designed in such a way to answer questions that it asks. It is beyond the remit of a short chapter to describe all the different research methods, but what follows will instead be an overview that highlights the most relevant issues.

Single-Case and Small Sample Designs

These methods are generally considered as unrigorous and unscientific by empirical researchers, because they do not provide statistically analyzable data. They can be of use in appropriate circumstances as they offer the opportunity for fine-grained investigation, which is necessary to explore the rich and complex domain of subjectivity. They can for instance be used in the examination of the process of psychoanalytic psychotherapy, where the focus is the complex interactional sequences between therapist and patient, in order to explore the elaborate changes in the patient–therapist interaction. The patient's responses to the therapist's interventions can be monitored by audio recording techniques, and rating scales have been devised that follow the changes in the transference and counter-transference patterns (see Kernberg 1994).

Changes are measured within the individual(s) over time, the subject(s) acting as their own control, measures being performed temporally, before, during, and after treatment. Without a control group it is impossible to be certain that an observed change is due to the intervention of psychotherapy, and not due to other confounding factors or the natural history of personality disorder.

Studies utilizing small numbers do not produce results of statistical confidence, but they do instead create a forum for ideas to emerge and hypotheses be created, which can then be tested clinically and by further research, with larger groups. In the early stages of forensic psychotherapy research such studies could contribute enormously to our understanding of the psychopathology of offenders: a detailed exploration of the internal world of the offender – particularly around the time of the offence – would greatly enhance our understanding of criminal behaviour and its treatability. Bowlby's (1947) classic study of a series of juvenile delinquents has shown how deprivation, trauma, and loss contributed to their personality disorder and offending.

Research on small numbers of subjects can be improved in terms of reliability by using a research group who independently rate the data. Sandler (1995) has described a method in which the research group discussed the data with the therapists, in order that an objective consensus of the observed material could be reached. It was found to be very helpful in clarifying and re-defining clinical concepts in psychoanalysis.

The generalizability of findings from small samples is limited, but can be improved – and replication made possible – by using operationalized diagnostic criteria at baseline, and by using standardized measures of known reliability and validity in order to allow comparisons to be drawn.

Group Comparison Studies

The **Randomized Controlled trial** (RCT) is generally considered the gold standard for treatment evaluation research. The purpose of the controlled study is that it provides a level of certainty that a significant difference between the groups is due to the intervention given to one group, in comparison to a matched group receiving no treatment. Matching of the groups is required to limit the influence of confounding variables, such as age, IQ, sex and ethnicity. Randomization ensures that any potential differences are randomly distributed between both groups. It will not automatically produce equal groups, but the likelihood that the groups are equivalent increases as a function of the sample size.

There are a number of serious impediments to using the RCT in psychotherapy outcome research, especially for long-term psychodynamic psychotherapy. The creation of a control group has evaded the attempts of researchers. It is not ethical to use randomization to select the control group, as psychotherapy has been shown to be of greater benefit than no treatment (Bergin and Garfield 1994). The control group has therefore to be selected from patients who are not receiving treatment, but this will introduce distortion as there may be a reason for treatment having been witheld. If such a control group is selected, the subjects may for understandable reasons not be compliant for long-term intensive research. RCTs tend to reflect ideal rather than real circumstances, consisting of well-motivated patients and therapists, which may be poorly representative, limiting generalizability. The limitations of the RCT for psychotherapy evaluation studies have been reviewed by Fonagy and Higgitt (1989), who conclude that naturalistic observational studies, prospectively on a large scale, using operationalized criteria and standardized measures is the way to proceed. Inter-service comparisons can then be made if the same measures are used across centres, and the findings can be generalized to other populations.

There are some important issues in large group studies that have to be handled carefully. **Attrition** – the drop out of cases – is a problematic factor in psychotherapy outcome research. It can de-randomize the groups (poor prognostic patients defaulting, or patients with a specific type of disorder withdrawing from one treatment more than another). This will limit the generalizability of the results as the samples are no longer representative of the population from which they were drawn; and by reducing sample size, attrition lessens the statistical power. Many factors will contribute to attrition, including factors relating to the patient (e.g. personality disorder), the therapy (e.g. the length of treatment and the confrontation of psychic pain) and the setting (the prison culture may interfere with psychotherapy). For these reasons the attrition rate will be high in forensic psychotherapy, and in addition, the patients are from a very mobile population and so will be difficult to follow up. This problem needs to be anticipated when designing a study, in terms of deciding upon the required sample size and having sufficient resources to follow up patients lost to the study. Attrition is best dealt with by retrospectively analyzing the reasons for the patients' leaving treatment, for which good baseline data is necessary.

The **statistical significance** of the results is another factor that requires consideration. It is commonly over-emphasized in the interpretation of results. The conventional level of significance (alpha) is set at $p < 0.05$, which provides an agreed level of confidence that the difference between groups has not just occurred by chance, and is therefore due to the intervention. It is, however, an arbitrary level, and before starting the study another level may be chosen. The emphasis placed on statistical significance is unsatisfactory as it depends on the **statistical power**, which is a function of sample size, the effect size (the difference between groups) and the level of alpha. The statistical power of the study is therefore important as it provides confidence in the results, and is conventionally set at 0.8. If the power is low, there is less confidence in the results even in the face of a statistical difference. Non-significant results should not be dismissed as meaningless, but need to be carefully interpreted: there may be no difference between the groups, or the difference may not have been discovered due to low statistical power or poor methodology.

A further reservation about statistical significance is that it may not reflect **clinical significance**. There may be a change found in the variable being measured (e.g. recidivism), but the patient's psychiatric symptomatology, social functioning and quality of life may not be improved. Measures of clinical relevance need to be incorporated, and may be supported by subjective reports of the patient and significant others. The goal of the research must therefore be aligned with the clinical aims of treatment and multidimensional measures need to be employed.

THE WAY TO PROCEED

It is a privileged position to be creating a new area of research and we need to make use of it. Further epidemiological studies are required to provide a baseline of the prevalence of personality disorder and degree of psychological disturbance in different forensic settings (see Dolan 1994).

The essential factor for research is the *quality of the design* of the methodology: this will make the results meaningful whether or not they attain statistical significance. Where the aim is to investigate the **internal world** of the offender, including the minutiae of intrapsychic and interpersonal processes, small numbers will probably be required to conduct multiple and intensive measures. The design should, however, still include operationalized diagnostic criteria, standardized measures of known reliability and validity, and inter-rater reliability tests, to enable replication and improve generalizability. Measures need to be repeated at frequent enough intervals to record change. A sufficient follow-up period is required that reflects the time expected for further change to occur after the end of treatment and that tests the endurance of that change.

For **outcome studies** where the objective is to evaluate the effectiveness of psychotherapy some principles should be observed:

(1) Sufficient sample sizes to give statistical power.

(2) The sample needs to be carefully described by demographic profile and diagnostic baseline data. It should be as homogeneous as possible to allow matching and replication.

(3) The use of operationalized diagnostic criteria for DSM-IV or ICD-10.

(4) Standardized measures of known reliability and validity.

(5) Multi-dimensional measures covering the levels of *intrapsychic processes*, e.g. the Adult Attachment Interview (George, Kaplan and Main 1985), symptomatology, e.g. The Symptom Checklist-90 (Derogatis 1973), and *inter-personal and social functioning*, e.g. the Social Adjustment Scale (Weissman 1975) and The Global Assessment Scale (Endicott, Spitzer, Fleiss and Cohen 1976). *Recidivism* should be measured from objective reports (e.g. Home Office files) as well as the subject's self-report. Subjective reports from patients and significant others improves clinical significance.

(6) A prospective design measuring changes temporally, before, during and at the end of treatment, as well as follow-up.

(7) For psychodynamic psychotherapy long-term follow up is required in order to reflect the long-term nature of treatment and potential for change to continue after treatment. Shorter forms of therapy, including behavioural, cognitive and brief focal psychotherapy do not require so long a follow-up period as the changes they aim to produce are more immediate. However, if they are to be compared with long-term psychotherapy there must be a long follow-up period to prevent bias.

(8) Comparison studies with a control group need to be done and remain a challenge for the future, due to the difficulties in constructing a control group.

CRITICAL ISSUES FOR FORENSIC PSYCHOTHERAPY RESEARCH

Ethical issues can be especially sensitive in the field of forensic psychotherapy research. The subjects may be held involuntarily either in prison or hospital. This could influence the quality of their consent in terms of its voluntary nature, as they may feel under pressure to co-operate. The researcher must be sensitive to these personal and legal issues and written consent is as always necessary, but special consideration will need to be given to the confidentiality of material. Ethical permission will need to be granted by the local health authority and the Home Office, as appropriate.

The **reliability** of information given by offenders has to be treated with caution. Subjects who are on remand will be liable to deny the alleged charges, thereby inhibiting their cooperation or distorting information. Wherever possible other sources of information should be tapped, for instance Home Office files and significant others (including partners, family of origin, employers and school reports). Witnesses are especially valuable to inform upon the mental state of the subject at or around the time of the offence.

The effect of the **setting** should be considered. It may affect the subject's mental state, it may influence the researcher's style of work and how the subject responds to questioning. This may restrict the generalizability of findings to other settings.

The **population** of offenders will largely consist of severe personality disorder and some perversions, for instance sex offenders. There has been insufficient research on these forms of mental disorders, although models for the causation of personality disorder have emerged (Bowlby 1988; Herman, Perry and Bessez 1989). We need preliminary studies to show that what we know of personality disorders in other settings can be generalized to secure settings (for instance prisons and special hospitals) and the prevalence of these mental disorders in the various settings. We will then be in a position to do more detailed studies and evaluate treatment.

Follow-up is an essential component to outcome studies and the difficulties that are likely to arise with the forensic population should be anticipated and planned for.

NEW DIRECTIONS FOR FUTURE RESEARCH

The sections above set out important methodological issues in the design of research. This section focuses on the area that should be most exciting for forensic psychotherapy to explore: the *internal world of the offender* – the internal object relations and mental representations – in particular at the time of the offence. Research in this area will be of fundamental value to clinical work, as legal issues centre on patients' accountability which depends on their mental state at the time of the offence. It is an area sometimes neglected in assessment, where judgements are too readily made based on the offender's pre-existing mental disorder, rather than their mental state at the specific time of the offence. Such research will extend our understanding of offenders' psychopathology and the reasons for and meaning of their behaviour.

At present, the main instrument available to us to investigate intrapsychic processes is the Adult Attachment Interview (AAI) (George, Kaplan and Main 1985). Attachment theory was developed by Bowlby, observing childrens' responses to separation and loss, as well as theories from ethology and cognitive science. The AAI has provided us with a measure of adults' internal representations of attachment figures and related experiences, and how they understand the effect of these experiences on their current functioning. It is audio recorded and transcribed verbatim. The transcripts are rated by trained raters on a number of scales of experience – including love, rejection and neglect, and states of mind – including idealization, derogation, passivity and coherence. The attachment classification is derived from these scales. The three main classifications are autonomous, dismissive, and preoccupied.Superimposed upon these is a fourth classification, unresolved to trauma or loss; and a fifth, cannot classify, which has recently been discovered and which reflects a mixed defence strategy of dismissal and preoccupation.

The importance of the AAI is that it has been shown to have external validity: there is 75 per cent concordance between adult attachment classification and their infants (Main, Kaplan and Cassidy 1985) and pre-natally it can predict infants' attachment patterns (Fonagy 1991). It has also been found to have cross-cultural validity (Main 1990). The AAI has therefore provided us with an instrument of known reliability and validity that measures the internal world with respect to attachment. Attachment theory provides us with a model to understand the transgenerational transmission of attachment-related pathology, including maltreatment (Crittendon and Ainsworth 1989).

We are now in a position to develop other scales that can be applied to AAI transcripts to measure specific dimensions of the internal world. One such instrument is the Reflective-Self Function (RSF) scale (Fonagy 1991) which operationalizes the capacity for empathy and insight. RSF is the capacity of an individual to think about their own state of mind and that of others, in terms of feelings, thoughts, beliefs and intentions. It has its derivatives in Baron-Cohen, Tager-Flusburg and Cohen's (1993) Theory of Mind, Dennett's (1978) theory of intentionality, and Main's (1991) concept of metacognitive monitoring. It is an attachment-related capacity and has been shown to be the key determinant in predicting attachment security in the adult and transgenerationally in their infant (Fonagy 1991).

In our own study (Levinson and Fonagy, in press) we have applied the AAI and RSF scale to a series of prisoners, matched and compared with a group of severe personality disordered patients, and a group of normal controls. There was a higher incidence of childhood maltreatment, specifically physical abuse and neglect, in the prison population. They were, paradoxically, found to be less unresolved to this trauma than the inpatients were, according to the Main and Goldwyn classification (1994). We understood this finding in terms of the prisoners' tendency to disavow defensively attachment-related experiences. This strategy will make them less likely to be assessed as requiring psychological help than the patients were, and instead they will be considered as 'bad'. We also found that criminals have an impairment in their capacity for RSF compared with the personality disordered patients, matched for severity of psychiatric and personality disturbance. The more violent criminals who offended against persons had a greater deficit in RSF than the less violent who offended against property. We have proposed that prisoners represent a different developmental line of psychopathology, in which they tend to disavow attachment related experiences and have an inhibition of their RSF, which is thought to develop as a defence against childhood trauma by caregivers (Fonagy and Higgitt 1989). The lack of RSF and accompanying deficit in symbolic functioning removes a critical barrier that would normally prevent individuals from offending, and makes the individual experience feelings in physical and even bodily terms, which can lead to the violent act.

This would be one area of research that would be very interesting to extend. It could be achieved by adding a further question to the AAI, regarding the subject's mental representations of the victim, which would allow us to explore the subject's state of mind in respect of the victim at the time of the offence. The revised interview could be rated with the RSF scale and other scales rating the subject's internal object relations. Examples of other such scales are first, the Social Cognition and Object Relations Scale (SCORS-Q) (Western 1994) and second, the Personal Relatedness Profile (Patrick and Hobson 1996). Meloy (1992) describes splitting and projective identification as being at the core of the violent act: the individual attacks the split off intolerable aspect of themselves which they have come to identify in another. The violent act may be conceived of as a way of destroying the mental representations of self and other. By examining the intrapsychic processes of offenders, our knowledge from research may start to converge with, and develop, our understanding from clinical experience.

38

Audit

Rachael Davenhill

INTRODUCTION

This chapter aims to provide a useful, practical introduction to audit for those new to the area at both clinical and management level. It is written within the context of the British National Health Service, and for the purposes of readers of this book in other countries I hope will translate effectively if you bear in mind your own experience as clinicians with public sector settings.

WHAT IS AUDIT?

Audit, at its best, *is fundamental in supporting good clinical practice.*

In her excellent paper, Parry (1992) highlights audit along with research, service evaluation, quality assurance and total quality management as conceptual tools which can be used in combination to improve psychotherapy services:

> They all serve the principle of service practitioners or service planners reflecting on practice to learn from experience, embodied in the concepts of the reflective practitioner (Schon 1983), the learning organization (Garratt 1987) and the self-evaluating organization (Wildavsky 1972).(p.9)

Parry's (1992) definition of audit is based on:

> reflective practice within a self-evaluating psychotherapy service and a systemic approach which can take account of the perspectives of patients, purchasers, service managers, referrers and practitioners. (p.3)

In looking at this definition, along with your own clinical experience, it may become clear that your own service already has an implicit understanding of the basic components of audit. These components include the capacity to reflect, to look in detail at one area systematically, to maintain an open mind, and to give meaning to data which in itself holds no life and has to be understood within the complexities of human relationship.

The success or failure of audit will very much depend on how it is used and understood by the individual clinician, the multi-disciplinary team, and the clinical service in relationship to its external environment. Successful audit can facilitate dialogue and communication around areas of joint interest. Unsuccessful audit is experienced by clinicians as a constant criticism imposed from without containing the 'never-feel-good' factor. Guinan (1995) writes vividly of the perception by many clinicians of clinical audit and total quality management as containing 'the implication that nothing is ever going to be good enough'. Certainly for those working within the NHS there is now a formal requirement inbuilt within the purchaser–provider relationship for audit to take place, and where there are tensions within this relationship, the danger is of audit operating at an extremely concrete level, driven purely by contracting pressures.

THE AUDIT SETTING

The development of a successful audit approach will be determined by the kinds of issues clinicians, patients and managers are either interested, preoccupied or troubled by. As such, the starting point for the reader interested in implementing audit in their workplace is to clarify:

(1) What is the nature of the service offered?

> e.g. o Inpatient/Outpatient?
>
> o Access to beds or not?
>
> o NHS/Probation/Social Services

(2) Who is it aimed at?

> e.g. a service dealing with patients who are required to attend as part of a court order will have to deal with a different set of tensions regarding the provision of psychotherapy treatment from an outpatient clinic where self-referrals can be made.

(3) Who is it staffed by?

All of the above will inform what areas of interest are potentially audit interest areas. They also clarify what audit is not. Not research, which is to do with establishing a more generalizable 'truth', nor the broader area of quality or total quality management. Audit can be a supplement to but not a substitute for either. Audit priorities will be determined by their direct relevance locally, and results may not, therefore, automatically generalize to other services.

'HOW TO' AUDIT

Audit can take place at various levels and serve to communicate across these levels. These may include:

- **Self-audit**, i.e. what occurs between the patient and therapist.
- **Service audit**, i.e. what occurs within the service.
- **Management audit**, i.e. what occurs within the broader overall management of services.

(1) The Audit Circle

The most popular description of 'how to' audit is contained in what is commonly referred to as the 'Gold Standard' *Audit Circle*.

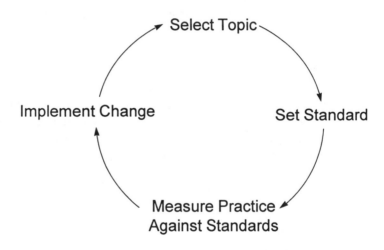

Figure 38.1 The Audit Circle

The framework here is that the therapeutic unit may decide to look at a particular area of interest. The 'Gold Standard' approach involves clinicians agreeing amongst themselves a particular 'standard' they feel is appropriate to their service, then measuring practice against it. This can then lead either to a change in practice, *or* a change in the standard if it proves unrealistic.

A common starting point for many units would be to carry out a service audit, in other words a manageable 'snap-shot' of what is actually occurring within the service. This commonly involves charting 'patient flow', that is

(i)   How referral takes place into the service.

(ii)   Referral letter.

(iii) How referrers are communicated with.

(iv) How patients are communicated with.

(v) Appointment.

(vi) First visit.

(vii) Treatment.

(viii) Case closure/discharge

(ix) Outcome.

Each of these points can be looked into via the process of audit. For example, you may want to find out the breakdown of patients coming through your service in terms of gender, race, age, and so on, and who refers into your service. To take as a simple example Point (i) 'How referral takes place into the service' – this in itself can give a great deal of information about the referrer's assumptions about which patients are suitable for treatment. It is clear, for example, that young Afro-Caribbean men are more likely to receive medication, custodial sentences, or more coercive forms of treatment over and above psychotherapy. It may be that your service is not suitable. It may be that it had not crossed a referrer's mind to refer on to you.

(2) The Audit Spiral

Whilst the audit circle, as described above, is by now a standard, well-known and well-tried approach to audit within the NHS, it does have its dangers in being experienced, at times, as a vicious circle. Godwin, de Lacey and Manhire

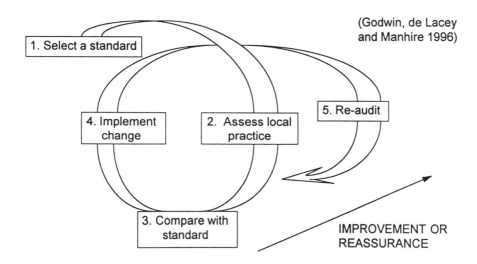

Source: Clinical Audit in Radiology. Godwin, R., de Lacey, G. and Manhire, A. Royal College of Radiologists, 1996)

Figure 38.2 The Audit Spiral

(1996) have addressed this dilemma most succinctly in their development of the audit cycle as a spiral of repeating cycles as follows:

> It is customary to emphasise that continuous improvement is the *raison d'être* for completing the audit cycle. This implies that whatever we achieve is not good enough. When accompanied by an undue emphasis on an unremitting need for change this can also be dispiriting to those who find that many of their audits indicate that no change is necessary. For this reason the spiral illustration used... places as much emphasis on the word reassurance as on the words continuous improvement. (Godwin, de Lacey and Manhire 1996)

The audit spiral allows in the possibility of movement, freedom to support, freedom to think.

(3) The Audit Triangle

Building on the importance of movement and space created by the spiral described above, the audit triangle again brings in a different perspective but one which will be instinctively familiar to the psychodynamic practitioner. The audit triangle is a helpful visual aid developed by Cape (1994), originally

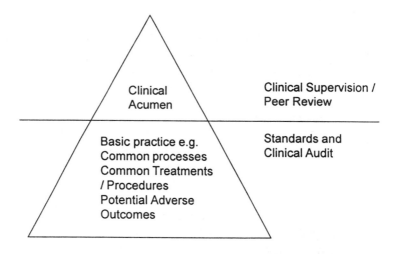

Source: Cape 1994.

Figure 38.3 The Audit Triangle

for use in clinical psychology. It is reproduced and adapted here for the use of services incorporating forensic psychotherapy by kind permission of the author.

The 'tip of the iceberg' with which readers of this book will be familiar refers to the area most visible to you and your patients which is the area of clinical experience. This is an area usually gained over many years of accumulated experience both as individual clinicians and as members of a clinical team.

'Clinical acumen' refers to what is commonly called the process of 'peer review', in other words case presentation and peer supervision which provides inbuilt containment by a service for the individual clinician with their patient. Whilst psychotherapy generally and forensic psychotherapy in particular can be managed very effectively via the process of peer review, it is clear that it does not provide change over time when used as a form of service evaluation.

It is in this area that the Audit Triangle can make a useful contribution, whereby the setting of standards and the process of clinical audit within a well-functioning multidisciplinary team can provide a solid service base within which individual clinicians can be supported in their clinical work with patients.

Under 'Basic Practice' at the base of the triangle you may want to consider looking at the following areas, using the setting of standards and clinical audit as one frame to think within.

Standards for:

(i)   Common Processes, e.g.

    ○ Assessment

    ○ Selection for treatment

    ○ Treatment length

    ○ Communication with referrers

    ○ Case notes.

(ii) Common Treatments/Procedures, e.g.

    ○ Length of assessments

    ○ Allocation of patients to individual/group long/short term therapy

    ○ Handling of D.N.As (patients who did not attend)

(iii) Potential Adverse Outcomes, e.g.

    ○ Management of violence

    ○ Management of suicide risk

    ○ Management of suspected child abuse.

CONCLUSION

I want to finish by returning to my main starting point concerning audit as a fundamental concept in the support of good clinical practice. All clinicians will have an experience of internal reflection and self-monitoring. Those of you treating forensic patients in psychotherapy may well have undergone, or be undertaking, your own personal psychotherapy. This is extremely valuable and, I would suggest, necessary. It enables you to reflect at first hand on the personal experience of being a patient and understand the dynamic of a therapeutic scrutiny that, whilst necessary, can be full of repetition and difficulty as well as rewards. From experience, there will be a hard won understanding that when push comes to shove and real change is necessary, there is inevitable conflict.

The audit process is no different. Certainly all audits of the audit process indicate that the 'impasse' in audit usually arises at the point of implementing and seeing through real change in an enduring way as a result of detailed audit work. If you have not undertaken any formal audit work before, then it can be helpful to bear this in mind ahead of time as a way of reducing the potential for omnipotent expectations of yourself or the clinical team or the audit process in itself as a 'solve-all' for the broader service and the external demands on it.

In conclusion, I would suggest that whilst audit has a useful contribution to make to the area of forensic psychotherapy, it needs to be introduced and implemented in a thoughtful manner if it is not to be experienced as a cynical pressure on clinicians. Small, manageable projects are good beginnings, the results of which will inevitably lead onto the next question. I wish you luck and refer you onto key papers you may wish to read if you intend to pursue the area further.

References

Adshead, G. (1991) 'The forensic psychotherapist: dying breed or evolving species?' *Psychiatric Bulletin/British Journal of Psychiatry 15*, 410–12.

Adshead, G. (1994) 'Damage: trauma and violence in a sample of women referred to a forensic service.' *Behavioural Sciences and the Law 12*, 235–249.

American Psychiatric Association (1994) *Diagnostic and Statistical Manual of Mental Disorders, Fourth Edition – Revised (DSM IVR)*. Washington, DC.: American Psychiatric Press.

Ammerman, R.T., Van Hasselt, V.B., Hersen, M., McGonglie, J.J., and Lubetsky, M.J. (1989) 'Abuse and neglect in psychiatrically hospitalised multihandicapped children.' *Child Abuse and Neglect 13*, 3, 335–343.

Arroyave, F. (1984) 'Group analytic treatment of drinking problems.' In T.E. Lears (ed) *Spheres of Group Analysis*. Eire: Leinster Leader Ltd.

Arroyave, F. (1986) 'Some implications of transference and counter-transference in the treatment of dependence.' *Journal of Analytical Psychology 31*, 119–216.

Asher, R. (1951) 'Munchausen's syndrome.' *Lancet I*, 339–341.

Bailey, S. (1996) 'Adolescents who murder.' *Journal of Adolescence 19*, 19–39.

Bally, G. (1931) 'Die Wahrnehmungslehre jaenschs und ihre Bezehung zu den psychoanalytischen Problemen.' *Imago 17*.

Baron-Cohen, S., Tager-Flusburg, H. and Cohen, D.J. (eds) (1993) *Understanding Other Minds: Perspectives from Autism*. Oxford: Oxford University Press.

Becker, J.V. (1990) 'Treating adolescent sex offenders.' *Professional Psychology: Research and Practice 21*, 5, 362–365.

Bentovim, A. (1992) *Trauma Organised Systems. Physical and Sexual Abuse in Families*. London: Karnac Books.

Berg, I.K. and Miller, S.D. (1992) *Working with the Problem Drinker: A Solution Focused Approach*. New York: W.W. Norton.

Bergin, A.E. and Garfield, S.R. (1994) *The Handbook of Psychotherapy and Behaviour Change*. New York: John Wiley and Sons (pp.10–11).

Bion, W.R. (1959) 'Attacks on linking.' *International Journal of Psychoanalysis 40 (5 and 6)*, 308–115.

Black, D. and Newman, M. (1995) 'Television violence and children.' *British Medical Journal 310*, 273–274.

Black, D., S., Wolkind and Hendricks, J.H. (eds) (1991) *Child Psychiatry and the Law* 2nd edition. London: Royal College of Psychiatrists, Gaskell.

Blom-Cooper, L., Grounds, A., Guinan, P., Parker, A. and Taylor, M. (1996) *The Case of Jason Mitchell: Report of the Independent Panel of Inquiry.* London: Duckworth.

Bluglass, R. (1990) 'The scope of forensic psychiatry.' *Journal of Forensic Psychiatry 1*, 7.

Bluglass, R. and Bowden, P. (eds) (1990) *Principles and Practice of Forensic Psychiatry.* Edinburgh: Churchill Livingstone.

Bools, C. Neale, B. and Meadow, R. (1994) 'Munchausen syndrome by proxy: a study of psychopathology.' *Child Abuse and Neglect 18*, 773–788.

Booth, B. and Grogan, M. (1990) *People with Learning Difficulties who Sexually Offend.* Community Resource Centre, Thameside General Hospital, Ashton Under Lyne.

Boston, M. and Szur, R. (eds) (1983) *Psychotherapy with Severely Deprived Children.* London: Routledge and Kegan Paul.

Bowden, P. (1995) 'Psychiatry and criminal proceedings.' In D. Chiswick and R. Cope (eds) *Practical Forensic Psychiatry.* London: Gaskell.

Bowlby, J. (1947) *Forty Four Juvenile Thieves, Their Characters and Home Life.* London: Bailliere, Tindall and Cox.

Bowlby, J. (1988) 'The role of attachment in personality development.' In J. Bowlby (ed) *Parent Child Attachment and Human Health Development.* London: Routledge.

Breen, T. and Turk, V. (1991) 'Sexual offending behaviour by people with learning disabilities: prevalence and treatment.' Unpublished paper. Kent: University of Canterbury.

Brenton, M. (1985) 'Women who steal.' *Cosmopolitan,* May, 285–287, 340.

Brezinka, C., Huter, O., Biebl, W. and Kinzl, J. (1994) 'Denial of pregnancy – obstetrical aspects.' *Journal of Psychosomatic Obstetric Gynaecology 15*, 1–8.

Briere, J. and Zaidi, L. (1989) 'Sexual abuse histories and sequelae in female psychiatric emergency room patients.' *American Journal of Psychiatry 146*, 1602–1606.

British Medical Association (1989) *Guide to Alcohol and Accidents.* London: British Medical Association.

Brooke, D., Taylor, C., Gunn, J. and Maden, A. (1996) *Mental Disorder in Remand Prisoners.* London: HMSO.

Brown, R., Domingo-Perez, l. and Murphy, D. (1989) 'Treating "impossible" children: A therapeutic group on a children's ward.' *Group Analysis 22*, 283–298.

Buchanan, A. and Oliver, J.E. (1979) 'Abuse and neglect as a cause of mental retardation.' *Child Abuse and Neglect 3*, 467–75.

Butler Report (1975) *The Report of the Committee on Mentally Abnormal Offenders.* Cmnd 6244. London: HMSO.

Campbell, D. and Hale, R. (1991) 'Suicidal acts.' In J. Holmes (ed) *Textbook of Psychotherapy in Psychiatric Practice.* London: Churchill Livingstone.

Cape, J.D. (1994) 'Clinical audit, clinical effectiveness and clinical psychology.' Unpublished paper.

Chiswick, D. and Cope, R.(eds) (1995) *Practical Forensic Psychiatry.* London: The Royal College of Psychiatry, Gaskell.

Coen, S.J. (1995) 'The excitement of sadomasochism.' In M.A.F. Hanly (ed) *Essential Papers on Masochism.* New York and London: New York University Press.

Coltart, N. (1988) 'Diagnosis and assessment for suitability for psychoanalytic psychotherapy.' *British Journal of Psychotherapy 4,* 2, 127–134.

Coltart, N. (1996) 'Why am I here?.' In *The Baby and the Bathwater.* London: Karnac.

Cooke, P. and Craft, A. (1995) *Annotated Bibliography, Supplement One on Sexual Abuse and Learning Difficulties.* Nottingham: NAPSAC.

Cordess, C. (1994) *Munchausen by Proxy: Concepts, Phenomenology and Dynamics in Current Issues in Forensic Psychiatry.* A Schering Symposium: Merit Publishing International.

Cordess, C. and Cox, M. (eds) (1996) *Forensic Psychotherapy: Crime, Psychodynamics and the Offender Patient.* London: Jessica Kingsley Publishers.

Cordess, C., Riley, W. and Welldon, E. (1994) 'Psychodynamic forensic psychotherapy: an account of a day-release course.' *Psychiatric Bulletin 18,* 88–90.

Cox, M. (1986) 'The "holding function" of dynamic psychotherapy in a custodial setting: a review.' *Journal of the Royal Society of Medicine 79,* 162–164.

Cox, M. (1992) 'Forensic psychotherapy: an emergent discipline.' In *Proceedings of the 17th International Congress of the International Academy of Law and Mental Health,* Leuven, Belgium (first published 1978).

Crittendon, P. and Ainsworth, M.D. (1989) 'Childhood maltreatment and attachment theory.' In D. Cicchetti and V. Carlson (eds) *Childhood Maltreatment: Theory and Research on The Causes and Consequences of Child Abuse and Neglect.* Cambridge: Cambridge University Press. (pp. 432–463).

Dartington Conference (1995) 'Psychodynamic practitioners – the family justice system.' 23–25th September. List of papers.

Davenhill, R., Patrick, M., and Price, T. (1996) *National NHS Audit and Psychotherapy Service Bibliography/ Database.* Available c/o The Tavistock Centre, 120 Belsize Lane, London, NW3 5BA.

Davis, G. and Leitenberg, H. (1987) 'Adolescent sex offenders.' *Psychological Bulletin 101,* 417–427.

Dennett, D.C. (1978) *Brainstorms.* Cambridge, MA: MIT Press.

Department of Health (1990) Health Circular – HC (90)23/LASSL(90)11 (The Care Programme Approach). London: Department of Health.

Department of Health (1992) *Report of the Committee of Inquiry into Complaints about Ashworth Hospital.* London: HMSO.

Derogatis, L.R. (1973) 'The Symptom Checklist-90: An out patient psychiatric rating scale – a preliminary report.' *Psychopharmacology Bulletin 9,* 31–27.

Dobmeyer, J.A.N. (1971) 'The sociology of shoplifting: avocation and vocation'. Dissertation, University of Minnesota.

Docker Drysedale, B. (1990) *Therapy and the First Year of Life: Provision of Primary Experience.* London: Free Association.

Dolan, B. (1994) 'Personality disorder and psychological disturbance of female prisoners: A comparison with women referred for NHS treatment of personality disorder.' *Criminal Behavior and Mental Health 4,* 130–143.

Dolan, M., Hollaway, J. and Bailey, S. (1996) 'Psychosocial characteristics of a series of 121 child and adolescent sex offenders.' *Medicine, Science and the Law.*

Dyer, A.R. (1988) *Ethics and Psychiatry: Toward Professional Definition.* Washington, DC: American Psychiatric Association Press.

The Economist (1996) 'Crime in America.' *The Economist,* June 8th, 339, 7969.

Ellenberger, H. (1966) 'The pathogenic secret and its therapeutics.' In *Beyond the Unconscious. Essays in the History of Psychiatry.* Princeton, NJ: Princeton University Press.

Elliott, B. (1995) *Development of a New Approach to the Treatment of Serious Alcohol Dependency.* ACCEPT Publications, ACCEPT, 724 Fulham Road, London SW6 5SE.

Endicott, J., Spitzer, R.L., Fleiss, J.L. and Cohen, J. (1976) 'The global assessment scale: a procedure for measuring overall severity of psychiatric disturbance.' *Archives of General Psychiatry 33,* 766–772.

Etchegoyen, R.H. (1991) 'Transference perversion.' Chapter in *The Fundamentals of Psycho-Analytic Technique.* London: Karnac Books.

Fairbairn, W. (1944) 'Endopsychic structure considered in terms of object relationships.' In W. Fairbairn (ed) (1952) *Psychoanalytic Studies of the Personality.* London: Tavistock.

Fairbairn, W.R.D. (1952) *Psychoanalytic Studies of the Personality.* London: Routledge and Kegan Paul.

Faulk, M. (1988) *Basic Forensic Psychiatry.* Oxford: Blackwell Scientific Publications.

Feldman, M. (1992) 'Audit in psychotherapy: the concept of Kaizen.' *Psychiatric Bulletin.* Royal College of Psychiatrists *16,* 6.

Finklehor, D. (1986) 'Abusers: special topics.' In D. Finklehor (ed) *A Sourcebook on Child Sexual Abuse.* London. Sage Publications, pp.119–141.

Fonagy, P. (1991) 'Thinking about thinking: some clinical and theoretical considerations in the treatment of a borderline patient.' *The International Journal of Psycho-Analysis 72,* 4, 639–656.

Fonagy, P. and Higgit, A. (1989) 'A developmental perspective on Borderline Personality disorder.' *Review Internationale de Psychopathologie 1*, 125–159.

Fonagy, P. and Higgit, A. (1989) 'Evaluating the performance of departments of psychotherapy.' *Psychoanalytic Psychotherapy 4*, 2, 121–153.

Fonagy, P., Steele, M. and Steele, H. (1991) 'Maternal representations of attachment during pregnancy predict organisation of infant–mother attachment at one year of age.' *Child Development 62*, 880–893.

Fonagy, P., Steele, H., Moran, G., Steele, M. and Higgit, A.C. (1991) 'The capacity for understanding mental states: The reflective self in parent and child and its significance for security of attachment.' *Infant Mental Health Journal 13*, 200–216.

Foulkes, S.H. (1975) 'The conductor in action: functions as administrator.' Chapter in *Group Analytic Psychotherapy: Method and Principles.* London: Maresfield Library.

Freud, S. (1914) 'On narcissism: an introduction.' In J. Strachey (ed) *The Standard Edition of the Complete Psychological Works of Sigmund Freud, Vol. 14.* London: Hogarth Press.

Freud, S. (1916) 'Criminals from a sense of guilt.' *The Standard Edition of the Complete Psychological Works of Sigmund Freud, Vol. 12.* London: Hogarth Press.

Freud, S. (1923) 'The Ego and the Id.' *The Standard Edition of the Complete Psychological Works of Sigmund Freud, Vol. 19*, pp 1–59. London: Hogarth Press.

Freud, S. (1953) 'Three essays on the theory of sexuality.' *The Standard Edition of the Complete Psychological Works of Sigmund Freud, Vol. 7.* London: Hogarth Press.

Freund, K., Scher, H. and Hucker, S. (1983) 'The courtship disorders.' *Archives of Sexual Behaviour 12*, 369–379.

Gallwey, P. (1990) 'The psychopathology of neurosis and offending.' In R. Bluglass and P. Bowden (eds) *Principles and Practice of Forensic Psychiatry.* London: Churchill Livingstone.

Gallwey, P. (1991) 'Social maladjustment.' In J. Holmes (ed) *Textbook of Psychotherapy in Psychiatric Practice.* Edinburgh: Churchill Livingstone.

Gallwey, P. (1992) 'The psychotherapy of psychopathic disorder.' *Criminal Behaviour and Mental Health 2*, 159–168.

Garelick, A. (1994) 'Psychotherapy assessment: theory and practice.' *Psychoanalytic Psychotherapy 8*, 2, 101–116.

Garratt, B. (1987) *The Learning Organisation and the Need for Directors Who Think.* London: Fontana.

General Medical Council (1995) *Duties of a Doctor.* London: General Medical Council.

George, C., Kaplan, N. and Main, M. (1985) 'The adult attachment interview.' Unpublished manuscript. University of California at Berkeley.

Gilby, R., Wolf, L. and Goldberg, B. (1989) 'Mentally retarded adolescent sex offenders, a survey and pilot study.' *Canadian Journal of Psychiatry 34*, 542–8.

Gilligan, J. (1996) *Violence: Our Deadly Epidemic and its Causes.* New York: Grosset/Putman.

Glasser, M. (1979) 'Some aspects of the role of aggression in the perversions.' In I. Rosen (ed) *Sexual Deviations.* Oxford: Oxford University Press, pp.278–305.

Glasser, M. (1994) 'Violence: a psychoanalytical research project.' *Journal of Forensic Psychiatry 5*, 2, 312–320.

Godwin, R., de Lacey, G., and Manhire, A. (1996) *Clinical Audit in Radiology – One Hundred Plus Recipes.* London: Royal College of Radiologists.

Green, C.M. and Manohar, S.V. (1990) 'Neonaticide and hysterical denial of pregnancy.' *British Journal of Psychiatry 156*, 121–123.

Griffiths, D., Hingsburger, D. and Christian, R. (1985) 'Treating developmentally handicapped sexual offenders: the York behaviour management services treatment program. *Psychiatric Aspects in Mental Retardation Review 4*, 49–52..

Grubin, D. (1996) 'Intervention and recidivism: some facts and some problems.' *The Derwent Initiative Newsletter Communique 4*, 1, 1–3.

Grunebaum, H. and Klerman, G. (1967) 'Wrist slashing.' *American Journal of Psychiatry 124*, 527–534.

Grunn, J. and Taylor, P.J. (eds) (1993) *Forensic Psychiatry: Clinical, Legal and Ethical Issues.* London: Butterworth-Heinemann Ltd.

Guinan, P. (1995) 'Through the looking glass.' *The Psychologist 8*, 10, October.

Gunn, J., Robertson, G., Dell, S. and Way, C. (1978) *Psychiatric Aspects of Imprisonment.* London: Academic Press.

Guntrip, H. (1968) *Schizoid Phenomena Object Relations and the Self.* London: Hogarth Press.

Hambridge, J.A. (1990) 'The grief process in those admitted to regional secure units following homicide.' *Journal of Forensic Sciences 35*, 5, 1149–1154.

Harding, T. (1992) 'Research and evaluation in forensic psychotherapy.' *First International Conference Association of Forensic Psychotherapy*, London.

Harris, D.P., Cole, J.E. and Vipond, E.M. (1987) 'Residential treatment of disturbed delinquents. Description of centre and identification of therapeutic factors.' *Canadian Journal of Psychiatry 32*, 579–583.

Hawkes, C., Jenkins, J. and Vizard, E. (1996) 'Roots of sexual violence in children and adolescents.' In V. Varma (ed) *Violence in Children and Adolescents.* London: Jessica Kingsley.

Herman, J.L. (1992) 'Complex PTSD: A syndrome in survivors of prolonged and repeated trauma.' *Journal of Traumatic Stress 5*, 3.

Herman, J.L. and van der Kolk, B. (1987) 'Traumatic antecedents of borderline personality disorder.' In B. van der Kolk (ed) *Psychological Trauma.* Washington: American Psychiatric Press.

Herman, J.L., Perry, C. and Bessez, A. (1989) 'Childhood trauma in borderline personality disorder.' *American Journal of Psychiatry 146*, 4, 490–495.

Hinshelwood, R. (1993) 'Locked in a role: a psychotherapist within the social defence system of a prison.' *Journal of Forensic Psychiatry 4*, 3, 427–440.

Hinshelwood, R.D. (1994) 'The relevance of psychotherapy.' *Psychoanalytic Psychotherapy 8*, 3, 283–294.

HMSO (1988) *Report of the Enquiry into Child Abuse in Cleveland 1987* Cm Paper 412. London: HMSO.

Home Office (1983) *Mental Health Act 1983*. London: HMSO.

Home Office (1985) *Police and Criminal Evidence Act 1984 (S.66) Codes of Practice*. London: HMSO.

Home Office (1994) *Statistics on Crime*. London: HMSO.

Home Office/Department of Health/Department of Education and Science/Welsh Office. (1991) *Working Together Under the Children Act 1989. A Guide to Arrangements for Inter-Agency Co-Operation for the Protection of Children from Abuse*. London: HMSO.

Hopper, E. (1991) 'Encapsulation as a defence against the fear of annihilation.' *International Journal of Psychoanalysis 72*, 4, 607–24.

Hopper, E. (1996) 'A psychoanalytical theory of drug addiction.' *International Journal of Psychoanalysis 76*, 6, 1121.

Howarth, J. and Lawson, B. (1995) *Trust Betrayed*. National Children's Bureau, 8 Wakley Street, London, EC1V 7QE.

Hoxter (1990) Chapter in M. Boston and P. Szur (eds) *Psychotherapy with Severely Deprived Children*. London: Maresfield Libarary

Hyatt Williams, A. (1986) 'A masterpiece on murder.' Book review of *Killing for Company: Two Cases of Dennis Nilsen*, by Brian Masters. *Free Associations 7*, 26–37.

Innes, R. (1996) 'An art therapist's inside view.' In C. Cordess and M. Cox (eds) *Forensic Psychotherapy, Vol. I: Mainly Practice*. London: Jessica Kingsley Publishers.

Jackson, M., Pines, M. and Stevens, B. (1986) 'Borderline personality: psychodynamics and treatment.' *Neurologia et Psychiatria, 66–88.*

Jacques, E. (1955) 'Social systems as a defence against persecutory and depressive anxiety.' In M. Klein, P. Heimann and R. E. Money-Kyrle (eds) *New Directions in Psychoanalysis*. London: Tavistock.

James, D.V. and Hamilton, L. (1992) 'Setting up psychiatric liaison schemes to magistrates' courts: problems and practicalities.' *Medicine, Science and the Law 32*, 2, 167–176.

Joseph, B. (1985) 'Transference: the total situation.' *International Journal of Psycho-Analysis 66*, 447–54.

Jung, C.G. (1968) 'The archetypes and the collective unconscious.' In H. Read, M. Fordham and G. Adler (eds) *C.G. Jung The Collected Works: Volume 9, Part 1*. Trans. R.F.C. Hull. London: Routledge and Kegan Paul Ltd.

Karpman, B. (1957) *The Sexual Offender and his Offences.* Washington, DC: Julian Press.

Kempe, R. and Kempe, C. (1978) *Child Abuse.* London: Fontana Books.

Kennard, D. (1983) *Introduction to Therapeutic Communities.* London: Routledge and Kegan Paul.

Kennard, D. (1988) 'The therapeutic community.' In A. Aveline and W. Dryden (eds) *Group Therapy in Britain.* Milton Keynes: Open University Press.

Kerngerg, D.F. (1984) *Severe Personality Disorders: Psychotherapeautic Strategies.* New Haven, CT: Yale University Press.

Kernberg, O. (1975) *Borderline Conditions and Pathological Narcissism.* New York: Jason Aronson.

Kernberg, O. (1994) 'Identity diffusion and structured change: research findings.' Paper presented at the fourth IPA Conference on Psychoanalytic Research in London, March 1994.

Khan, M.M.R. (1986) 'The concept of cumulative trauma.' In G. Kohen (ed) *The British School of Psychoanalysis: The Independent Tradition.* London: Free Association Books.

Klein, M. (1932) 'The sexual activities of children.' In *The Psychoanalysis of Children, The Writings of Melanie Klein, Vol.2.* London: Hogarth, Institute of Psycho-Analysis.

Klein, M. (1940) 'Mourning and its relation to manic depressive states.' In M.R. Kahn (ed) *Collected Works I.* London: Hogarth Press.

Klein, M. (1946) 'Notes on some schizoid mechanisms.' In M. Klein (ed) (1980) *Envy and Gratitude and Other Works.* 1946–1963, pp.1–24. London: The Hogarth Press.

Kohut, H. (1977) *The Restoration of The Self.* Madison, CT: International Universities Press.

Kolb, L.C. (1977) *Modern Clinical Psychiatry.* Philadelphia, PA: W.B. Saunders and Co.

van der Kolk, B., Perry, C. and Herman, J. (1991) 'Childhood origins of self-destructive behaviour.' *American Journal of Psychiatry 148,* 1665–76.

Kolman, A.S. and Wasserman, C. (1991) 'Theft groups for women: a cry for help!' *Federal Probation 55,* 1, 48–54.

Kroll, J. (1993) *PTSD/Borderlines in Therapy.* London: W.W. Norton.

Langevin, R. and Lang, R.A. (1987) 'The courtship disorders.' In G.D. Wilson (ed) *Variant Sexuality: Research and Theory.* London: Croom Helm.

Laufer, M. (1974) *Adolescent's Disturbance and Breakdown.* London: Pelican Books.

Levinson, A. and Fonagy, P. 'Criminality and attachment: the relationship between interpersonal awareness and offending in a prison population.' Unpublished paper.

Lewis, D.O. (1992) 'From abuse to violence: psychophysiological consequences of maltreatment.' *Journal of American Academy Child and Adolescent Psychiatry 31*, 383–391.

Libow, J.A. and Schreier, H.A. (1986) 'Three forms of factitious illness in children: when is it Munchausen syndrome by proxy?' *American Journal of Ortho Psychiatry 56*, 602–611.

Liebling, A. (1992) *Suicides in Prison*. London: Routledge.

Limentani, A. (1986) 'On the psychodynamics of drug dependence.' *Free Associations 5*, 48–64.

Limentani, A. (1987) 'Perversions: treatable and untreatable.' *Contemporary Psychoanalysis 23*, 3, 415–437.

Lindemann, E. (1944) 'Symptomology and management of acute grief.' *American Journal of Psychiatry 101*, 141–149.

Livingston, R. (1987) 'Maternal somatisation disorder and Munchausen syndrome by proxy.' *Psychosomatics 28*, 213–217.

Loth, H. (1994) 'Music therapy and forensic psychiatry – choice, denial and the law.' *British Journal of Music Therapy 8*, 2.

Macleod, R.J. (1982) 'A child is charged with homicide. His family responds.' *British Journal of Psychiatry 141*, 199–201.

McDougall, J. (1990) 'Creation and sexual deviance.' In J. McDougall (ed) *Plea for a Measure of Abnormality*. London. Free Association Books.

McGauley, G. (1996) 'Therapeutic communities.' In S. Stein, J. Pearce and R. Haigh (eds) *Essentials of Psychotherapy*. London: Butterworth Heinemann (in press).

McKeown, O., Forshaw, D.M., McGauley, G., Fitzpatrick, J. and Ruscoe, J. (1996) 'Forensic addictive behaviours unit: a case study.' *Journal of Substance Misuse 1*, 27–31 et seq.

Main, M. (1990) 'Cross cultural studies of attachment organization: recent studies, changing methodologies, and the concept of additional strategies.' *Human Development 33*, 48–61.

Main, M. (1991) 'Metacognitive knowledge, metacognitve monitoring, and singular (coherent) vs. multiple (incoherent) models of attachment: Findings and directions for future research.' In P. Harris, J. Stevenson-Hinde and C. Parkes (eds) *Attachment Across the Life Cycle*. New York: Routledge.

Main, M. and Goldwyn, R. (1991) 'Adult attachment classification system. Version 5.' Unpublished manuscript, University of California, Berkeley.

Main, M. and Hesse, E. (1992) 'Disorganised/disorientated behaviour in the strange situation, lapses in the monitoring of reasoning and discourse during the parent's Adult Attachment Interview, and Dissociative States.' In M. Ammanati and D. Stern (eds) *Attachment and Psychoanalysis*. Rome: Guis, Laterza and Figli.

Main, M., Kaplan, N. and Cassidy, J. (1985) 'Security in infancy childhood and adulthood: A move to the level of representation.' In I. Bretherton and E.

Waters (eds) *Growing Points of Attachment Theory and Research. Monographs of the Society for Research in Child Development 50*, (1–2, serial no.209,), 66–104.

Main, T. (1957) 'The ailment.' *British Journal of Medical Psychology 30*, 129–145.

Main, T. (1975) 'Some psychodynamics of large groups.' In L. Kreeger (ed) *The Large Group.*

Main, T.F. (1983) 'The concept of the therapeutic community: variations and vicissitudes.' In M. Pines (ed) *The Evolution of Group Analysis.* London: Routledge and Kegan Paul.

Marlatt, G.A. and Gordon, J.R. (1985) *Relapse Prevention.* New York: Guilford Publications.

Marleau, J.D. (1995) 'Homide d'enfant commis par la mère.' *Canadian Journal of Psychiatry 40*, 142–149.

Martin, G. and Waite, S. (1994) 'Parental bonding and vulnerability to adolescent suicide.' *Acta Psychiatrica Scandinavica 89*, 246–254.

Matano, R. and Yalom, I.D. (1991) 'Approaches to chemical dependency: chemical dependency and interactive group therapy – a synthesis.' *International Journal of Group Psychotherapy 41*, 3.

Meadow, R. (1977) 'Munchausen syndrome by proxy: the hinterland of child abuse.' *Lancet II*, 343–345.

Meadow, R. (1979) 'What is, and what is not, Munchausen syndrome by proxy.' In 'Controversy', *Archives of Disease in Childhood 72*, 534–538.

Meloy, J.R. (1992) *Violent Attachments.* New York: Jason Aronson.

Menzies Lyth, I. (1959) 'The functioning of social systems as a defence against anxiety.' In I. Menzies Lyth (ed) *Containing Anxiety in Institutions.* London: Free Association Books.

Miller, A. (1983) *For Your Own Good: Hidden Cruelty in Child Rearing and the Roots of Violence.* London: Virago.

Miller, W.R. and Rolnick, S. (1991) *Motivational Interviewing: Preparing People to Change Addictive Behaviours.* New York: The Guilford Press.

Milton, J. (1994) 'Abuser and abused: perverse solutions following childhood abuse.' *Psychoanalytic psychotherapy 8*, 243–255.

Monck, E. and New, M. (1995) *Sexually Abused Children and Adolescents and Young Perpetrators of Sexual Abuse who were Treated in Voluntary Community Facilities.* London: HMSO.

Morley, C. (1995) 'Practical concerns about diagnosis of Munchausen by proxy.' In 'Controversy', *Archives of Disease in Childhood 72,* 528–530.

Mrazek, P.B., Lynch, M. and Bentovim, A. (1981) 'Recognition of child sexual abuse in the United Kingdom.' In P.B. Mrazek and C.H. Kempe (eds) *Sexually Abused Children and Their Families.* Oxford: Pergamon Press, pp.35–50.

National Research Council (1993) *Understanding Child Abuse and Neglect.* Washington: National Academy Press.

National Society for the Prevention of Cruelty to Children (1992) *Trends in Child Abuse: Fourth Report on NSPCC Special Unit Registers.* London: NSPCC.

NCH (National Children's Home) (1992) *Children who Abuse Other Children.* London: National Children's Home, 85 Highbury Park, London, N5 1UD, U.K.

Norton, K. (1992) 'Personality disordered individuals: the Henderson Hospital model of treatment.' *Criminal Behaviour and Mental Health 2,* 180–191.

Norton, K. and Dolan, B. (1995) 'Acting out and the institutional response.' *The Journal of Forensic Psychiatry 6,* 2, 317–332.

Norwood East, W. (1927) *Introduction to Forensic Psychiatry in the Criminal Courts.* London: J&A Churchill.

Obholzer, A. and Zagier Roberts, V. (1994) *The Unconscious at Work.* London: Routledge.

Orbach, S. and Eisenbaum, L. (1981) *What do Women Want?* London: Penguin.

d'Orban, P.T. (1990) 'Female homicide.' *Irish Journal of Psychological Medicine 7,* 64–70.

Orton, R. (1992) 'From improvisation to composition.' In Paynter, Howell, Orton and Seymour (eds) *The Companion to Contemporary Musical Thought.* London: Routledge.

Parry, G. (1992) 'Improving psychotherapy services: applications of research, audit and evaluation.' *British Journal of Clinical Psychology 31,* 3–19.

Patrick, H. and Hobson, P. (1996) Personal communication.

Perkins, D. (1996) 'The Cognitive–Behavioural Appraoch.' In C. Cordess and M. Cox (eds) *Forensic Psychotherapy: Crime, Psychodynamics and the Offender Patient,* Vol. I, 57–65. London: Jessica Kingsley Publishers.

Pfäfflin, F. (1993) 'What is in a symptom? A conservative approach in the therapy of sex offenders.' *Journal of Offender Rehabilitation,* Department of Sex Research, Psychiatric Clinic, Universitätskrankenhaus Eppendorf, Hamburg (in press).

Pierce, D. (1986) 'Deliberate self harm: how do patients view their treatment?' *British Journal of Psychiatry 4,* 149, 624–626.

Pilgrim, D. (1987) 'Psychotherapy in British Special Hospitals. A case of failure to thrive.' *Free Associations 11,* 59–72.

Pines, M. (1978) 'Group analytic psychotherapy and the borderline patient.' *Group Analysis 11,* 2, 115.

Platt, S. and Salter, D. (1987) 'A comparative investigation of health workers' attitudes towards parasuicide.' *Social Psychiatry 22,* 202–208.

Podvoll, E. (1990) *The Seduction of Madness.* New York: HarperCollins.

Power, M. (1994) *The Audit Explosion.* London: Demos.

Rapoport, R. (1960) *The Community as Doctor.* London: Tavistock.

Raspe, R.E. (1944) *The Surprising Adventures of Baron Munchausen.* New York: Peter Pauper.

Reed, J. (1996) 'Psychopathy: a clinical and legal dilemma.' *British Journal of Psychiatry 168*, 1, 4–9.

Reed Report (1992) *Report of the Academic Advisory Group 1992*. London: Department of Health/Home Office.

Reiss, D., Grubin, D. and Meux, C. (1996) 'Young "psychopaths" in special hospital: treatment and outcome.' *British Journal of Psychiatry 168*, 99–104.

Resnick, P.J. (1969) 'Child murder by parents – a psychiatric review of filicide.' *American Journal of psychiatry 126*, 325–334.

Richardson, J. (1993) 'Eeking out his little existence.' Unpublished paper.

Robarts, J. and Sloboda, A. (1994) 'Perspectives on music therapy with people suffering from anorexia nervosa.' *British Journal of Music Therapy 8*, 1.

Robinson, A. and Duffy, J. (1989) 'A comparison of self-injury and self-poisoning from the regional poisoning treatment centre, Edinburgh.' *Acta Psychiatrica Scandinavica 80*, 272–279.

Robertson, I. and Heather, N. (1986) *Let's Drink to Your Health: A Self Help Guide to Sensible Drinking*. London: BPS.

Rosen, I. (1979) *Sexual Deviation*. Oxford: Oxford University Press.

Rosen, I. (1979) 'Exhibitionism, scopophilia, and voyeurism.' In *Sexual Deviation*. Oxford: Oxford University Press.

Rosen, I. (1996) *Sexual Deviation*, 3rd edition. Oxford: Oxford University Press.

Rosenfeld, H. (1971) 'A clinical approach to the psychoanalytic theory of the life and death instincts: an investigation into the aggressive aspects of narcissism.' *International Journal of Psycho-Analysis 52*, 169–78.

Rosenfeld, H. (1982) 'The psychopathology of drug addiction and alcoholism, (a critical review of the psycho-analytical literature).' Chapter in *Psychotic States – A Psycho-Analytic Approach*. London: Karnac Books.

Roy, A. (1978) 'Self-mutilation.' *British Journal of Medical Psychology 51*, 201–203.

Royal College of Psychiatrists (1985) Working paper from the forensic psychiatry section: 'Confidentiality and Forensic Psychiatry'. London: Royal College of Psychiatrists.

Ryan, G. (1986) 'Annotated bibliography: adolescent perpetrators of sexual molestation of children.' *Child Abuse and Neglect 10*, 125–131.

Rycroft, C. (1968) *A Critical Dictionary of Psychoanalysis*. London: Penguin Books.

Samuels, M.P., McLaughlin, W., Jacobsen, R.R., Poets, C.F. and Southall, D.P. (1992) 'Fourteen cases of imposed upper airway obstruction.' *Archives of Disease in Childhood 67*, 162–170.

Sandler, J. (1976) 'Countertransference and role-responsiveness.' *International Review of Psycho-Analysis 3*, 43–7.

Sandler, J. (1995) 'Research without numbers: an approach to conceptual research in psychoanalysis.' Paper presented at the British Psycho-Analytic Society's Research Lecture, London, 5 July 1995.

Sapsford, R.J. (1983) *Life-Sentenced Prisoners – Reaction, Response and Change.* Milton Keynes: Open University Press.

Sartre, J.P. (1995) *Being and Nothing.* London: Routledge.

Scharff, J. and Scharff, D. (1994) *Object Relations Theory of Physical and Sexual Trauma.* New York. Jason Aronson.

Schierse Leonard, L. (1989) *Witness To The Fire-Creativity and the Veil of Addiction.* Boston, MA: Shambala Publications.

Schon, D.A. (1983) *The Reflective Practitioner.* London: Temple Smith.

Schreier, H.A. and Libow, J.A. (1993) *Hurting for Love (Munchausen by Proxy Syndrome).* New York: Guilford Press Publications.

Scott, P.D. (1973) 'Parents who kill their children.' *Medical Scientific Law 13,* 120–126.

Selby, M. (1991) 'HMP Grendon – The care of acute psychiatric patients: a pragmatic solution.' In K. Herbst and J. Gunn (eds) *The Mentally Disordered Offender.* Oxford: Butterworth–Heinemann Ltd.

Sgroi, S. (1982) *Handbook of Clinical Intervention in CSA.* Lexington, MA: Lexington Books.

Sinason, V. (1986) 'Secondary mental handicap and its relationship to trauma.' *Psychoanalytic Psychotherapy 2,* 2, 131–154.

Sinason, V. (1988) 'Richard III, Echo and Hephaestus: sexuality and mental/multiple handicap.' *Journal of Child Psychotherapy 14,* 2.

Sinason, V. (1992) *Mental Handicap and the Human Condition.* London: Free Association Books.

Sinason, V. (1993) 'The special vulnerability of the handicapped child and adult: with special reference to mental handicap.' In C.J. Hobbs and J.M. Wynne (eds) *Bailliere's Clinical Paediatrics, Child Abuse.* London: Bailliere.

Sinason, V. (1995) 'Prison poetry reading.' In *Night Shift: New Poems.* London: Karnac Books.

de Smit, B. (1992) 'The end of beginning is the beginning of the end: the structure of the initial interview in forensic psychiatry.' *Proceedings of the 17th International Congress of the International Academy of Law and Mental Health.* Leuven, Belgium.

Sohn, L. (1995) 'Unprovoked assaults on waking sense of apparently random violence.' *International Journal of Psychoanalysis 76,* 3, 565–575.

Steiner, J. (1993) *Psychic Retreats.* London: Routledge.

Stevenson, B. and Ruscombe-King, G. (1993) 'Corking and uncorking: a reflection on group-analytic treatment for alcoholics.' *Group Analysis 26,* 3, 213–224.

Stewart, J.T., Myers, W.C. and Burnet, R.C. (1990) 'A review of one pharmacotherapy of aggression in children and adolescents.' *Journal of American Academic Child and Adolescent Psychiatry 29,* 269–277.

Stoller, R.J. (1975) *The Erotic Form of Hatred.* London: Maresfield Library.

Stoller, R.J. (1976) *Perversion: The Erotic Form of Hatred.* Brighton: The Harvester Press.

Stoller, R.J. (1986) *Perversion: The Erotic Form of Hatred.* London: Maresfield Library.

Stoller, R. (1991) 'The term perversion.' In G.I. Fogel and W.A. Myers (eds) *Perversions and Near-Perversions in Clinical Practice.* New Haven and London: Yale University Press.

Stone, M. (1987) 'A psychodynamic approach: some thoughts on the dynamics and therapy of self-mutilating borderline patients.' *Journal of Personality Disorders 1,* 347–349.

Storr, A. (1964) *Sexual Deviation.* Harmondsworth: Penguin.

Strachey, J. (1930) 'Some unconscious factors in reading.' *International Journal of Psycho-Analysis 11,* 322–331.

Symington, N. (1996) 'The origins of rage and aggression.' In C. Cordess and M. Cox (eds) *Forensic Psychotherapy: Crime, Psychodynamics and the Offender Patient.* London: Jessica Kingsley.

Tantam, D. and Whittaker, J. (1992) 'Personality disorder and self wounding.' *British Journal of Psychiatry 161,* 451–464.

Taylor, L.B. (1982) 'Shoplifting: when "honest" women steal.' *Ladies Home Journal,* January, 88–102.

Taylor, P.J. (1985) 'Motives for offending among violent and psychotic men.' *British Journal of Psychiatry 147,* 491–498.

Thornton, D. and Hogue, T. (1993) 'The large-scale provision of programmes for imprisoned sex offenders: issues, dilemmas and progress.' *Criminal Behaviour and Mental Health 3,* 371–380.

Tustin, F. (1987) *Autistic Barriers in Neurotic Patients.* London: Karnac Books.

Vanicelli (1988) 'Group therapy aftercare for alcoholic patients.' *International Journal of Group Psychotherapy 38,* 3, 37–353.

Vizard, E. (1996 in press) *The Mind of the Abuser. The Dynamic Origins of Perversion.* Based on a talk given to the British Institute of Psychohistory, November 1995.

Vizard, E., Monck, E. and Misch, P. (1995) 'Child and adolescent sex abuse perpetrators: a review of the research literature.' *Journal of Child Psychology and Psychiatry 36,* 731–756.

Vizard, E., Wynick, S., Hawkes, C., Woods, J. and Jenkins, J. (1996) 'Juvenile sexual offenders: assessment issues.' *British Journal of Psychiatry 168,* 3, 259–262.

Weintrobe, S. (1995) 'Violence and mental space.' *Bulletin of the Anna Freud Centre 18,* 149–164.

Weisman, D. (1972) *On Dying and Denying.* New York: Behavioural Publications.

Weissman, M.M. (1975) 'The assessment of social adjustment.' *Archives of General Psychiatry 32,* 357–365.

Welldon, E.V. (1988) *Mother, Madonna, Whore: The Idealisation and Denigration of Motherhood.* London: Free Association Books.

Welldon, E.V. (1992) *Mother, Madonna, Whore: The Idealisation and Denigration of Motherhood.* New York: Guilford Press.

Welldon, E.V. (1994) 'Forensic psychotherapy.' In P. Clarkson and M.R. Pokorny (eds) *The Handbook of Psychotherapy.* London: Routledge.

Westen, D. (1994) 'Social cognition and object relations scale Q-sort (SCORS-Q) for interview and narrative data.' Unpublished document. Cambridge Hospital, Massachusetts.

Widiger, T.A. and Trull, T.J. (1994) 'Personality disorders and violence.' In J. Monahan and H.J. Steadman (eds) *Violence and Mental Disorder.* London: University of Chicago Press.

Williams, G. (1983) *Textbook of Criminal Law,* (second edition). London: Stevens and Sons.

Williams-Saunders, J. (1996) 'In search of containment: dramatherapy in prisons.' Unpublished paper given at the Arts Therapies Forensic Seminar.

Wildavsky, A. (1972) 'The self-evaluation organisation.' *Public Administrative Review, 32,* 509–520.

Winnicott, C., Shepherd, R. and Davies, R. (eds) *Deprivation and Delinquency.* London: Routledge.

Winnicott, D.W. (1960) *Maturational Processes and the Facilitablility Environment.* London: Karnac Maresfield Library.

Winnicott, D.W. (1965) *The Maturational Processes and the Facilitating Environment: Studies in the Theory of Emotional Development.* London: Hogarth Press.

Winnicott, D.W. (1969) *Playing and Reality – Transitional Objects and Transitional Phenomena.* London: Routledge.

Winnicott, D.W. (1984) 'The absence of a sense of guilt.' In C. Winnicott, R. Shepherd and M. Davies (eds) *Deprivation and Delinquency.* London: Tavistock.

Wolf, M.S. (1977) 'A review of literature of milieu therapy.' *Journal of Psychiatric Nursing 15,* 7–12.

Woollcott, R.C., Aceto, T., Rutt, C., Bloom, M. and Glick, R. (1982) 'Doctor shopping with the child as proxy patient: a variant of child abuse.' *Journal of Paediatrics 101,* 297–301.

Yalom, I. (1960) 'Aggression and forbiddenness in voyeurism.' *Archives of General Psychiatry 3,* 305–319.

Yalom, I.D. (1985) *The Theory and Practice of Group Psychotherapy.* London: Basic Books.

Zacune, J. and Hensman, C. (1971) *Drugs, Alcohol and Tobacco in Britain.* London: Heinemann.

de Zulueta, F. (1993) *From Pain to Violence. The Traumatic Roots of Destructiveness.* London: Whurr Publishers.

The Contributors

Gwen Adshead is Lecturer in Forensic Psychiatry at the Institute of Psychiatry, and Senior Registrar at Broadmoor Hospital.

Lynn Aulich is an Art Therapist at the Adolescent Forensic Service, Mental Health Services of Salford.

Sue Bailey is Adolescent Forensic Psychiatrist for Mental Health Services of Salford.

Penelope Barrett is a Barrister at Law at Gray's Inn.

Kerry Bluglass is a Consultant Psychiatrist, Deputy Medical Director of the Woodbourne Clinic and Senior Clinical Lecturer at the University of Birmingham.

Christine Bradley is Psychotherapist and Training Consultant for NCH Action for Children, and a freelance Child Care Consultant and Analytical Psychotherapist.

Fiona Caldicott DBE is immediate past President of the Royal College of Psychiatrists, and Principal of Somerville College, Oxford.

Jo-anne Carlyle is Clinical Psychologist in Psychoanalytical Psychotherapy in the Adult Department at the Tavistock Clinic.

Jenifer Anne Clarke works at the Caswell Clinic, Glanrhyd Hospital, for the Bridgend and District NHS Trust.

Rachael Davenhill is a Psychoanalyst at the Institute of Psychoanalysis and a Consultant Chartered Clinical Psychologist in Psychotherapy in the Adult Department at the Tavistock Clinic and a Member of the Association for Psychoanalytical Psychotherapy in the NHS.

Sheilagh Davies is a Consultant Psychiatrist/Psychoanalyst in the Department of Psychiatry at the Royal Free Hospital.

Marisa Dillon-Weston is a Group Therapist in the Psychotherapy Department at St Peter's Hospital, Chertsey, and has her own private practice.

Barbara Elliott is Director of ACCEPT Services and member of the Group-Analytic Society and Institute of Group Analysis.

Christine Foy is Associate Specialist in Psychiatry at Mid Wales Hospital.

Caroline Garland is a Consultant Clinical Psychologist/Psychoanalyst in the Adult Department at the Tavistock Clinic.

Ü. Elif Gürişik is a Consultant Psychotherapist at the Portman Clinic.

Maggie Hilton is a Consultant Clinical Psychologist at the Henderson Hospital, and a Chartered Clinical and Forensic Psychologist.

Francesca Hume is a Clinical Psychologist in Psychoanalytic Psychotherapy at the Tavistock Clinic.

Rein Innes is Art Psychotherapist Senior I at the Fromeside Clinic.

Helena Kennedy QC is Chancellor of Oxford Brookes University.

Jane Knowles is a Consultant Psychotherapist for West Berkshire Psychotherapy Service, and is a member of the Institute of Group Analysis.

Alice Levinson is Senior Registrar in Psychotherapy at the Parkside Clinic, NWL Mental Health (NHS) Trust.

Gill McGauley is a Consultant and Senior Lecturer in Forensic Psychotherapy at Broadmoor Hospital and St George's Hospital Medical School.

Jane Milton is Consultant Psychotherapist at the Tavistock Clinic and has a private practice as a Psychoanalyst.

Carine Minne is a Senior Registrar at the Portman Clinic.

Valerie Sinason is a Consultant Child Psychotherapist at the Anna Freud Centre at the Tavistock Clinic, Research Psychotherapist at St George's Hospital Medical School, and is a Consultant in the Psychiatry of Disability Department at the Portman Clinic.

Ann Sloboda is Head Music Therapist at Three Bridges RSU.

Julie Stone is a member of the Department of Biomedical Ethics at the Medical School at the University of Birmingham.

Caecilia Taylor is Senior Lecturer in Forensic Psychiatry at the Institute of Psychiatry and Honorary Consultant in Forensic Psychiatry at Broadmoor Hospital.

Debbie Taylor is a Barrister at Law at the Hardwicke Building in Lincoln's Inn.

Judith Trowell is a Consultant Psychiatrist in the Child and Family Department at the Tavistock Clinic.

Cleo Van Velsen is Consultant Psychotherapist in the Psychotherapy Department at the Maudsley Hospital.

Eileen Vizard is a Consultant Child and Adolescent Psychiatrist for the Simmons House Adolescent Service, Clinical Director of the Young Abuser's Project, and Honorary Senior Lecturer at University College London.

Estela V. Welldon is a Consultant Psychotherapist at the Portman Clinic, and Honorary Lecturer in Forensic Psychotherapy at University College London.

Judith Whale is Senior Registrar in Psychotherapy for Addenbrookes NHS Trust, and a Member of the Royal College of Psychiatrists.

Jessica Williams-Saunders is a Consultant Dramatherapist and Supervisor at Broadmoor Hospital.

Anne Zachary is a Consultant Psychotherapist at the Portman Clinic, and a member of the British Psychoanalytical Society.

Felicity de Zulueta is a Consultant Psychotherapist and Honorary Senior Lecturer at Charing Cross Hospital. She is also a Group Analyst and Family Therapist.

Subject Index

References in italic indicate figures or tables.

Author Index